history of the American fin de siecle run the contrasting themes of continuity and change, faith and rationalism, despair over the meaninglessness of life and, ultimately, a guarded optimism about the future.

THE AUTHOR

George Cotkin is professor of history at California Polytechnic State University, San Luis Obispo. He received his B.A. from Brooklyn College and his M.A. and PhD from Ohio State University. He is the author of *William James: Public Philosopher* (1990) as well as numerous essays.

Twayne's American Thought and Culture Series, under the general editorship of Lewis Perry, Vanderbilt University, provides an in-depth survey of American intellectual and cultural history. Each volume draws on a wide range of sources to examine the birth and influence of major ideas and cultural trends and the historic events to which they are connected.

RELUCTANT
MODERNISM

TWAYNE'S
AMERICAN THOUGHT
AND CULTURE SERIES

Lewis Perry, General Editor

RELUCTANT MODERNISM

American Thought and Culture, 1880–1900

GEORGE COTKIN

Twayne Publishers • New York
Maxwell Macmillan Canada • Toronto
Maxwell Macmillan International • New York   Oxford   Singapore   Sydney

Reluctant Modernism: American Thought and Culture, 1880–1900
George Cotkin

Copyright 1992 by George Cotkin

Twayne Publishers   Maxwell Macmillan Canada, Inc.
Macmillan Publishing Company   1200 Eglinton Avenue East
866 Third Avenue   Suite 200
New York, New York 10022   Don Mills, Ontario M3C 3N1

Macmillan Publishing Company is part of the Maxwell Communication Group of
Companies.

Library of Congress Cataloging-in-Publication Data

Cotkin, George, 1950–
    Reluctant modernism : American thought and culture, 1880–1900 /
George Cotkin.
        p.   cm. — (Twayne's American thought and culture series)
    Includes bibliographical references (p. 174) and index.
    ISBN 0-8057-9054-3 (alk. paper) : $28.95. — ISBN 0-8057-9059-4
(pbk. : alk. paper) : $12.95
        1. United States—Intellectual life—1865–1918. 2. United States—
Civilization—1865–1918. I. Title. II. Series.
E169.1.C785   1992
973.8—dc20   91-34316
                                                                 CIP

The paper used in this publication meets the minimum requirements
of American National Standard for Information Sciences—Permanence
of Paper for Printed Library Materials, ANSI Z39.48-1984. ∞™

10 9 8 7 6 5 4 3 2 1 (hc)
10 9 8 7 6 5 4 3 2 1 (pb)

Copyediting supervised by Barbara Sutton
Typeset by Compset, Inc., Beverly, Massachusetts

Printed in the United States of America

For my friends

Illustrations

Contents

Foreword

The American Thought and Culture Series surveys intellectual and cultural life in America from the sixteenth century to the present. The time is auspicious for such a broad survey because scholars have carried out so much pathbreaking work in this field in recent years. The volumes reflect that scholarship as well as valuable earlier studies. The authors also present the results of their own research and offer original interpretations. The goal is to bring together books that are readable and well informed and that stand on their own as introductions to significant periods in American thought and culture. There is no attempt to establish a single interpretation of all of America's past; the diversity, conflict, and change that are features of the American experience would frustrate any such attempt. What the authors can do, however, is to explore issues that are of critical importance to both a particular period and the whole of American history.

Today the culture and intellectual life of the United States is a subject of heated debate. While prominent figures summon citizens back to an endangered "common culture," some critics dismiss the very idea of culture—let alone *American* culture—as elitist and arbitrary. The questions asked in these volumes are directly relevant to that debate, which concerns history but too often proceeds in ignorance of it. How did leading intellectuals view their relation to America, and how did their compatriots regard them? Did Americans believe that theirs was a distinctive culture? Did they participate in international movements? What were the links and tensions between high culture and popular culture? While discussing influential works, creative individuals, and major institutions, the books in this series place intellectual and cultural history in the larger context of American society.

In this book we hear a number of voices expressing alarm at the direction of American culture: religion is being stifled by evolutionary science; philosophy is losing coherence; ethnic diversity and female assertiveness threaten the premises of culture and education; materialism and conspicuous consumption debase the spirit. Other voices are much more optimistic about new directions in academic disciplines and social values. These are not voices of the 1980s and 1990s but 1880s and 1890s, and there are many differences between today's controversies and those of a century ago. Yet there are similarities too, as George Cotkin reveals in his exploration of the earlier era's "reluctant modernism." American intellectuals persistently tend to consider their doubts and quandaries of recent origin and to envy the certainties and harmony of earlier generations. Even those who take a longer view may date the origins of "modernity" to World War I or the 1920s. But Cotkin makes a strong case for the continuity between the end of the nineteenth century and the end of the twentieth. In examining a wide range of responses to "modernity," he acquaints us with some men and women who were confident about the progress of American culture, with many others who were cautious and ambivalent, and with a few who were exceedingly pessimistic. This book is a good example of how looking closely at a relatively short period of time can improve our perspective on issues of lasting importance.

LEWIS PERRY
Series Editor

Preface

In 1894 philosopher William James complained to his brother, novelist Henry James, that "the only terms on which modern life offers a man anything are those of *all* or *none*."[1] By the turn of the century Gertrude Stein, once a psychology student of James's, would come to exemplify—indeed, to celebrate—a modernist sensibility that forced one to choose either the new or the old, nothing in between. "Act so that there is no use in a center," wrote Stein. Moreover, Stein refused to wear the cultural garments of the past: "One must never forget that the reality of the twentieth century is not the reality of the nineteenth century, not at all."[2]

During the years 1880 to 1900 a generation of American intellectuals perceived the imperative to be absolutely modern, to reject the wisdom of tradition, as a dangerous notion, if not a downright silly one. Their favorite sword of thought was intended to cut out a center, a middle ground between what they perceived to be the comforting but weakening assumptions of Victorianism and the exciting but frightening implications of modernity. Even William James, who worried that the choice was either *"all* or *none,"* based his philosophy on accommodationist principles. Thus, American thinkers of this era were reluctant modernists, attempting to synthesize the traditions and ideals of Victorianism with the challenges and possibilities of modernist streams of thought.

The terms *Victorianism* and *modernism* cry out for definition. Each conceptualization helps to define a style or sensibility and an intellectual constellation. With them the historian may paint, albeit in an impressionistic manner, the general outlines of a distinctive historical period. Victorianism has been succinctly described by Henry F. May as resting confidently upon the bedrock of the ideals of progress, moralism, and culture.[3] Victorians also craved certitude, emphasized control, and proudly upheld a patriarchal view of the world.

Modernism is an elusive but compelling conceptualization. Sometimes modernism is conceived as a specific shift in styles of artistic representation that began around the turn of the century. When transformed into *modernity*, it may capture everything from the Cartesian philosophical revolution of the seventeenth century to the momentous change in the late nineteenth century that ushered in a bureaucratized and rationalized vision of the world. Modernism is often deemed an adversarial culture; in order to survive, it must challenge familiar assumptions and styles of thought. At the heart of the modernist temper, in this definition, was a feeling, verging on a certainty, that the world was an alien, confusing, and not altogether comfortable place to dwell. But all was not despair. Some modernists promoted the scientist no less than the artist as a cultural hero. By uncovering truths of nature or self, the scientist and the artist were engaged in the act of creating a new world.

For the purposes of this book, modernism and modernity will be considered as intimately connected with the Darwinian revolution in science, and especially with the concept of evolution. In modernist fashion, Darwinism posited change, process, and struggle as essentials; it promised little succor to those thinkers who craved a solid, unshifting foundation for values and beliefs. But the appeal of Darwinism was never absolute. Most thinkers worked hard to negotiate a compromise between their cherished ideals of progress, moralism, and culture and the concepts of ceaseless change and challenge to authority, which Darwinism appeared to substantiate strongly.

The upsetting possibilities of the Darwinian position, however, were lessened by a view that equated evolution with assured progress. In this vision, the more things changed, the more they remained the same. Traditional moral and cultural beliefs only seemed to grow stronger, many intellectuals announced, as the forces of evolution played themselves out. This synthesis largely defined the contours of American thought in the final two decades of the nineteenth century.

Reconciliation came at a price and did not pass unchallenged. Zealous in their pursuit of order and progress, evolutionary theorists sometimes put the complex world of experience and change into a comfortable but not always intellectually credible living room furnished with gross generalizations, absurd deductions, and racist hierarchies. Some thought these perspectives missed too much of what was occurring outside the drawing rooms of Victorian culture. The most challenging and original thinkers of the age—William James, John Dewey, Newman Smyth, Charlotte Perkins Gilman, and Franz Boas—attempted to jump into the flow of experience, change, and complexity, into the raging waters of modernity. Nonetheless, they continued to retain much of the order and system, the certitude and progress, that the Victorian mindset had promoted.

Victorian cultural proprieties would in time be questioned as well. Fin de siècle aestheticism, literary and artistic naturalism, and the acid-tinged, ironic cultural commentaries of Henry Adams, Thorstein Veblen, and Louis Sullivan melted the sensibilities that had informed Victorian culture. No less threatening was the shift from a culture of scarcity and production toward a culture of abundance and consumerism. For all of the changes charted, however, the proud ship of Victorian values continued to sail with a strong tail wind. Self-appointed custodians of culture, cognizant of the forces threatening to upset presumed cultural unity and truth, sought to develop and disseminate their cultural values to the population at large. Through the development of a literary and artistic canon and through the institutions of school and museum, custodians of culture desperately sought to weave the thread of Victorianism into the normative fabric worn by every American. This attempt to create a common public culture failed. In part, the cultural elite proved to be divided among themselves; a significant sector came to view Victorianism as a culture devoid of excitement, marked only by a *tedium vitae*. In evoking this imagery, they developed a discourse of heroism that promised cultural revitalization along lines quite distinct from those originally associated with Victorian idealism.[4]

Increasing cultural heterogeneity and class divisions made the ideal of a unified public culture into little more than a utopian dream. But dreams often come true, albeit in a slightly different version than initially anticipated. The force of consumerism, which horrified the custodians of culture, eventually came to promote social and cultural unity. With the rise of the department store and modern forms of entertainment, a culture based on the possibility of defining the self through desire and enjoyment seemed closer at hand. By the turn of the century this consumerist mentality helped to define modern American culture.

By 1880 America was being transformed from small-town communities, where individualism was a birthright as well as a commodity, into large cities, where the power and presence of the individual, as well as the unity of the self, came into question. The interdependencies fostered by a market society called forth social and economic explanations that seemed far removed from individual initiative. In the wake of this change, notions of causality and responsibility, of freedom and possibility, were questioned. Indeed, if America had seemed to an earlier generation to be blessed with the calm of certitude and homogeneity, the multitudes of immigrants to America's shores promised heterogeneity and cultural conflict. As the workshop of the preindustrial age gave way to the massive factory and the corporation (thanks to the climate of competitive capitalism), the rise of class conflict threatened to topple the established order. Changes in the social and economic structure of society hardly stand apart from shifts in the intellectual and cultural realm. Not surprisingly, the intellectual and cultural life of the era 1880–1900 reflected the constancy of change and the presumption of a new world dawning.

Reluctant modernist intellectuals were, in essence, engaged in what might conveniently be referred to as a "search for order" in the domain of thought and culture.[5] Intellectuals developed systems of thought that attempted to recognize fully, even if painfully, the ubiquity of change and the possibility of chaos, while seeking to impose or to create unity and order, sometimes through a new synthesis in thought. The foundations that had upheld the structure of Victorian thought eventually crumbled in the face of intellectual as well as economic change. Reluctant modernists played a role in this momentous transition through their willingness to entertain new ideas, to think seriously about the challenges of modernity. But these thinkers also showed themselves unwilling to revel in the destruction of values associated with modernity; they refused to applaud the chaos and disorder. Instead, most of the thinkers studied in this volume attempted to reconcile as best they could the values of an earlier period with the ideals of a new era. In the process, of course, nothing would remain the same.

Acknowledgments

Writing, usually the most solitary of occupations, can also be a wonderfully communal enterprise. Each chapter finds its way into the hands of a colleague or friend, there to be criticized or complimented or simply acknowledged. Craig Harlan and Robert Rydell have read this entire book and offered useful hints, proper admonitions, and great support. They are the best of friends. I have been immensely aided by the sage prescriptions of Paul Jerome Croce, Sarah Elbert, and Ann Schofield regarding individual chapters or clusters of chapters. All five of these scholars should bask in the sunlight of this volume's successes; they bear none of the blame for its problems. David A. Hollinger and James Hoopes are thanked for their general support, insight, and example.

I have been appreciably and oftentimes materially aided by the generosity and support of the Department of History and the School of Liberal Arts at California Polytechnic State University. My research has been made easier by the efficient and friendly offices of the Interlibrary Loan Division at Cal Poly.

Strong appreciation goes to my wife, Marta Peluso, for her splendid and never-ending encouragement, and to my parents, Morris and Estelle Cotkin, for their consistent support. My wife's family, Louis, Pat, and especially Patti Peluso, have also contributed to this project.

Lewis Perry has been a model editor, carefully and critically reading the manuscript. I owe much to his sagacious and demanding editorial eye. Anne Jones, executive editor at Twayne, has been supportive at all times. Regina Morantz-Sanchez, an outside reader of the manuscript, helped me with her favorable comments.

This book is dedicated to the friends listed above and to many others un-named in these acknowledgments. Their presence in my life helped in various ways in the composition of this book. I thank all of them for their friendship and support.

one

The "Tangled Bank" of Evolution and Religion

Charles Darwin closed his justly famous *Origin of Species* (1859) with a convincing metaphor of nature as a "tangled bank," full of different and complex forms, informed by confusing yet compelling laws. The diversity and complexity of nature's world, so emphatically described in Darwin's account of the process of evolution, would in time come to serve as an apt description for interpretations of his own text. In the eyes and especially in the hearts of many late-nineteenth-century American intellectuals, ministers, and scientists, the meaning and significance of the laws and implications of *Origin of Species* represented a "tangled bank" of interpretation.

Darwinism is now read as positing that the evolutionary development of the species from common ancestors was an agonizingly slow process. Continuity and change coexist as the double doors into Darwin's system. Variations are selected for survival or demolition according to their value or inutility in the struggle for existence. While Darwin himself admitted that he was weak on what caused the variations that occurred from generation to generation (bereft as he was of a modern doctrine of genetics and heredity), natural selection figured centrally in his theory, if not exclusively, as the mechanism that determined which variations would survive. And in the common understanding, Darwinism posed a fundamental and perhaps unresolvable challenge to religious belief by emphasizing a world of purely natural laws without apparent direction. It is in that challenge that Darwinism's proximity to the essence of modernist thought—the idea of ceaseless, undirected change—may be seen most fully.

The foregoing account may seem particularly straightforward to today's reader. Many Americans in the final third of the nineteenth century, how-

1

ever, did not have our present-day comprehension of Darwinism. Instead, they fished at the "tangled bank" of his text and reeled in a more traditional, less challenging message. Why? To begin, Darwin's scientific work was bathed in a host of elusive metaphors and theoretical uncertainties. The text of *Origin of Species* left ample room for interpretation of crucial points: How do variations occur? Are mechanisms in addition to natural selection at work in the process of evolution? Are design, order, and progress inherent in the process of evolution?

According to the readings of various American interpreters, Darwin promoted order and design in the natural world. Plenty of room remained for the guiding and beneficent wisdom of God in the process of evolution. Whether scientists or theologians, most American thinkers in the period 1880–1900 used Darwinism, as well as other doctrines of evolutionary development, to support and extend traditional beliefs. These thinkers were reluctant modernists, quite willing to open their worldviews to the logic and language of modern evolutionary science but not willing to abandon their traditional beliefs in the process. True, they saw *Origin of Species*, and science in general, through glasses tinted by their most cherished assumptions, but they did not consciously misrepresent Darwin and evolutionary theory to fit their own needs. Indeed, Darwin, the great evolutionist, actually shared some of their assumptions.

Consider the central metaphor of natural selection. Darwin initially encountered it when examining how plant and animal breeders selected certain desired variations for cultivation. Variations that breeders allowed to be passed on to future generations eventually created new varieties of plants and animals. Darwin simply inserted the environment into the role of the professional breeder: nature as selector of variations. Natural selection's inherent problems as a metaphor stemmed from its presupposition of a breeder—someone or something that actively selects variations for survival or demise. Ultimately, as Darwin came to regret, the metaphor suggested an anthropomorphic vision of nature. Adam Sedgwick communicated to Darwin in 1866, "You write of 'natural selection' as if it were done consciously by the selecting agent."[1] Describing and defining the possible meaning and nature of this consciously selecting agent would become a major imperative for intellectuals on both sides of the Atlantic.

While Darwin's great accomplishment was his emphasis on natural selection as the mechanism for instituting change within species, he never ruled out a role for other mechanisms in the evolutionary process. Indeed, with each successive edition of *Origin of Species*, Darwin conceded more credibility to the logic of inheritance of acquired characteristics, a doctrine now discredited but popular at the time of Darwin's writing. Finally, while Darwin generally was loath to suggest that the development of the species led toward any progressive or predesigned end, he was guilty of alluding to a beneficial direction for natural development in crucial passages of his work.

Darwin, after all, had been greatly impressed by the ingenuity of William Paley's famous early-eighteenth-century argument in favor of design in nature. Darwin followed in the wake of a long tradition of natural theologians who had maintained that nature was defined by the ubiquity and genius of God's hand. How else, Paley and others had inquired, might one explain the incredibly complex mechanism of the eye? While Darwin preferred to see the eye as developing from natural causes, he nonetheless discovered utility in nature, even to the extent that he allowed that a role for God existed within the rules of nature: "I have said that Natural Selection is to the structure of organised beings what the human architect is to a building. The very existence of the human architect shows the existence of more general laws; but no one, in giving credit for a building to the human architect, thinks it necessary to refer to the laws by which man has appeared."[2] Thus, even when celebrating the singular necessity of natural laws, Darwin left room for the idea of a Creator acting behind the scenes, albeit by regular laws rather than by divine, occasional interdictions.

Initial Reception of Darwinism

The nineteenth century was an era marked by monumental changes. Earthshaking political revolts in France and America toppled entrenched monarchies and conceptions of the polity. The century was marked by nothing so much as political, intellectual, and physical movement—hurried, intense, exciting, frightening, and confusing. The industrial and transportation revolutions transformed concepts of time and space in both theory and practice. In the process of transformation, traditional ideals and realities of community, caste, and class were also damaged. In the world of ideas, new modes of thought undermined traditional foundations for knowledge. Confidence in the religious and secular verities of an earlier age trembled and sometimes disappeared.

Not surprisingly, the middle class—which in many ways was responsible for, or at least implicated in, initiating the monumental changes central to that century—sought security in the belief that nature and life had an essential design and order.[3] In the face of the all-too-apparent chaos surrounding the era, paeans to progress became intellectually respectable and emotionally necessary. Church and society enthusiastically espoused a religion of progress. The intellectual and emotional edifice of Victorian confidence in order, design, and progress generated the expectations crucial in directing the interpretation of evolutionary ideas in America.

Evolutionary ideals arrived at an American shore already receptive to science. In the antebellum period, scientists in laboratories and amateur students of nature exulted in the empirical, practical, and comforting realities of science. Each careful scientific examination of nature apparently demonstrated the regularity of law and the impressive hand of the Divine in the universe. Science in antebellum America attached its flag to the pole of American democracy and individualism. As presented in popular lyceum lectures, science upheld a vision of truth as a birthright of the multitude; responsibility, tinged with care and moderation, was presumed to govern the scientific frame of mind.

Most important, scientific truth in general was not regarded as counter to religious truth. Relations between science and theology in the age of scientific empiricism and natural theology before 1859 were invariably pleasant. Even when Charles Lyell's *Principles of Geology* (1830–33) challenged the literalness of the Bible on the age of the earth and the antiquity of man, religious leaders had not succumbed to a know-nothing antagonism to science. Nor, for that matter, did the researches of Germans Friedrich Schleiermacher and David Friedrich Strauss on the historicity of the Bible have any apparent debilitating effects on religion. American theologians deftly maneuvered the Bible into a position that would agree in spirit, if not always in letter, with the latest in scientific or historical research. On the eve of the Darwinian revolution, Oliver Wendell Holmes, Sr., found that science demonstrated the world's "premeditation, power, wisdom, greatness, prescience, omnipotence, providence." To the familiar melody of natural religion, Holmes sang out that "all these facts in their natural connection proclaim aloud the One God, whom man may know, adore, love; and Natural History must, in good time, become the analysis of the thoughts of the Creator of the Universe as manifested in the animal and vegetable kingdoms."[4]

The introduction of Darwinian ideas into America was a slow process—less a storm than a gentle sprinkle. Discussion of Darwinism in the newspapers was largely confined to its newsworthiness. Thus, analysis of Darwinism in the popular press peaked in 1876, during the visit of staunch evolutionist Thomas Huxley to America, and again in 1882, the year of philosopher Herbert Spencer's tour and Darwin's death. More pages were devoted to analyses of Darwinism from 1880 to 1900 than from 1860 to 1880. This delayed reaction may be explained by historian Jacques Barzun's hypothesis that the ideas of an elite group become the concepts of middlebrow intellects in the next generation before becoming the common assumptions of society by the third generation. Also, Darwinism's birth coincided with the years of the American Civil War and Reconstruction; the educated public was therefore distracted from Darwinism and its possible implications for traditional religious and secular ideas. Many recognized the troubling challenges that Darwinism might pose to religious views that depended on the immutability of the species, the reality of design and order in nature, and, of course, the veracity of the Biblical story of creation as contained in the book of Genesis—but no one seemed to perceive a need to respond immediately to Darwin's volume. After all, responsibility for the initial evaluation of Darwin's ideas had fallen into the capable and pious hands of America's scientific community. Sustained theological and cultural wrestling with Darwin's ideas would not commence before the scientists' verdict was in.[5]

By the mid-1870s evolution, variously interpreted, had cleared most hurdles of opposition within the scientific community in England and America. Certainly, pockets of absolute resistance still existed, but by and large the doctrine of evolution by either natural selection or the inheritance of acquired characteristics had come to seem compelling, if not obvious. Emphasis on natural laws appealed to the professionalizing requirements of a developing community of scientific professionals. Paleontologic research into the development of the horse, conducted separately by O. C. Marsh and Edward Drinker Cope, helped to lend plausibility to the idea of the evolution of the species. Many scientists switched allegiance, from the antievolutionism of Louis Agassiz, famed professor of geology and zoology at Harvard's Lawrence Scientific School, to the evolutionism of Charles Darwin. Many of America's most influential scientists—Nathaniel Southgate Shaler, Joseph LeConte, Alpheus Hyatt, and even Alexander Agassiz (son of Louis Agassiz)—converted to some form of an evolutionary hypothesis. Once this mass conversion process had become apparent within the scientific community, the ground was cleared for a full, public evaluation of the implications and import of Darwinism.[6]

Science occupied a seat of honor in American culture, thanks to its conquests in the physical and material realm and its long connection with a natural theology that had viewed all scientific advances as proof positive of order and logic in the natural world. Its function was at once normative and authoritative. The scientist had become a hero in American society, a dedicated sentinel of truth. In the words of Charles Peirce, America's greatest technical philosopher, "It is the man of science, eager to have his every opinion regenerated, his every idea rationalized, by drinking at the fountain of fact, and devoting all the energies of his life to the cult of truth, not as he understands it, but as he does not yet understand it, that ought properly to be called a philosopher. To an earlier age knowledge was power, merely that and nothing more; to us it is life and the summum bonum."[7] The modern scientific frame of mind, committed to analyzing the concrete, to demanding rigorous inductions as opposed to weak idealizations, constituted the mark of cultural sobriety, a sign of modernity as opposed to superstition. Josiah P. Cooke, professor of chemistry and mineralogy at Harvard University and a man who wore his religious orthodoxy proudly, spoke glowingly of a "scientific culture." He pronounced, "I must declare my conviction that no educated man can expect to realize his best possibilities of usefulness without a practical knowledge of the methods of experimental science."[8]

Science and religion were joined as the siamese twins of nineteenth-century America. "The similarity between scientific and religious values," writes historian Charles Rosenberg, "made it natural for most Americans to move fluidly from one intellectual and emotional realm to another. Science, like religion, offered an ideal of selflessness, of truth, of the possibility of spiritual dedication—emotions which in their elevating purity could inspire and motivate."[9] A desire for truth, for the power it bestowed in both science and culture, necessitated a full accounting with Darwinism. But the openness of the scientific position and the horizon of assumptions shared by most American thinkers largely helped to define the interpretation of the text of evolution in both scientific and religious circles. There was no monologue with Darwinism; various voices competed for acceptance. All possessed scientific credibility, and all accepted evolutionary outlines for development.

Religious Opposition to Darwinism

Those who would accept evolutionary ideas in the 1880s had first to confront opposition to Darwinism. Overall, firm opposition to evolutionary ideas was minimal in America. But biblical and theoretical assumptions often combined to spell antagonism toward the Darwinian theory of evolution. Some orthodox religionists, armed with a literal interpretation of the Bible, found it difficult to reconcile Darwinism with the book of Genesis. Anti-Darwinians shared a common emotional and intellectual adherence to a scientific method that stressed empirical investigation and careful ordering of facts. They were uncomfortable with the apparent leaps of scientific logic and hypothesis formation that supported the structure of Darwinism's message. Thus, some anti-Darwinians were moved less by theological concerns than by competing philosophies of science.

Theological and philosophical opposition to Darwinism continued to exist among American intellectuals well after Louis Agassiz's powerful attacks against evolution had been launched in the 1860s. Anti-Darwinians were convinced that acceptance of Darwin's ideas meant inhabiting a world without deity, design, or direction. Ironically, in some ways their understanding of *Origin of Species* corresponds closely to Darwin's stated intentions and to what has since become a commonly accepted reading. But oppositional reading left little room for interpretive license or the play of the intellect.

Rigid anti-Darwinians occasionally refused to countenance dissent within the ranks of the true believers in religion. In the name of theological purity, they sought to resist the tide of challenge and change. Religiously oriented evolutionists faced censure. James Woodrow's address "Evolution," delivered to the Alumni Association of the theologically conservative South Carolina Theological Seminary in 1884, was benign on evolution and fervent on religion. Woodrow gently asserted that "every word" of the Bible remained sacred and divinely inspired even when the truth of evolutionary doctrines appeared to contradict it directly. Woodrow assured his listeners that design was central in the universe; evolution simply represented God's way of working within the world. Nevertheless, these sentiments proved controversial, and Woodrow was forced out of his position as professor of natural science. Similarly, Alexander Winchell, an important geologist at Vanderbilt University, in his address "Man in the Light of Geology," presented a mild version of Darwinism. In response, the Methodist leadership of the university fired Winchell. Although the controversy over evolution was muted within American Catholicism, Father John A. Zahm, professor of physics at Notre Dame University, also suffered for his espousal of evolution. In *Evolution and Dogma* (1896), Zahm calmly proclaimed "evolution a theory which is in perfect accordance with science and Scripture." Nonetheless, in 1889 Zahm was forced to withdraw his book from circulation when he learned of opposition from Rome.[10]

Charles Hodge, professor of theology at Princeton University, in *What Is Darwinism?* (1874), presented the most famous and succinct condemnation of evolutionary ideas. Darwin's implicit questioning of biblical literalism troubled Hodge less than Darwin's "reject[ing] all teleology, or the doctrine of final causes. He denies design in any of the organisms in the vegetable or animal world." Hodge refused to jettison his belief in a final cause—a natural order and progression in nature and life. Since the notion of design, or predetermined ends, was central to any religious cosmology, Hodge concluded that "no teleologist can be a Darwinian." In his famous summing-up of objections to Darwinism, Hodge answered the question "What is Darwinism?" with the thunderous pronouncement, "It is Atheism."[11]

Darwin's evolutionary message bothered other American thinkers as well. George Ticknor Curtis's *Creation or Evolution?* (1887) and Luther Tracy Townsend's *Bible Theology and Modern Thought* (1883) condemned Darwinism as a dangerous doctrine of materialistic atheism. Also at stake was what form of scientific analysis would rule—Baconian empiricism or hypothetical induction. Such considerations figured most strenuously in the work of Francis Bowen, Alford Professor of Philosophy at Harvard University from 1853 to 1889. Bowen found *Origin of Species* to be deficient in logic, an example of bad science that had easily transformed itself into a dangerous philosophy of modern pessimism and infidelity. Bowen referred to Darwinism as a "dirt philosophy" that debased social stability and undermined happiness. He declared that "civilization which is not based upon Christianity is big with elements of its own destruction."[12]

Christian Darwinists

Most American intellectuals attempted to reconcile their religious assumptions with a theory of evolutionary development. The structure and content of such accommodations varied widely. At one extreme stood "Christian Darwinists," who embraced many of the controversial tenets of Darwinism without flinching in their religious devotion. A small circle of scientists and religious believers who supported Darwin fully, including Asa Gray and George Frederick Wright, attempted to demonstrate that Darwinian ideas posed no threat to traditional theology; indeed, they claimed that Darwinism actually updated and improved the idea of design. Yet for every Gray and Wright, scores of other intellectuals virtually ignored Darwinism. Nonetheless, they identified themselves as confirmed evolutionists, albeit of a non-Darwinian denomination. The interpretive banks of evolution were tangled indeed.

Asa Gray, in the preface to his important defense of evolutionary ideas, *Darwiniana* (1876), described himself as "a Darwinian, philosophically a convinced theist, and religiously an acceptor of the 'creed commonly called the Nicene,' as the exponent of the Christian faith." Gray, who was known as the "American bulldog" in support of Darwinian evolution, had slowly converted to the evolutionary hypothesis. His own scientific work in classifying the flora of eastern North America and Japan had established the geographic distribution of species with evidence of their transmutation over time. Gray's botanical studies had also proved helpful to the development of Darwin's own thesis. It would be going too far, at least in Gray's case, to suggest that he was untroubled by the implications of Darwin's theory for religious truths. Compartmentalization of knowledge translated into a form of reluctant modernism: Gray accepted Darwinism in his scientific work, but he did not fully incorporate it into his theological ruminations.[13]

Gray asserted that true science must be metaphysically neutral; essential scientific ideas, based as they were on the functioning of natural laws, could be given either a theistic or an atheistic slant. Gray noted that Darwin himself was not atheistic and that his science teemed with proofs of design and teleology in the natural world. Although Darwin hesitated to pursue these arguments fully in *Origin of Species*, Gray's reading of the text brought them into full view. Gray contended that design reigned supreme in the natural world. He even proclaimed that Darwin had successfully reintroduced the concept of design and purpose into the organic world by suggesting that natural selection had utilitarian ends. Gray peppered his letters to Darwin with evidence of direction and purpose in nature. Darwin's responses to Gray's teleological interpretations were initially warm, but they grew progressively colder: "I am inclined to look at everything as resulting from designed laws, with the details, whether good or bad, left to the working out of what we may call chance."[14] Nevertheless, in 1883—more than 20 years after that statement by Darwin on the role of chance in the development of the species—Gray still proclaimed that an intelligence was behind the development of variations and the direction of adaptation, if not for all of the parts of nature, then certainly for nature as a whole.

Gray was not alone in reading an "evolutionary teleology" into Darwin in this fashion. Many scientists and theologians saw in Darwin's metaphor of natural selection the hand of a designer—and design implied purpose. In the essay "Evolutionary Teleology" (1876), Gray attributed order and chance to nature. If the traditional argument for design faltered in the face of apparently useless organs, the doctrine of evolution demonstrated how those organs had once served a perfectly utilitarian, and hence designed, purpose.

Darwinian teleology has the special advantage of accounting for the imperfections and failures as well as for successes. It not only accounts for them, but turns them to practical account. It explains the seeming waste as being part and parcel of a great economical process. Without the competing multitude, no struggle for life; and without this, no natural selection and survival of the fittest, no continuous adaptation to changing surroundings, no diversification and improvement, leading from the lower to higher and nobler forms. So the most puzzling things of all to the old-school teleologists are the *principia* of the Darwinian.[15]

George Frederick Wright followed the path laid out by Gray. A Calvinist minister, Wright was associated first with the Andover School and its New England Theology, and later with Oberlin College. For thirty years he was editor of *Bibliotheca Sacra*, an important and orthodox theological journal. Wright's geological excursions earned him the respect of leading scientists, and his textbook *The Ice Age in North America* (1889) was the standard work in the field. Thus, his impassioned and educated defense of the affinity between Darwinian science and Calvinist theology had an air of authority.

Lest readers of his spirited defense of Darwinism in *Studies in Science and Religion* (1882) be wary of its author's orthodoxy, Wright introduced himself as an "evangelical Christian," a committed follower of the doctrinal beliefs of Augustine and Calvin. What followed was a tour de force of close analysis and a series of judgments that usually came down positively on the side of Darwinian hypotheses.[16] Wright argued that critics of Darwinism, such as Charles Hodge of Princeton University, had failed to comprehend the essential epistemological assumptions central to modern science. Science did not pretend to embrace absolute knowledge, to explain everything, to account for every uncertainty. Modern science rested upon a foundation of hypothesis, generalization, and induction. No one sensibly claimed that the laws of gravitation were wrong as general theorems, even though they failed to account for the irregular tidal movements in the Bay of Fundy. In like manner, Darwinism, despite its occasional hesitations and confusions, offered the best available explanation of the diversity of species and the obvious facts of their historical development.

The utility of Darwinism presented no threat to orthodox theology, in Wright's opinion. He agreed with Gray that properly drawn scientific hypotheses were metaphysically neutral. Speculative philosophies of science, such as those developed by Herbert Spencer, the most popular philosopher of evolution in the nineteenth century, based their interpretations on an initial prejudice or assumption. In contrast, Darwin's science was empirical and careful; its truth, like all scientific fact, avoided the metaphysical or religious questions of the beginning or end of things. These concerns remained the venue of theologians and philosophers. By focusing on the laws and regularities of development, Darwin's challenge confined itself to questioning other scientific theories. Christians were required simply to indicate how Darwin's theories matched religious beliefs. Wright, in the most interesting part of his book, the chapter "Some Analogies Between Calvinism and Darwinism," proposed to demonstrate precisely how the two views were friendly to each other.

Wright constructed a series of parallel structures—a comparative anatomy—between the tenets of Calvinism, as outlined by Jonathan Edwards, and the ruling conceptions of Darwinism. Calvinist principles asserted that God alone was self-existence, and the universe the unfolding of His ideas. Wright's traditionalist belief posited God "behind everything, be it the fall of a sparrow . . . or the fate of each particular hair on our head." Little in these views was controversial for Christians of varied denominational affiliations; even theists such as Agassiz, with his doctrine of special creation through ideal forms, might adhere to this theology.

Interestingly, Wright's Calvinism refused to bow down to the era's predominant beliefs in sustained progress and the perfection of man. Sin existed in the world because of the events that had transpired in the Garden of Eden; the reality of the inheritance of original sin was reflected in the sad truth that many "will be consigned thereby to endless punishment." Some might have been better off never to have been born. Happiness was not man's lot in this life: "the universe is so vast that it is unsafe to assume that the happiness of particular individuals, or generations, even, much less of animals, is a prominent object of the existing order of things." Nevertheless, Wright acknowledged that the process of creation seemed to betoken a salutary end for the whole of humanity. Finally, rejecting the typical Victorian reverence toward man's powers of rational thought, Wright sternly recognized the imperfection of man's claims to understanding: "God's ways, though not absolutely unknown, are often inscrutable, compelling men to walk by faith and not by sight."

On the basis of these theological principles, Wright evaluated the implications of Darwinism for religious belief. He appreciated Darwin's hesitancy to posit progress as the essential thrust of evolution. Indeed, he observed, Darwinian development could result in "either advancement or degradation." Wright noted that the Calvinist idea of the inheritance of original sin paralleled the Darwinian concept of transmission, or continuity of variations from generation to generation. The ubiquity of strife in the natural world, carefully described by Darwin, actually supported Calvinist assumptions concerning man's fall from grace. Moreover, the entire process of natural development often appeared to occur in an utterly willy-nilly fashion. The fall from grace, in Wright's theology, rendered nature a shattered mirror of God's plan and turned the Bible into a sometimes confusing rendition of God's wisdom. Wright therefore approached the Bible and nature without the confidence and certitude that Hodges so complacently assumed. Wright's brand of theological modernism rested on a foundation of ancient doubt in the face of God's mystery and power.

Yet Wright did believe, both as a scientist and as a minister, that God worked through laws and according to an ordered and progressive design. Although nature might be "red in tooth and claw," marked by struggle and strife, Wright continued to maintain that the hand of divine guidance worked behind its horrific veil. In Wright's estimation, the apparent inutility of certain human organs served a purpose within God's mind. Everything that transpired was a fragment of a final cause—"the good of being." All rested on a bottom-line induction of God's ultimate benevolence. Old-time Calvinism—with its rejection of sentimental optimism and proud reason, according to Wright—accorded perfectly with the explanations and metaphorical images expressed in Darwin's *Origin of Species*. Gray summed it all up in 1883: "It is not *chaos* but *cosmos* that the true Darwinian has in mind, common though the contrary impression be."[17]

Gray and Wright were Christian Darwinians. While embracing Darwin's theory, they engaged in a process of revision. Gray's correspondence with Darwin reveals a sustained attempt to read Darwin's metaphor of natural selection as marked by the presupposition of an outside intelligence. This presumption necessarily placed design within the structure of Darwinism. Even Wright's acceptance of Darwinism had its limits. He readily acknowledged the validity of evolution as a slow process, and he suggested that the many criticisms of Darwin's hypothesis that rested on the failure to discover missing links would eventually be proved specious—but as a trained geologist, Wright remained open to the un-Darwinian possibility of sudden transformations. Following the work of American geologists Clarence King and Joseph LeConte, Wright entertained the idea of "paroxysmal evolution," which filled in some of the gaps in Darwinian theory and reintroduced God into the process of evolution: "He who believes in a providential Ruler can easily grant that the Creator, through the combination of the forces which produce a natural selection, may hasten the development of a variation even more rapidly and surely than man [as breeder] can do by his combination of these forces." In assigning indeterminacy to the rate of evolutionary change in nature, Wright continued to posit the influence and design of God behind the laws of nature. Thus, while Wright and Gray were champions of Darwinian modes of explanation, they also deviated from their scientific master's doctrines in favor of their Heavenly master's prerogatives. Each was reluctant to give up theological truisms in return for scientific modernism.[18]

Not all thinkers attempted to grapple with Darwinism as seriously as did Gray and Wright. For many intellectuals, the task was less to defend the scientific essentials of Darwinism than to demonstrate how a general evolutionary perspective could easily be reconciled with religious and moral presumptions. The road away from a theological rejection of evolutionary science is illuminated by the shifting thought of the old-school Presbyterians at Princeton. One of the leaders of the Princeton theology, Charles Hodge, had strongly dismissed Darwinism as atheism. Even before Hodge's death in 1878, however, Princeton theologians had initiated a full-scale reconciliation between Darwinism and evolution that became their credo throughout the 1880s and 1890s.

In 1868 James McCosh arrived in the United States from Scotland to assume the presidency of Princeton. He brought with him an orthodox Scottish Common Sense theology and a firm belief in the necessity of design in nature. Well before the first flash of the Darwinian revolution, McCosh had sought, in *The Method of the Divine Government* (1850), to move away from mechanical and particular analogies that proposed to demonstrate design in nature, and toward a system sustained in its whole by a pattern of shifting relationships and adjustments between all aspects of the natural world. With the dawning of the age of evolution, McCosh simply began to fit Darwin into this already well-drawn picture.[19]

In his fullest exposition, *The Religious Aspect of Evolution* (1890), McCosh revised Hodge's contention that Darwinism was atheism by arguing that "there was nothing atheistic in it if properly understood." If one recognized divine law operating behind and within evolution, then atheism was untenable. This logic required that one keep in mind God's role as First Cause. From this all secondary causes might be understood, and order and design in the universe discerned. Chance and chaos, the chief stumbling blocks to a religious adherence to Darwinism, were removed as obstacles when one recognized the beneficent ends toward which evolution proceeded. Not a strict Darwinian by any means, although he understood the doctrine quite well, McCosh combined a variety of developmental theories designed to prove order and design. He massaged biblical descriptions to make them fit with scientific exposition. Genesis and Geology were not contradictory, McCosh submitted, but analogous. He believed that he had solved the problem of understanding how the world could have been created in less than a week, simply by interpreting a biblical day as a geological epoch. McCosh marveled at how precisely scripture had been able to comprehend and demonstrate the essential structure of evolutionary development.[20]

In volume after volume, McCosh painted evolution in generally positive terms, and always as conducive with order and design. McCosh defined *de-*

velopment (he preferred the term to *evolution* and rarely considered natural selection the sole mechanism operating in the process of change) as marked by "progression"; in sum, "the tendency of animal life is generally upward." God, McCosh was convinced, had chosen to act through the process of development, transforming even the harsh doctrine of the survival of the fittest into "certainly a good provision." But McCosh did not intend to limit God's reign over the process of evolution to secondary or natural causes alone. God could have created species by direct acts of intervention as easily as through a slow process of development. Lest the orthodox shadow of Charles Hodge condemn him for overlooking the scientific lapses in Darwinism, McCosh noted that evolutionary doctrines failed to comprehend fully the ultimate origins and direction of development. A "mist" of mystery prevented science from gaining access to the divine mind or power behind everything. The explanation that natural law was the sole factor in development faltered: "Evolution of itself cannot give us the beneficent laws and specific ends we see in nature." Finally, seconding the generally held position of most theologians and many scientists, McCosh held that the mind could not, as certain Darwinians maintained, have developed from mechanical actions within the process of evolution or from inanimate matter. The introduction of mind required the direct intervention of God.[21]

McCosh was hardly a lonely voice in the Princeton acceptance of Darwinism. The distance covered in the movement away from Charles Hodge's wail of derision and toward a general acceptance of evolutionary doctrines can readily be seen in the work of Hodge's son, Archibald Alexander Hodge. After studying physics with Joseph Henry, A. A. Hodge became a minister; he accepted his father's theology, without major deviations, in his own *Outlines of Theology* (1866). There he rejected the Darwinian thesis of the transmutation of the species. A quarter of a century later, A. A. Hodge had made his peace with evolution. As did McCosh, Hodge viewed God as First Cause and proceeded to show how God's will might be accomplished through the working of natural laws. Seizing upon Darwin's metaphor of natural selection, Hodge found that if in "artificial breeding, man selects," then in natural selection one must assume that "nature selects." If this process of selection results in "the most careful adjustments to effect purpose," then there must be intelligence involved in nature, either in an immanent fashion or by virtue of the machinery having been made originally by "an intelligent Creator." Thus Hodge used an open but not unfair reading of *Origin of Species* to defend religious orthodoxy and to blunt more challenging interpretations of evolutionary doctrine. McCosh and Hodge were only two of the Princetonian voices effecting a reconciliation between science and religion. In *Theism and Evolution* (1886), Joseph Van Dyke, a onetime student of Charles Hodge at the Princeton Theological Seminary, proclaimed that progressive evolution was not at all atheistic or even challenging to religious orthodoxy. In fact,

Van Dyke confidently concluded, along with McCosh and Hodge, that religion had nothing to fear from the doctrine of evolution.[22]

Liberal Theology

Calvinistic theology of the type adhered to by Gray, Wright, and the Princetonians was on the wane in America after the Civil War, increasingly displaced by a sentimental religiosity that stressed the rationality and order, as well as the essential justice and beneficence, of God's creation. The theological effusions of famous minister Henry Ward Beecher accorded nicely with the secular beliefs of middle-class Americans in progress, prosperity, and reason. Optimism pushed Calvinistic pessimism to the side. Not surprisingly, a vision of science that stressed order over chaos, peace over struggle, would also become popular in this period.

Darwinism appeared on the American religious horizon at an opportune moment. American theologians were, at the time, attempting to make their theologies and practices more consonant with the new and pressing realities of urbanization, industrialization, and immigration. In addition to these tumultuous social concerns, specifically intellectual problems engaged the minds of many theologians. New methods of biblical exegesis and an increasingly critical understanding of history as a process of development and interpretation contributed to a revamping of traditional religious beliefs. In England and America a New Theology without firm denominational lines arose as a liberal response to issues intimately associated with the swirling currents of modern society and thought.[23]

The golden age of liberal theology in America spanned the second half of the nineteenth century; it was marked by an imperative to retain religious belief while propping it up with rational explanation. In light of the challenges of Darwinism, naturalism, and history, liberal theologians held to a system of beliefs that understood God as immanent in the development of culture and that maintained that society was progressing toward the Kingdom of God. Tied to these views, liberal theological modernism questioned biblical literalism. Finally, through either the Social Gospel of minister Walter Rauschenbusch or the Gospel of Wealth as preached by Beecher, these ministers were united in recognizing that religious ideas must not remain stagnant, divorced from the new forces transforming modern culture and ideas. Religious ideas had to confront scientific ideas, especially regarding evolution.

Recent historical research suggests that the more liberal the theologian, the greater the difficulty that individual had in reconciling religion with Darwinism. Thus, religious conservatives Gray and Wright, and to a lesser degree the Princetonians, were able to look with complacency at Darwinism's emphasis on the apparent chaos of the struggle for existence, as well as its rejection of progress. Such views corresponded closely to traditional Calvinist concepts of the limitations of man, knowledge, and progress. Yet acceptance of Darwinism was rarely wholehearted. Conservative theologians, along with liberals, worried about Darwin's antagonism toward the idea of design and order in the universe. While it is true that liberal ministers who supported an optimistic theology of progress and reason received relatively little sustenance from Darwinism's table, they did come to eat heartily from the menu of evolutionary ideas. The evolutionary theory digested, however, was not purely Darwinian (if such a species of theory existed at that time). Instead, these liberal theologians patched together ideas that allowed them to have the essentials of their revised theology without needing to cast science out of their Garden of Eden of religious belief. They could be modern but still traditional.

Henry Ward Beecher was typical of many who embraced evolution without inflicting any damage on cherished religious ideals. Although no one ever accused Beecher of being a great thinker, it might be fair to say that the strength of his mind was proportional to its familiarity with the intellectual and cultural desires of middle-class Americans. From his podium at the prestigious Plymouth Congregational Church in Brooklyn, New York, Beecher preached a theology marked by alternate doses of Victorian strenuousity and sentimentalism, along with an unshakable faith in man, reason, and progress. During much of his adult life Beecher attempted to banish the harsh and unloving God of his Calvinist upbringing in favor of a nurturing God of salvation and happiness. Highly ecumenical and beneficent toward everyone, sometimes to the point of excess and controversy, Beecher possessed ideals that are helpful in understanding American religion's acceptance of evolutionary doctrines.

Beecher discussed evolution in a vague manner. His lectures on *Evolution and Religion* (1885) rarely mentioned Darwin by name. Perhaps illustrating the general acceptance of evolutionary doctrines in American intellectual and cultural life, Beecher simply grafted some aspects of evolutionary doctrines borrowed from the natural sciences onto his longstanding belief in a historical and developmental interpretation of the Bible, humanity, and the moral sense. Not thoroughly versed in the details of Darwinism, Beecher pirouetted around the controversial issue of man's descent from other mammals with the statement that man had evolved from a lower, indeterminately defined form. Although the struggle for existence explained much about the process of development, Beecher focused on the importance of the introduction of the moral faculty among humans, which motivated men and women to care for those less able to provide for themselves. Beecher did, however, emphasize that struggle made the individual sharper and more successful. Nonetheless, the American businessman struggled in a nicer jungle than had his ancient ancestors.

Evolution became an explanatory principle for Beecher, valuable in tracing the development of religion from polytheism to modern Christianity. While people should not perceive God as subject to evolutionary development, their ideas or concepts of God certainly continued to thrive under the influence of evolution. Over the ages, people had increasingly cast off visions of God as stern and vengeful; notions of damnation and depravity as the birthright of humans were no longer widespread. Beecher proclaimed that "this wild heathenism, this outrageous paganism is lurking in the blood of the Church yet, but will be purged away by Evolution." Evolution became the merry mechanism of progress in the hands of this grand apostle of progress. Likewise, modern science became the method for analyzing the development of modern religion. In outlining the direction of social development, Beecher used evolutionary terminology in its most general sense, as promoting a world of comfort, amusement, and happiness. Indeed, Beecher's world, brought about by social and moral evolution, represented nothing so much as a Chautauqua campground meeting at which the middle class were lectured to and immersed in an ideology and a reality of comfort, calm, and complacency.[24]

Beecher was hardly alone in using evolutionary ideas to support a polite, optimistic type of religion. His disciple Lyman Abbott, who disagreed with Beecher on social issues, seconded his mentor on the efficacious nature of evolution: God worked within the world through evolution; God operated by secondary causes in the development of the natural and moral world; design and order reigned. In *The Theology of an Evolutionist* (1897), Abbott stated, "As God makes the oak out of the acorn, and the rose out of the cutting, and the man out of the babe, and the nation out of the colony, and the literature out of the alphabet, so God has made all things by the development of higher from lower forms. . . . God is never a manufacturer, but always does His work by growth processes."[25]

Growth and change, through scientific theories of evolution, quickly became central elements in the New Theology popularized by Beecher, Abbott, and others. One of the more liberal New Theologians, Octavius Brooks Frothingham, employed evolutionary ideas in the fight against dogmatic theology. Everything became subject to the scientific reality of ceaseless change. Recognizing in 1891 that "ours is a scientific age," Frothingham viewed modern science as enlarging and beautifying the world. Never veering too far from the reassuringly beneficent world of antebellum natural theology, Frothingham maintained that evolutionary theory had increasingly painted the world as it should be, in colors "orderly, harmonious, poetic." This picture, owing little to Darwin, illustrated the ability of thinkers to use evolutionary terminology in a way that maintained traditional theological beliefs while undermining "old-fashioned," dogmatic Calvinist views. Frothingham's reluctant modernism posited the centrality of evolutionary change in conceiving the world, without leaving his readers adrift in a sea of undirected, chaotic change. The final criteria for science, philosophy, and even truth might never be positively known until God revealed them, but everyone could rest assured that religion in America would be "emotional and enduring" as well as intellectual and reasonable. The force of directed evolution demanded nothing less.[26]

One hardly sees in Beecher, Frothingham, or even Abbott a sincere desire to come to terms with troubling implications of Darwinism for order and progress in the natural world. Greater minds than theirs, however, upon encountering the doctrines of Darwin, came to strikingly similar conclusions; the concept of evolution did little damage to the cherished and necessary ideals of design and order in the universe.

Newman Smyth was an important and energetic thinker. He was determined to be knowledgeable as both a theologian and a scientist. Thus, he worked in Yale University's biological laboratory to gain experience in experimental science. In a course of Lowell Lectures delivered during 1900 and 1901, Smyth attempted to demonstrate the unity, order, progression, and design of nature within an evolutionary framework that accorded well with the essentials of liberal New Theology.[27]

In the published version of his turn-of-the-century lectures, *Through Science to Faith* (1902), Smyth presented the progressive, developmental essence of revelation as the "one continuous course of nature."[28] Nature's path resembled a work of literature in its design: "Evolution is a novel with a plot." Smyth approached evolution from a recapitulationist perspective, positing that the later stages of the human species's development from lower to higher had largely recreated those that had come earlier until human development had finally reached its apogee as a "fulfilled prophecy" of progress.

Smyth believed that the concept of pure chance, which some considered essential to a Darwinian framework, was nothing more than an illusion. Smyth's proofs ranged from anecdote to analysis. He engagingly related a story involving the astronomer Kepler and his wife at their dinner table. A good salad, someone remarked, might come together simply by a chance meeting of lettuce, tomato, olives, and other ingredients. But, remonstrated Kepler's wife, it would not be "so nice and well dressed as this [salad] of mine is." Smyth observed that "If it requires intelligence to make so nice a salad, perhaps we may find good reason to suspect that Mind may have had considerable part to play in the evolution of such a world as ours."

Design, in the making of a salad or of the world, was the inherent reality of nature. With the polymath Lester Frank Ward as one of his guides, Smyth noted that while progress might not always be linear, it remained reassuringly certain. Chance played an important role, as Darwin and others suggested, but Smyth held that all atoms occupied a necessary place in God's monumental plan: "There is no limbo in nature for lost atoms. There is no apparent waste of energy in aborted possibilities of worlds." In contrast, one of the most troubling of Darwin's conclusions was that unbelievable waste occurred in the process of adaptation.

Yet Smyth did not find nature to be "a slovenly work-basket." Order existed in the physical and chemical structures of atoms, in the relationship between energy and stability, and in the higher organisms, in which structural order was coupled with a conscious intelligence that directed and (in the case of humans) interpreted life. In every more elevated stage of life, Smyth uncovered greater order, less chance, and fuller evidence of "the supreme fact of the one harmonized evolution of all the orders of nature."

Smyth realized that evolution might not be progressive—a concept that certainly represented a challenge to the essentials of his progressive theology. Degeneration theories promoted a Calvinist view that questioned the optimism of the New Theologians. Smyth acknowledged that "the most awful doctrine of the possibility of fall is opened by an evolutionary philosophy." In his view, while degeneration (whether in Calvinist terms of sin or in a biological sense) could affect the individual, it did not apply to the species as a whole. Man fell as an individual personality, perhaps by toppling out of his "type." Retrogression was analogous to individual sin. Happily, ultimate advance for humanity was preplanned into the process of evolution. As Smyth put it, "Man by his own motion cannot escape the rising sun. So the movement of evolution, the divine moment of it as a whole, shall bear man's personal history of sin on with it to the coming day of the Lord."

Smyth also considered, certainly more fully than Beecher, the variety of mechanisms that might be involved in the process of evolutionary development. He weighed contradictory evidence that variations might be either determined or haphazard. The convenient answer to the quarrel concerning the mechanisms behind evolution transcended biology and pointed in the direction of the spirit. Smyth contemplated the possibility that adaptation resulted from an "internal growth-force or a perfecting or progressive principle with real meaning." Yet his quasi-mystical effusions on the "other arrows in [nature's] quiver" were balanced by his recognition that natural selection was the fundamental method of evolution. Thus, for Smyth, Darwin's doctrine of natural selection became invested with spiritual, perfecting principles. The value of natural selection, its teleologic effect, was in keeping up a standard of excellence: "Natural selection acts thus as a perfecting principle of life."

If Smyth failed to engage the issue of waste and chaos fully, he simply followed Beecher and most other American thinkers in presuming that evolutionary development beneficently led to happiness and morality. In general, Smyth's theology of evolution was, as historian Sidney Ahlstrom has described it, a "benign naturalism." Nature's laws, originally crafted by God, had "worked well." When perceived in this light, they appeared to be moral in character and orderly in substance. Even the touchy subject of the struggle for existence took on a gentler coloring. The necessary severity of nature in eliminating the weak so that the strong might prosper gave way to unadulterated sweetness: "Play has entered in as a part of the very struggle for existence." In good Darwinian terms, Smyth proceeded to explain how play functioned in that struggle, how it represented a spiritual gift. Play presaged greater things that would come as evolutionary progress replaced evil with love.

Some materialist theories of evolution seemed to posit that humans were lost in an inexorable mechanistic process of evolutionary development. These theories robbed man of the capability or responsibility to act morally or ethically. In contrast Smyth, along with William James and other philosophers impressed with Darwin's doctrine on the development of the mind, found that the law of natural selection had led man to attain the power of consciousness. With consciousness, a critical factor in the evolutionary process, came responsibility—the ability to make choices. Man's conscious will promised to speed evolution's course. A more perfect adaptive harmony between individual and environment, the completion of man's social and spiritual evolution, greater individuality (*personality* was Smyth's favored term), and immortality loomed on the horizon.[29]

American Neo-Lamarckians

Liberal theologians were not alone in their attempts to join evolution to progress. Many important scientists were actively engaged in the 1870s, and especially in the 1880s, in developing the vibrant and influential American School of evolutionary science. American School leaders—scientists Edward Drinker Cope, professor of geology and mineralogy at the University of Pennsylvania; Alpheus Hyatt of the Boston Museum of Natural History; A. S. Packard, professor of zoology and geology at Brown University; and later, Henry Fairfield Osborn, president of the American Museum—labored hard to resuscitate the reputation of Jean-Baptiste de Lamarck, an evolutionist of the early nineteenth century. Lamarckian hypotheses stressed the inheritance of acquired characteristics and the use and disuse of organs. In contrast to Darwinian theories, they suggested that changes acquired through the exertions of a biological organism could be passed on to its progeny. This view accepted evolutionary development but did not see it as subject to the harsh laws of natural selection. American neo-Lamarckian scientists reintroduced Louis Agassiz's concept of ideal types with predetermined linear development, thus once again promoting the concepts of design and divine guidance in the process of evolution.

The scientists of the American School of neo-Lamarckianism were often former students of Agassiz, now converts to evolution. They were by no means outside the mainstream of American science; they occupied positions at prestigious universities (Harvard, Berkeley, and Chicago) and institutions (Boston Museum of Natural History) and controlled important publications *(American Naturalist)*. For nearly three decades, until the pivotal challenge mounted under the impetus of Mendelian genetics, which demonstrated the purely statistical nature of evolution, the American School presented alternatives to certain aspects of Darwinism while supporting an evolutionary framework.

Although members of the American School of evolution differed on the ultimate implications of a Lamarckian or Agassiz-oriented evolutionary schema, much of their work supported the thrust of the liberal theologians in attempting to reconcile evolution with religion. Evolutionists of the American School generally posited that design operated within the internal logic of each species, through what Cope described as "bathmism" or, more popularly, as "growth force." Faith in progress was buoyed by the suggestion that evolution was based on internal forces that initiated changes in a particular predesigned direction. Thus, change was marked by regular and predictable progress along linear paths of development, at least within certain parameters.

Acceptance of notions of the inheritance of acquired characteristics and the use or disuse of functions was commonly viewed as reintroducing responsibility, or willpower, to the organism or to its "type." This directed thinking away from the apparently helter-skelter evolution of Darwinism toward an evolution that followed a sustained, logical pattern that accorded more comfortably with both religious and secular teleologies of progress. Evolutionary theory thus established the importance of mind and culture as inherited factors in the process of evolution—a development that owed much to the formulations of Herbert Spencer's *Principles of Biology*. American scientist A. S. Packard wrote in 1894 that progress throughout human history had been due to the "principle of the inheritance of mental traits, [which] caus[es] the intellectual efforts of one generation to pass down and thus to have finally a cumulative effect." How else, asked Packard, "could there be any progress in human society"? In the work of the respectable scientists of the American School, discussions of the evolution of the species were never distinctly separated from considerations of social utility and possibility.[30]

The theories spun by the American School were scientifically credible and sufficiently Darwinian in essentials to be accepted by a wide audience of scientists, intellectuals, and theologians. For those unable to accept fully the Darwinian emphasis on the natural history of mind, the neo-Lamarckian view explained mind in more idealistic terms. In *The Theology of Evolution* (1887), E. D. Cope wrote that "mind was one at the start; and all this evolution has been simply due to the active exercise of mentality, or of mental qualities." This tautology allowed Cope to posit consciousness and design of mind in even the simple amoeba. Mind controlled matter; it was primal, although its development was beholden to conditions furnished by the environment. Purely natural selection, Cope asserted in his popular *The Origin of the Fittest* (1886), did not explain how variations occurred, only how they were selected by the environment. For Cope, whose view was echoed by many religious authorities, the appearance of useful variations—consciousness or morality, for example—was best explained as the result of either internal or external growth forces of a designing nature—not, as proposed by certain Darwinians, as the haphazard outcome of natural selection.[31]

Joseph LeConte

No scientist played a larger, more sustained role than Joseph LeConte in making evolutionary thought accessible and acceptable to the religious-minded. He masterfully combined many of the ideals of the liberal theologians with the scientific premises of the American-School theorists. His most important scientific work was done in geology (his *Elements of Geology* written in 1878 was a standard text) and binocular vision; he also demonstrated impressive range and familiarity with biological science. Although deeply religious by nature and inclination, LeConte was not affiliated with any particular denomination. Born in the South, he was deeply affected by the Civil War. After attending the Lawrence Scientific School at Harvard, where he studied with Louis Agassiz, LeConte moved west and taught at the University of California at Berkeley from 1869 until 1901. Although he later rejected his mentor's fierce antagonism toward the concept of evolution, LeConte always credited Agassiz for pointing toward an evolutionary understanding of the world. This desire to be conciliatory toward his antievolutionist former advisor was replicated in LeConte's approach regarding both religion and evolutionary theory.

By the 1880s the battle between the idealistic system of Louis Agassiz and the scientific view of Darwin had ended; victory belonged to the evolutionists. Some, like LeConte, refused to declare an absolute winner of the fracas. To be sure, Agassiz had lost the battle over evolution; his finest students—Cope, Hyatt, and LeConte—all became confirmed evolutionists. LeConte tried to save Agassiz's reputation by announcing that without Agassiz there would have been no Darwin. He maintained that Agassiz, despite his firm opposition to the hypothesis that the human species had undergone transmutation, had proved geologic and embryonic succession to be analogous, had demonstrated the progress of the universe as a whole, and had developed the inductive method to such a degree that it had become the recognized mode of modern scientific inquiry. Agassiz had simply not been able to follow the evidence and theory toward a doctrine of evolution. Moreover, Agassiz's religious beliefs, in LeConte's interpretation, prevented the great scientist from seeing the truth of evolution.

In many ways LeConte summarized the key ideas of his advisor and placed them within an evolutionary framework. Design and order were central to the universe. Movement of the whole was toward greater progress and increased spirituality; the law of succession correlated nicely with Darwinian perceptions of adaptation. Agassiz's idealistic system remained intact as LeConte announced that "design, purpose, adjustment, *adaptation* are not material things, but relations or intellectual things, and therefore perceivable only by thought, and conceivable only as the result of thought."[32]

LeConte's analysis in *Evolution: Its Nature, Its Evidences, and Its Relation to Religious Thought* (1888) was a pastiche of theories, at times strongly Darwinian in hue, at other times resolutely Lamarckian. LeConte's intent was not to defend Darwinian natural selection. He wanted to demonstrate that the doctrine of evolution, in any of its mechanisms, was decidedly compatible with a religious view of the world. At the beginning of *Evolution*, LeConte wrote that "the universal mistake of the age" was to imagine that a conflict necessarily existed between evolution and religion.

Admitting that some scientists had attempted to add a materialistic edge to evolutionary biology, LeConte countered by making it strongly idealistic. Development occurred through natural processes, yet divine agency was always intimately involved. This pushed LeConte in the direction of a doctrine of immanence, or a philosophy of pantheism. Although some thinkers had attempted to retain God by making Him once again the great Clockmaker who had developed through natural laws a universe in perfect motion, LeConte rejected any division between primary and secondary forces in evolution. Instead, he proposed that God not only had created the laws of natural development but also was "resident *in* Nature." Thus, "there is no real efficient force but spirit, and no real *independent* existence but God." God operated in nature through regular processes and acted on the spirit by revelation. LeConte backed away from a strong pantheism that might conflate God with every fallen leaf or drop of dew. God was a personality, not in the anthropomorphic sense of earlier theology but as "personal will immanent in Nature, and determining directly all its phenomena."

LeConte's spiritual theism was not successful in reconciling his often contradictory ideas—for example, the notion of God as immanent within yet separate from nature. But the theological gaps in his system were less important than the intent and scope of his analysis. LeConte attempted to show how what might at first glance appear to be chaos and tumult was in actuality part of a larger movement of the universe—on the whole, if not always in its parts—toward progress. His metaphysics of evolution left no doubt in readers' minds that evolution represented a new set of positive possibilities. In

Evolution, design was reintroduced into the universe along lines as beneficent as Paley's yet more scientifically respectable: "To the uncultured there is a distinct and separate design in every separate work of Nature. But, as science advances, all these distinct, separate, petty, man-like designs are merged into fewer and grander designs, until, finally, in evolution at last, we reach the conception of the one infinite, all-embracing design, stretching across infinite space, and continuing unchanged through infinite time, which includes and predetermines and absorbs every possible design. There is still design in everything, but no longer a separate design—only a separate manifestation of the one infinite design."

If this explication was too grand for comprehension, then LeConte returned to the issue of design a few pages later to reiterate that God, as the divine mind, was not simply one of many factors of evolution. Instead "All is mind or none; so also all is mechanics or none. It *is all mind through mechanics.*" All was God's mind; all would be under divine direction, with divine ends of immortality, happiness, and spirituality assured.

LeConte could not countenance the Darwinian view of natural selection that appeared to him to imply that cultural achievements, the mental baggage acquired by the individual and society, were not cumulative, capable of becoming the natural inheritance of future generations. To suggest otherwise indicated that each individual would have to recapitulate or rebuild the earlier stages of social and cultural development. To reclimb continuously the steps already taken meant that progress would be substantially slowed and the world rendered less hopeful. LeConte's Lamarckianism was reflected in his statement that "all our hopes of race-improvement, therefore, are strictly conditioned on the efficacy of . . . the fact that useful changes, determined by education in each generation, are to some extent inherited and accumulated in the race."

LeConte's fervent attempts to reconcile change and progress, religion and evolution, were popular—as indicated by the many favorable references to his work in volumes composed by theologians and scientists between 1880 and 1900. There was something for everyone in LeConte's work. But even he could not satisfy all religious believers. One minister from a Baptist church in Oakland, California, accused LeConte of "ruining" the minds of young people with his forthright allegiance to evolution. Such attacks were the exception rather than the rule. LeConte's public theology was appealing precisely because of its vagueness and sweet rationality. In private, his religious views were more controversial. In "A Brief Confession of Faith," written in 1890 and revised in 1897, LeConte expanded on the religious ideals he had initially outlined in *Evolution.* Much remained consistent, especially his firm belief that God was immanent in nature and the cause of everything spiritual and physical. If in his published works LeConte had been largely silent on the issue of the veracity of the Bible, in private he wrote that it "is not a divine word-book, but a record of the growth of the divine idea in the mind of man." The Bible was mired in its own historicity and reflected the "misconceptions characteristic of the age and of the writer." Neither the Bible nor nature were to be worshiped as entities; each was to be adored as a receptacle through which God revealed Himself.[33]

LeConte used his credibility as a scientist and as a devout believer to reconcile religion and evolution, without threatening traditional faith in reason or design. He placed spirit throughout the universe and drove narrow materialism against a philosophical wall. Progress and hope exude from his pages. The historical and scientific evidence of the increasing ability of humans to employ their power of reason and their spirit over their base animal inheritance promised that the direction of evolutionary development threatened nothing sacred in the realms of religious or secular belief.

Evolutionary Religion and the Crisis of Faith

Conservative theologians such as Gray, McCosh, and Wright, along with liberal theologians like Beecher and Smyth, linked arms with respected scientists such as Joseph LeConte to transform the "tangled bank" of evolutionary theory into a comforting cultural, scientific, and religious ideal. Traditional religious ideas were packaged by them in the wrapping paper of modern science. If perhaps the specifics of Darwinism suffered in the process, the strength of the developmental ideal grew stronger. Theology adapted evolution and science to its own ends. But did this wedding between science and religion actually weaken religious belief?[34]

Historians commonly speak of a "spiritual crisis," a period of "unbelief," as central to America between 1880 and 1900.[35] Although many reasons might be offered to explain this state of affairs (one could even argue that religion was not in a state of crisis in this period), it is clear that a scientific perspective might actually have weakened religious doctrines in a variety of ways. After all, in this period many individuals from the elite classes wore their cloak of agnosticism in full view, while small-town agnostics and freethinkers readily flocked to the lectures of the great unbeliever of the age, Robert Ingersoll, who maintained that science and logic disproved the superstitions of religious belief.

But the infiltration of the virus of science into the lifeblood of religion may have occurred in a more subtle manner. Indeed, one argument goes, religious thinkers all too willingly succumbed to the virus. Well before the arrival of Darwin or evolutionary doctrines, Christian theology had begun to be harmed when it had attempted to incorporate into traditional dogma the new philosophy and mathematics of Descartes and Newton. Assimilation slowly moved religion away from its emphasis on the mysteries of grace, the sanctity of the individual's relationship with God, and the unfathomable experience of religious belief, and toward a theology that demanded a reconciliation between modern science and religion. And this reconciliation, many believed, had to be based as much on reason as on faith. What was gained in intellectual credibility in the short term may have eroded the long-term emotional power of religion. Science and religion became so closely connected as to become nearly indistinguishable. Why would an individual relish the power of religion, certain intellectuals argued, when the powers of science and reason presented themselves without the dogmatism and sectarian baggage that had historically accompanied religion?

In addition, many in this era of science maintained that a truly scientific perspective could only undermine the religious sensibility. Doubt, at least as interpreted by such popular sages of scientific wisdom as British scientists Thomas Huxley and W. K. Clifford, seemed to be the only properly scientific attitude to adopt on questions of religion. Rigorous doubt even questioned the right of the individual to hold any beliefs unsupported by empirical evidence, except those of the most narrow variety. Thus it became apparent that the intellectual credibility of a scientific age could require the suspension of religious belief.

In the minds of some analysts of the era, the negative impact of an evolutionary perspective, tinged with the colors of doubt, might undermine the permanency of religious values and demonstrate the historicity of all cherished assumptions. Moreover, an evolutionary perspective raised fundamental questions about authority and threatened to break down distinctions, at least in a functional sense, between the religion of an Episcopalian and the beliefs of a Maori. And—at least in comparison with the strenuous wrestling match between the intellect and the emotions of certain earlier Calvinist thinkers—the easy reconciliation effected by the ministers of 1880–1900 between evolution and religion appeared at times to have a stale air of moralism, of what Boston Brahmin intellectual Charles Eliot Norton once called "intellectual incompetence or exhaustion."[36]

Despite the logic of arguments for the deadening effects of science on religion, evolutionary perspectives often functioned to shore up religious beliefs. Such terms of derision as Norton's hardly seem to capture the intellectual inquisitiveness and honesty, as well as the emotional power and desire, that were written into the work of many of the era's religious thinkers. Smyth and LeConte, for example, wanted desperately to convert souls, but they also recognized the need for the mind to be convinced—especially in an age of scientific credulity—that an evolutionary perspective might strengthen religious belief rather than undermine it. The power of science was to accompany comfortably the strength of grace. Heightened awareness of the implications of evolutionary thought brought forth a fuller interplay between the traditional demands of religion and the changing realities that were moving America into the modern era.

American Protestant intellectuals had little choice but to seek reconciliation and accommodation. For them it was impossible to ignore the allure of science; that would have been intellectual apostasy. Likewise—especially given the hundred-year-old tradition of reconciling science and religion—it would have been absurd for them to pronounce suddenly that scientific explanation and religious belief occupied absolutely separate spheres. Cognizant of the problems involved in retreating into anti-intellectualism or pure emotionalism, American Protestant thinkers, by and large, happily took up evolutionary science and demonstrated that it accorded perfectly—perhaps too perfectly—with their theological perspectives.

To no less a degree than their theological brethen, American philosophers would be forced to confront the deep implications of evolution. They too would seek to reconcile philosophy's traditional quest for truth, order, and progress with the modern tendency of evolution to suggest that truth was by definition open to revision, never firmly established on a secure foundation. In grappling with this issue, the best minds in America sought to defend a viable tradition of security while opening thought to the process and change of modernity.

two

The Experiences of American Philosophy

The challenges of Darwinian and evolutionary ideas were extremely valuable in helping to develop and direct American philosophy in the closing decades of the nineteenth century. Influenced by scientific explanation and method, American philosophers reevaluated many conceptions that had long been taken for granted. This reexamination inspired these philosophers to move away from their discipline's traditional moorings in theology and to become excited about a scientific perspective, a new set of questions, and perhaps a different set of answers to some of the perplexing problems of life and thought.

Philosophical giants such as William James, Josiah Royce, John Dewey, and Charles S. Peirce, along with other less famous compatriots, began to reexamine the traditional foundations on which knowledge had been based. The classical philosophical presumption that truth, in order to be meaningful, must be predicated on ideal and nonshifting grounds, came to be replaced by a more evolutionary perspective—one that considered truth to be a process. The empiricism of modern science, its emphasis on careful observation of the specific processes and mechanisms operative in nature, moved American philosophers and psychologists toward a perspective that promoted experience over abstraction, adaptation over stasis. This imperative would result in the New Psychology associated with William James, John Dewey, and G. Stanley Hall. Finally, challenged by science to defend the ideals of religious belief rather than specific theological doctrines, American philosophers developed original and creative approaches that allowed religion to thrive without compromising the explanatory power of science.

Although the influence of Darwinism on American philosophy helped to

27

make it more modern in its methods and conclusions, such a shift must not be viewed as absolute. Like many of the theologians and scientists studied in the previous chapter, American philosophers sought to accommodate traditional ideals with modern notions whenever possible. Despite the sense of flux and uncertainty in the universe that evolutionary theory promoted, American thinkers managed to indicate that order was still a realistic hypothesis. Some held that order and logic were imposed on an open universe by the individual; others, following the lead of the German philosopher Hegel, saw a logic of development behind the facade of disorder. Thus, the challenges of new modes of thought led American thinkers to develop more creative, and perhaps more impressive, arguments to defend deeply entrenched American ideals and desires: the necessity of freedom and individualism, the validity of both science and religion, and the possibility of order and unity in the universe.

Philosophers accomplished these goals within a developing context of the rise of the modern university, but that did not mean that their considerations became overly technical or were isolated behind the ivy-covered walls of colleges, untouched by public concerns. Quite the opposite: between 1880 and 1900, as philosophy gained academic credibility, it strengthened its role as a public enterprise. This must be kept in mind, for it helps to explain the tremendous implications of philosophical rumination in this period. Public philosophy required that the philosopher consider perennial philosophical questions in a sophisticated manner, but it also expected the philosopher to be able to communicate his or her answers to a public audience. This not only gave power and sweep to the questions and answers that American philosophers contemplated; it also gave them a public role and a cultural resonance. In many ways, even when they were highly abstract, the ideas of philosophers were anchored in a set of social realities and cultural questions that were momentous to Americans in all walks of life.

The Rise of Professional Philosophy

Just after the conclusion of the Civil War, the production and distribution of knowledge in America exploded. Indeed, all aspects of American life changed in this period. Entrance into a modern age of industrial capitalism brought forth new demands, new realities. As Karl Marx put it, "All that is solid melts into air."[1] The transformations associated with this period—urbanization, industrialization, immigration, and the destruction of traditional lines of connection and causality—strongly indicated that the life of the mind would not escape unchanged.

No institution reflected monumental change more than the modern university. In 1870 there were 563 institutions of higher learning in the United

William James and Josiah Royce. *Courtesy of the Harvard University Archives*

States; by 1890 the number had swelled to 998. The growth of universities brought about a concomitant increase in the number of teachers—from 5,553 in 1870 to nearly 16,000 in 1890.[2] Changes were qualitative as well as quantitative. While it is no doubt an exaggeration to stress the chasm separating the antebellum college from the modern university, the content and style of learning did become transformed. Before the Civil War, for example, professors of philosophy not only taught a wide range of philosophy courses but also instructed students in mental science and the natural and physical sciences; to a large extent, students memorized their teachings by rote. By the turn of the century, such an uninspired and fragmentary approach to learning was banished from the modern university. Experts, armed with the requisite Ph.D. degree, instructed their students in the mysteries of specialized knowledge. Questions of methodology and experiment became as important as the content of a course. If the imperative behind the antebellum college had been to produce classically trained, generally educated young Christian gentlemen, the modern university sought, especially in the proliferation of advanced degree programs, to produce and train technically specialized professionals. These graduates with a scientific point of view would add to the sum of knowledge in a host of developing disciplines and professions.

In many ways, the rise of the modern university system, with its emphasis on secular education, dedication to science and public service, professionalization, and specialization, was the handiwork of a larger-than-life group of entrepreneurial educators. Just as robber barons like Jay Gould, John D. Rockefeller, and J. P. Morgan had transformed the landscape of American capitalism, an equally capable group of educational entrepreneurs—often in close collaboration with their counterparts from the business world—constructed a new academic environment for the expansion of knowledge. College presidents James B. Angell (at the University of Michigan from 1871 until 1909), C. W. Eliot (at Harvard from 1869 until 1909), Daniel C. Gilman (at Johns Hopkins from 1875 until 1902), and Andrew Dickson White (at Cornell from 1868 until 1885) helped to build the American university empire. They did little to upset the stock of ideas cherished by their institutions' wealthy benefactors, proud alumni, and the American public. Despite their conservative attachments, they erected a structure that would often house independent and creative thought.

The professionalization of philosophy lagged behind that of other university disciplines. The American Historical Association, American Economic Association, and Modern Language Association were all formed between 1883 and 1885, with the purpose of representing the interests of their respective disciplines. The exact nature of such interests was not always immediately clear, as amateurs and professionals within each field battled to define the direction and methods of study.[3] The American Philosophical Association did not achieve national status until 1901, although regional bodies had existed for a number of years. The disciplinary boundaries that were drawn between academic specializations in a host of fields in the 1880s were slower in coming to philosophy, perhaps because philosophers saw their practice as all-inclusive, as a necessary foundation for clear thinking and synthesis. Finally, around the turn of the century, psychology—increasingly dependent on laboratory research—broke away from its base within philosophy to become a self-contained discipline.

Philosophy was hardly immune from the general tendency toward professionalization. The field became academically successful once it began to follow the call of modern science and distanced itself from narrow theological concerns. The development and rise to prominence of the Harvard philosophy department, for example, required that its professors produce a steady stream of articles for publication in the leading professional journals. Increasingly, Harvard philosophy professors taught upper-division courses or seminars in their areas of specialization rather than general education courses, which were now taught largely by part-time faculty or graduate students.[4]

George Herbert Palmer, chair of the Harvard philosophy department, built his reputation less on the originality of his thought than on his ability to "sell" Harvard philosophy Ph.D.s around the country. The worth of a department's program sometimes came to be measured by its administrative power and influence. Not all in the Harvard department were delighted with academic professionalization, which also fostered the narrowly specialized seminar, the technicalities of philosophical discourse, and the arcane politics of academe. William James publicly derided the "Ph.D. Octopus" for strangling original thought with the tentacles of administrative logic and pedantry associated with the degree of doctor of philosophy. In James's eyes, and those of his colleague George Santayana, the increase of narrowly trained Ph.D.s signalled elitism and specialization; it threatened to remove philosophy from the arena of pressing public problems. In contrast, Palmer understood the advanced degree to be a mark of progress, standards, and directed thinking. As the evolution of the Harvard philosophy department in the twentieth century would indicate, movement was away from the quicksilver brilliance of James and Santayana and toward the direction of the technical virtuosity of philosophers like C. I. Lewis.[5]

Perhaps the university's support for independent thinking, for academic freedom, contributed most to the success of philosophical thought in America. In antebellum colleges, senior-level courses in moral philosophy usually had been taught by college presidents determined not to allow instruction in such an important subject to fall into the hands of unorthodox religious thinkers. Challenging questions were absent from such courses; only certitude and ethical absolutes were welcome. Secularization of learning allowed American philosophers to focus enthusiastically on religious questions without having to subscribe to specified theological formulas. University-supported philosophers, despite their personal religious doubts and troubled consciences, generally labored to renew religious faith.

The development of academic freedom and philosophical sophistication in America was not assured in this period. In 1883 Royce worried about outside interests interfering with freedom of thought: "the enemies of the freedom of teaching are numberless." Philosophers Charles Peirce and George Morris, for example, faced dim job prospects because of either their unusual life-style or religious unorthodoxy. In addition, the rate of progress and the depth of the secularization of philosophy in America was not sufficient in the eyes of young philosophers such as William James, Josiah Royce, and G. Stanley Hall. Writing in 1880, Hall found the vast majority of colleges in the United States still dominated by a rote method of teaching; philosophical instruction was impeded by a theological outlook that rarely allowed free and speculative thinking to prosper. The shaky financial resources of many colleges, in Hall's estimation, forced them to satisfy the theological and political assumptions of their private and public benefactors. James agreed with Hall, noting that college presidents dominated courses in moral philosophy. An aspiring philosopher consigned to Harvard's physiology department at the time, James hoped that philosophical study in America would cast off its reliance on theology and sail with the heady winds of German physiology and natural science. Cause for optimism did exist. James concluded his own evaluation of philosophy in America by recognizing that at Harvard College in the 1870s a student might just as easily study Kant's *Critique of Pure Reason* as Locke's *Essay concerning Human Understanding*, and that even the controversial views of philosophers such as Schopenhauer, Hartmann, and Spencer were increasingly to be found in the curriculum.[6]

The New Psychology

Many philosophers found that the university—with its ever-increasing demand that they direct their attention to the importance of Darwinism in particular and science in general—created an atmosphere of incredible energy in the development of thought. Philosophers in the years from 1880 until 1900 concentrated on a host of traditional philosophical problems: the meaning of truth, the relation between science and religion, the possibility of order and progress in the universe, and the problematic status of individual freedom. But they evaluated these traditional concerns with the tools of evolutionary science. Evolutionary theory in philosophy and psychology between 1880 and 1900 provided philosophers with a new way of understanding and describing the world. As John Dewey remembered most famously in 1909, Darwinism's importance for philosophy rested in its "laying hands upon the sacred ark of absolute permanency, in treating the forms that had been regarded as types of fixity and perfection as originating and passing away, the *Origin of Species* introduced a new mode of thinking that in the end was bound to transform the logic of knowledge, and hence the treatment of morals, religion and politics."[7]

Two separate articles, published in 1884 and 1885 by John Dewey and G. Stanley Hall, respectively, heralded the arrival of the New Psychology. Both Hall and Dewey had come to the study of psychology thoroughly convinced that the universe was essentially intelligible only as a mental construct. On the basis of this initial perception, Hall and Dewey expected to find connections that would make subject and object, knower and known, cohere—that would suggest that common distinctions between such entities were apparent, not real.

Both were also convinced that the science of psychology supported religious belief. Thus, Hall explicitly promoted the New Psychology as an aid to religious reflection. The "new method" associated with the philosophy of the New Psychology, Hall wrote, was "Christian to its root and centre." Rather than seeking, as had natural theologians in the antebellum period, "to trace petty harmonies and small adjustments between science and religion," the New Psychologists extended the reach of reason and offered "a new cosmos . . . with the old Scriptural sense of unity, rationality, and love beneath and above all."[8] Dewey agreed with Hall's religious enthusiasm, suggesting in his own essay "Psychology as Philosophic Method" (1886) that psychological insights proved the spiritual nature of man. Indeed, as Dewey phrased it in "Soul and Body" (1886), "Let it be no surprise that physiological psychology has revealed no new truth concerning the relations of soul and body" beyond those keen insights already presented by Aristotle and St. Paul.[9]

Evolutionary theory significantly influenced the New Psychology in the 1880s, and in turn that influence signaled a "rebirth of American thought."[10] The New Psychology rejected the formalistic psychology commonly associated with British empiricism's atomistic view of experience as structured by the mind in parcels of discrete sense impressions, one built on top of another. In this traditional view, experience was not a stream of events, one running into the next; it was only a series of connected fragments. The New Psychologists revised this conception of consciousness and developed a view of the adaptive role of mind; later, some of them would propose the important American philosophies of pragmatism and instrumentalism.

The proponents of the New Psychology did not represent a united front on all philosophical points. Hall, Dewey, and James could not necessarily agree on the exact contours of psychological science or even on how to describe it. For example, Dewey, in his *Psychology* (1886), placed too much emphasis (to both Hall's and James's tastes) on fitting the particulars of experience into a framework of Hegelian absolute idealism. Yet all were moving in a similar direction, toward making psychology a natural science. Nonetheless, each remained reluctant to drop the ideal of an active and purposeful subject.

The New Psychology, under the influence of naturalism and Darwinism, posited an activist view of mind, promoted a complex comprehension of experience, and emphasized the interaction between individual and environment. In his work of the 1880s and 1890s Dewey attacked the idea of a passive mind, a mind that simply received sense impressions. Instead, Dewey maintained, the mind was teleological, a seeker after ends; the will was dynamic, always in contact with life. The New Psychology not only [bore] the realistic stamp of contact with life" but also "[laid] large stress upon the will . . . as a living bond connecting and conditioning *all* mental activity."[11]

The New Psychology derived its particularly modern flavor from its emphatic espousal of experience. In the late nineteenth century, partly under the influence of evolutionary and historical modes of thought, thinkers in a variety of disciplines sought to throw out static conceptions of human nature and institutions, and to replace them with a more dynamic notion of experience. Oliver Wendell Holmes, Jr., a close confidant of William James, had in his groundbreaking *Common Law* (1881) asserted that "the life of the law has not been logic; it has been experience. The felt necessities of time, the prevalent moral and political theories, intuitions of public policy, avowed or unconscious, even the prejudices which judges share with their fellow men, have a good deal more to do than the syllogism in determining the rules by which men should be governed."[12] Similarly in revolt against formal logic and syllogism, John Dewey proclaimed in "The New Psychology" that "Experience is realistic, not abstract. Psychical life is the fullest, deepest, and richest manifestation of this experience. The New Psychology is content to get its logic from this experience, and not do violence to the sanctity and integrity of the latter by forcing it to conform to certain preconceived abstract ideas. It wants the logic of fact, of process, of life. . . . For this reason it abandons all legal fiction of logical and mathematical analogies and rules; and is willing to throw itself upon experience. . . . Thus the New Psychology bears the realistic stamp of contact with life."[13]

William James was more successful than Dewey in bringing all conceptions before the court of experience. James's *Principles of Psychology* (1890) abounded with analogies and examples that made it clear to readers that psychological theory must be anchored in the flux of experience. Indeed, James's willingness to reject older psychological theories of consciousness as discontinuous led him to coin a term that became famous: "stream of consciousness." Now experience was described as a continuous stream of relations marked by continuity as much as by discontinuity. In James's view, consciousness was not "chopped up in bits. . . . It is nothing jointed; it flows. A 'river' or a 'stream' are the metaphors by which it is most naturally described."[14]

The New Psychology not only promoted vibrant respect for the complexity and continuity of experience but also demanded an activist view of consciousness. In "The Muscular Perception of Space" (1878), and more fully in "The New Psychology" (1885), G. Stanley Hall argued that mind was active rather than passive: "All possible *truth* is practical." Rather than waste time on traditional epistemological questions regarding the reality of a chair or table as idealized essences or constructs of the mind, one should strive to understand conceptions in terms of "the uses to which they may be put." In effect, Hall emphasized, articulating what would become a credo of the New Psychology, "the Active Part of our nature is not only an essential part of cognition itself, but it always has a voice in determining what 1all be believed and what rejected."[15]

William James's deeply influential *Principles of Psychology* drew upon the laboratory results obtained by scientists around the world to support this view that the mind was active. Especially in the chapters dealing with habit, attention, and will, James promoted mind or consciousness as a seeker after ends. Facing the flux of experience, mind chose to attend to certain sense impressions as important and to reject or ignore others. Jamesian consciousness was part of the environment but was also responsible for changing that environment. As he phrased it in "Are We Automata?" (1879), "the mind is at every stage a theatre of simultaneous possibilities. Consciousness consists in the comparison of these with each other, the selection of some, and the suppression of the rest by the reinforcing and inhibiting agency of Attention."[16]

John Dewey agreed with Hall and James on this crucial point, especially after his own enlightening reading of James's *Principles*. In "The Reflex Arc Concept in Psychology" (1892) Dewey stressed the functional attributes of mind. Ideas became instruments, adapting the organism to the environment. But the relation was reciprocal; the mind and the environment were mutually interactive, always intertwined. Throughout the reflex arc, stimulus and responses were joined in a stream, and consciousness was capable of achieving its own desired ends.[17]

Darwinian Influences

The New Psychologists read Darwinism as situating man and mind as active entities within the context of the environment. Rather than following a popular strain of Darwinian naturalism that sometimes viewed man and mind as passively adapting to the environment, the New Psychology demonstrated that evolution had developed the mind as an activist organ designed to affect the environment. The New Psychologists found that the Darwinian emphasis on habit and instinct contributed to the understanding of the mind. Darwinian ideas on these concepts were incorporated into James's *Principles of Psychology*.

Habit, as explained by James, was a helpful mechanism that allowed organisms to adapt to the environment; it allowed the organism to organize thought (analyzed physiologically) and to retain actions or responses useful to survival. Lower forms of life were bound by biological habit and instinct. In contrast, man could, through the capacity of a highly developed consciousness, exercise acts of attention, instinct, and will when desired. Such changes could become habitual and might also achieve specified goals. This biological theorem was used by James to support Victorian moralism. He praised habit not only for aiding the survival of the race but also for ingraining morality in the individual: "Habit is . . . the enormous fly-wheel of society, its most precious conservative agent." By making useful actions habitual and automatic, the human species survived and thrived.[18] At every step of James's psychology, the Darwinian formula presented consciousness as an active, freedom-inducing agent.

Not all American philosophers of note were confirmed in their devotion to Darwinism, but none could ignore it. Although George Holmes Howison, professor of philosophy at the University of California at Berkeley, accepted the interpretive force and scientific validity of Darwinian evolution, he warned against a readiness to extend the scope of evolution into regions where it should not tread—for instance, into the realm of metaphysics, of a reality beyond that of sense impression.[19] Charles Sanders Peirce, whose influence had helped to relieve James of his early affection for Herbert Spencer's simplistic vision of the process of evolution and who, more than anyone else in America, was thoroughly conversant with the philosophy of science, was anything but a devout Darwinian. He believed that evolutionary development might sometimes be mechanical and slow, at other times unexpected and cataclysmic. He imbibed Lamarckian ideas nearly as much as he did Darwinian ones. Despite his eclecticism, Peirce greatly admired the scientific method and believed that only consensus by a community of scientists promised to establish valid truth claims.

Peirce, like many theologians, accepted evolution as a scientific fact of the utmost importance. He presented in Darwinian fashion a universe marked by chance, or by *tychism*, to use his preferred term. Darwin's emphasis on natural selection had helped Peirce to recognize the importance of statistical chance in the world of nature. Where chance existed, freedom of action was certain to be found. But happenstance in nature did not satisfy Peirce; he craved an order and logic to evolution. Though his doctrine of "evolutionary love" sounds strange to modern ears, the imperative behind it was plain: Peirce sought to ensure that evolutionary theory and tychism would lead to beneficial ends. The chance and violence in the Darwinian world of nature, paralleled by the "greed philosophy" and wastefulness that dominated modern American society, would be overcome by evolutionary love. Peirce believed that his evolutionary love doctrine—grounded in a desire for law and order, designed to promote an essentially moralistic vision—was superior to Darwin's theory of the struggle for existence, since its mechanism for progress was based on love and cooperation rather than competition and greed.[20]

Peirce was hardly alone in employing scientific and philosophical reasoning to support essentially religious and moral goals. Most of the religious thinkers mentioned in chapter 1 used evolutionary concepts to support the particulars of theology and the authority of the Bible. They hoped that science would not undermine, and that it might even aid, theological speculations. But they rarely turned to science to "prove" the necessity of religious belief.

William James creatively used the logic of the Darwinian argument for survival of the fittest to defend the efficacy of religious belief. He did this most fully and effectively in *The Varieties of Religious Experience* (1902). In that work James sought to extract the essence of the religious or mystical experi-

36

ence, to gauge its power in lifting the individual out of a state of stupor, to discern how religion bequeathed to a true believer the energy to persevere in the face of extreme opposition. Viewed in these terms, the experiences of intensely religious individuals left no doubt in James's mind as to the power of religious sentiments and the validity of belief. James proposed that the power of religion must be understood in Darwinian terms—that evolutionary theory supported rather than undermined the validity of religion. After all, what better argument for religion than the familiar Darwinian one of survival of the fittest? Religion had proved its fitness through its ability to help individuals to engage in a sustained and powerful interaction with the environment. "It is but the elimination of the humanly unfit, and the survival of the humanly fittest, applied to religious beliefs," James wrote. "If we look at history candidly and without prejudice, we have to admit that . . . Religions have *approved* themselves; they have ministered to sundry vital needs which they found reigning. When they violated other needs too strongly, or when other faiths came which served the same needs better, the first religions were supplanted."[21]

Freedom or Determinism

An evolutionary philosophy persuaded many Americans that all social and natural phenomena might be explained, and fitted together, by use of strikingly simple generalizations. In the hands of the most popular thinker of the era, the British polymath Herbert Spencer, the specifics of science often seemed less important than the sweep of his generalization. Spencer hypnotized many with his book *First Principles* (1862), wherein he proposed in a formula to capture the course of evolutionary development: "Evolution is definable as a change from an incoherent homogeneity to a coherent heterogeneity, accompanying the dissipation of motion and the integration of matter."[22] From this initial and vague (if not downright silly) principle Spencer produced a mountain of volumes on psychology, sociology, and biology, all demonstrating not only the explanatory power of evolutionary theory but also the logic of development in a predetermined direction.

John Fiske, in many lectures and books, interpreted social as well as biological phenomena through the laws of evolution, in part as developed by Spencer. As understood by Fiske, evolution could explain everything. For Fiske evolution demonstrated that sociability was destined to replace warfare as the means of selection, that human infants had a longer period of dependency on their parents than other animals, and that democracy was the highest stage of political organization. Despite the rosy predictions of Fiske's "cosmic philosophy," less appealing implications could be read into his formula. If the individual organism's survival depended on adaptation to the existing social formation—since what had developed was, by definition, what must be—then evolutionary philosophy seemed to consign the ideal of freedom into nothing more than a doctrine of necessity; freedom was the ability to adapt, nothing more and nothing less.

If the individual was simply expected to adapt, then plans for reform and change of the social or natural environment often seemed the dreams of dangerous utopians. Interference with natural laws could only lead to disastrous consequences; perhaps it would even push the hands of the clock of progress backward. This perception in turn served as the scientific underpinning for popular ideals of laissez-faire in the late nineteenth century. Noninterference, or passive adaptation to the natural laws of development, seemed to some to be the fastest and surest way to improve society. The most famous expression of this perspective came from William Graham Sumner, a professor of sociology at Yale University. Sumner's views synthesized Calvinism, Malthusianism, and Darwinism. He denounced "The Absurd Effort to Make the World Over" (1894), proclaiming that the powerful tide of evolution

will not be changed by us. It will swallow up both us and our experiments. It will absorb the efforts at change and take them into itself as new but trivial components, and the great movement of tradition and work will go on unchanged by our fads and schemes. . . . The men will be carried along with it and be made by it. The utmost they can do by their cleverness will be to note and record their course as they are carried along, which is what we do now, and is that which leads us to the vain fancy that we can make or guide the movement. That is why it is the greatest folly of which a man can be capable, to sit down with a slate and pencil to plan out a new social world.[23]

Affronts to the ideal of freedom and to the possibility that human beings could control their own destiny were not consigned to the experimental realm of scientific laws or to the heights of philosophical abstraction. The problem of determinism gnawed at the very structure of popular thought. In an older, more traditional America, notions of causality had rarely seemed arcane. But by the 1880s American society had become increasingly complex and complicated. Small towns, where interpersonal relations had been predictable, gave way to cities where people were increasingly subject to conditions and networks of authority beyond their control and, often, beyond their comprehension. The ideal of man as a free agent became problematic. Interdependency and complexity became the new keywords for social explanation.[24] The scissors of modernity seemed to cut out the traditional conception of man as the maker of his fate.

The famous trial of Charles Guiteau, assassin of President James Garfield in 1881, further drove home the possibility that human freedom was a declining proposition. The trial evaluated, in the light of modern scientific theories of human volition, whether Guiteau could be held accountable for his crime. The implications of the trial were obviously great for moral and ethical behavior. Although the prosecution maintained that Guiteau was morally culpable for the crime, defense lawyers brought forth psychologists who testified that Guiteau's hereditary insanity prevented him from distinguishing between right and wrong. This argument, and the contention that insanity might be due to social or environmental causes, threatened to remove ultimate responsibility from the individual and shift it to entities such as heredity or environment.[25] By the 1890s this vision came to the fore in the new genre of realistic, or naturalistic, fiction. In Frank Norris's *McTeague* (1899) the strength of heredity and environment create a saga of determined degeneracy, in which the individual is incapable of resisting the fate assigned to him by natural and hereditary forces.

The suspicion that freedom was an illusion became a numbing reality to some Americans. As a young man, William James had confronted the contradictory modern world of change and uncertainty and absolute determinism with fear and trembling. His metaphysical and personal demons forced him to retreat into a long period of illness and depression. Writing to a friend who was experiencing similar metaphysical uncertainties, James confided that under pressure from empirical philosophy, he had come to "feel that we are Nature through and through, that we are wholly conditioned, that not a wiggle of our will happens save as a result of physical laws; and yet, notwithstanding, we are *en rapport* with reason."[26]

In "Great Men and Their Environment," published in the *Atlantic* in 1880, and in "The Dilemma of Determinism" (1884), William James addressed some of his concerns about the problem of freedom. He was irked by the deterministic arguments that Spencerian philosophers purveyed under the guise of scientific certitude. The deterministic philosophy of Spencer placed the individual, even the individual of genius, at the mercy of the environment, passive before the predetermined sweep of historical development. In James's summation, determinism "professes that those parts of the universe already laid down absolutely appoint and decree what the other parts shall be. The future has no ambiguous possibilities hidden in its womb: the part we call the present is compatible with only one totality." Mechanical laws of development and the unbearable weight of past reality and future necessity conspired to diminish, if not to eliminate, individual responsibility.[27]

Determinism also boded ill for morality and ethics. Citing a sensational murder case, James feared that a determinist universe might absolve a man who had murdered his wife because she bored him. Regret for the horror of this crime would become superfluous: in a deterministic world this act of cruelty had to have happened, since all was determined by the weight of the past and the logic of preestablished laws of development. To accept determinism, then, as a philosophical explanation for all, removed responsibility and regret from the world—and thus removed the very possibility of morality. Everyone was lowered to the moral netherworld of Charles Guiteau.

James fired his own bullet of evolutionary philosophy into the heart of deterministic theory. Consciousness and mind, no less than individual genius, were spontaneous variations. The environment did not create the man of genius. James admitted that the environment did play a substantial role in determining whether the individual of genius would thrive or perish. But, he emphasized, "whenever [environment] adopts and preserves the great man, it becomes modified by his influence in an entirely original and peculiar way. He acts as the ferment, and changes its constitution, just as the advent of a new zoological species changes the faunal and floral equilibrium of the region in which it appears." Thus, in one stroke, by recourse to Darwinian logic, James had promoted a reciprocal relation between the individual and the environment. In so doing, he believed, he had salvaged the importance of the individual and promoted the exercise of freedom.[28]

Since the individual was free to act and could anticipate that his or her actions counted for something, morality was returned to the universe. Most memorably in *The Will to Believe* (1897), James implored his many readers to take responsibility for their spiritual well-being, to cast off the depressing aura of inactivity. To be moral meant to recognize that choices might be exercised among a variety of options, some better than others. To simply play a waiting game, to let the environment define everything, was as much a choice as to determine to do something active. In James's world of "Rembrandtesque moral chiaroscuro," the fight with evil took on real consequence; each individual actor and actress became transformed into a moral agent battling to make this "restless universe" a more humane place.[29]

Other important philosophers joined James in defending the possibility of freedom. Charles S. Peirce, in "The Doctrine of Necessity Examined" (1892), rejected the postulate that "every single fact in the universe is precisely determined by law" as a proper scientific inference. While Peirce certainly found laws and regularities operative in the universe, he did not believe that they determined individual actions in an "exact and universal" fashion. Regularity did not equal exactitude. Thus, mechanical laws of determinism failed to explain diversity and change. Speaking in Darwinian tones, Peirce, along with James, accepted variation and spontaneity as opportunities for the organism to develop habits that "produced all regularities."

Peirce believed that undermining the logic and implications of determinist views would leave room for the exercise of free will on the part of the individual. Individual responsibility would remain strong in a world teeming with chance and change: "By thus admitting pure spontaneity or life as a character of the universe, acting always and everywhere though restrained within narrow bounds by law, producing infinitesimal departures from law continuously and great ones with infinite infrequency, I account for all the variety and diversity of the universe, in the only sense in which the really *sui generis* and new can be said to be accounted for." Diversity served for Peirce as a proof of freedom and as a real possibility, thanks to philosophical logic and natural law.[30]

Arguments for individual responsibility and free will were central to American philosophy between 1880 and 1900. Even philosophers such as Josiah Royce, who emphasized a necessary plan or logic to the world, were forced to present the individual in the full light of individual responsibility and moral freedom. Royce's philosophical system, presented most impressively in *The Religious Aspect of Philosophy* (1885), began with an attempt to refute skepticism and doubt by focusing on a paradox concerning the existence of error. If error was true—that is, if error could be recognized—then there had to be an abstract standard or absolute truth against which to judge it. From this powerful logical argument, Royce proceeded to demonstrate that error was simply incomplete thought, part of a larger community of discourse understood as a fragment of the conversation of "Absolute Truth and Absolute Knowledge." Therefore, uncertainty and error became parts of a necessary order, a higher, more inclusive thought.[31]

In *Religious Aspect* Royce did support notions of individualism and freedom. But the terribly abstract and all-encompassing nature of his system pointed in the direction of the type of thinking that James regularly condemned as deterministic. For in the lush folds of Royce's absolute, regret seemed banished from the universe, since all parts of the universe, evil no less than good, had to serve their purposes as part of a larger whole. The individual surrendered to the group or to the Absolute: "The One Will must conquer."[32] And, in comparison with James, Royce emphasized community more than individualism in his social philosophy.

The perceived shortcomings of Royce's philosophical case for individual freedom were accentuated when in 1898 he participated in a symposium on "The Conception of God" at the University of California at Berkeley. Royce sought to demonstrate the "reality of the omniscient" in the presence of the Absolute. The contents of experience, while described by Royce as "indeed particular," or individual, were nevertheless to be viewed as necessary parts of "a self-determined whole." George Holmes Howison, organizer of the symposium, found that Royce's shuffling of the deck of the Absolute dealt a losing hand to the individual; the "self-active member of a manifold of persons" vanished. Howison wanted a true idealism in which the individual had responsibility and a "true personality."[33]

Stung by the force of Howison's animadversions against determinism and the ambiguity of his conception of Absolute idealism, Royce composed a rejoinder in "The Absolute and the Individual." In clear, sharp prose, Royce stated that his absolute left "room for ethical responsibility" and that "the very essence of ethical individuality brings it at last . . . into a deeper harmony with the concept of the Absolute . . . just *because* the ethical individual is sacred."[34] Thus, Royce and Howison, idealists to the core, and James and Peirce, empiricists after a fashion, reached consensus on the importance of human freedom and responsibility in a world that often appeared to negate the very possibility of human individuality and responsibility. In so doing, these philosophers accepted the flux of experience, recognized the reality of chance at the heart of modern thinking, and also promoted the possibility of progress through human volition or (for Royce) through an absolute ideal.

Pragmatism

American philosophers, like their European counterparts, not only worried about individuality and freedom; they were also greatly concerned about the untidy nature of truth. Science had not solved all the puzzles of the universe, as some philosophers of science had once anticipated it would. Science had only shown itself capable of constructing useful hypotheses. In a world where science displaced stability with uncertainty at every turn, where foundations for knowledge often seemed to crumble, and where social change rapidly transformed traditions, many hoped that scientific interrogation would bring forth stronger conceptions of truth. Although some philosophers, like Josiah Royce, believed that modern logic would demonstrate that higher truths still existed and that order still obtained, modern thought seemed to be moving toward a definition of truth that had no abstract props to hold it up, no firm or absolute foundations beneath it.[35]

American pragmatism, which posited that truth could be determined by experimental means, represented an original and powerful philosophical response to this situation. In part, pragmatism grew out of the New Psychology's emphasis on experiment and experience. This orientation toward experience and the recognition that all existence was in a state of process and change (perhaps the only premise common to all schools of evolutionary thought) promoted revisions in the traditional conception of knowledge as a representation of reality, a mirror of nature. The development of the American philosophy of pragmatism in the hands of Peirce and James in the closing years of the nineteenth century, and in Dewey's instrumentalism in the early twentieth century, represented a significant current in the river of modern philosophy.[36]

In "How to Make Our Ideas Clear" (1878), perhaps the first expression of the pragmatist frame of mind, Peirce dismissed Cartesian rationalism based on a priori categories of clarity and distinctness, along with Leibniz's abstract definitions of truth. While apprehension of clarity and abstract distinctness were acceptable as the initial steps toward meaning, Peirce posited another necessary level. The purpose of thought, he wrote, was to develop beliefs, to establish habits, to produce actions. Meaning, in Peirce's pragmatic usage, signified "simply what habits it involves." To quote his famous maxim, "Consider what effects, what might conceivably have practical bearings, we conceive the object of our conception to have. Then our conception of these effects is the whole of our conception of the object." Peirce illustrated this idea by discussing the concept of hardness as nothing more than the "conceived effects" of certain objects on other objects (e.g., whether or not an object scratches a surface). Abstract rationalist definitions offered little by way of meaning, according to Peirce; they were too vague. Inquiry helped the individual to produce belief and habit, and most of all to engage in useful discussions of truth. Only in this way, Peirce contended, would clarity be obtained and meaning rendered valuable in action.[37]

Avoiding a definition of meaning that pivoted around an abstraction and fixed terms, Peirce judged meaning by its effects in the realm of activity. Meaning was never to be evaluated according to its individual, particular value. But meaning was constituted as the logical and relevant result of a concept being put to the test. Peirce refused to follow his experimental and possibly relativistic hypothesis too far. He never intended to suggest that meaning was absolutely transitory or particular. Peirce fiercely held to the existence of universals or general ideas as necessary truths. The truth of a mathematical or logical theorem was unaffected by the actions or wishes of a particular individual or group. Especially in Peirce's later thought, his realism distinguished between what is true and what is useful. In the end Peirce asserted that the true was real, that in the long run truth would be found to exist. He envisioned a community of scientists, objective observers, who through long-term investigation and evaluation would arrive at an agreement about what constituted truth. Peirce's pragmatism thus retained its experimental flavor, undermined traditional conceptions of truth, and expressed itself in an evolutionary manner while retaining a certainty that truth would someday be attainable.

In 1898, after giving credit to Peirce for originating the idea, William James presented his own doctrine of pragmatism in "Philosophical Conceptions and Practical Results." Like Peirce before him, James attacked abstract systems of thought that presumed that "the belly-band of the universe must be tight."[38] In contrast, the pragmatic version of the universe was wild and teeming with possibilities. Pragmatism distanced itself from traditional epistemology. James found that many problems in philosophy, when examined according to their possible practical or theoretical effects, were meaningless disagreements or verbal quibbles. "If no future detail of experience or conduct is to be deduced from our hypothesis," he wrote, "the debate between materialism and theism becomes quite idle and insignificant. Matter and God in that event mean exactly the same thing."[39]

Jamesian pragmatism was available as a method that both "the common

43

man and the scientist" could use to test conceptions in the stream of experience. Pragmatism recognized the transitory nature of truth and realized that all ideas were not equal in their implications. Although pragmatism was directed toward the future, it did not neglect the past. For James, building upon Darwinian premises, pragmatism recognized that the fund of previous truths, often referred to as common sense, represented ideas that had survived, concepts that had proven useful. Jamesian pragmatism, then, was determined to combine previous perceptions with changing realities, to view truth as a process rather than as a finished piece of work. Pragmatism did not see truth as an individual possession; truth was communal and tied to realities that simply would not vanish, no matter how much the deluded individual or group wished them to. "Woe to him whose beliefs play fast and loose with the order which realities follow in his experience" wrote James in his *Pragmatism* (1907); "they will lead him nowhere or else make false connexions."[40]

James's mature description of pragmatism was congruent with the modernist ethos that truth was subject to revision. Experimentation served as the way of arriving at valid conclusions. Moreover, pragmatism fit in nicely with James's desire for an open world in which the individual added his or her fiat to the stuff of experience. As James put it, pragmatism was hardly a philosophy of "moral holidays"; rather, it suggested that the world was malleable, open to improvement.

American Hegelians

Not all American philosophers practicing in the final decades of the nineteenth century were content with a pragmatic philosophical perspective that failed to serve a fully satisfying main course of cosmic order, rationality, and progress. George S. Morris, William T. Harris, and George H. Howison supported a Hegelian approach to philosophy that was designed to accept the ubiquity of change but also to balance it with order.

American academic philosophy in the late nineteenth century was dominated by a various brands of idealism, many having affinities with a Hegelian perspective. These philosophies maintained that the universe was ultimately spiritual and rational. The presence of the idealist imperative was felt at Harvard, in the presence of Royce and Palmer, no less than at Cornell (Jacob Gould Schurmann and James Edwin Creighton), Princeton (John Grier Hibben and Alexander T. Ormand), University of Michigan and Johns Hopkins (G. S. Morris), Columbia (Nicholas Murray Butler), and Boston University (Borden Parker Bowne). The varieties of the idealist experience of philosophy ranged from the Speculative, or Objective, Idealism in vogue at Cornell to the Personalism of Bowne, the Dynamic Idealism of Morris, and the "Absolute Idealism" of Royce. (the latter being the most famous).[41]

Hegelianism reigned supreme among these forms of idealism. It promised unity, order, and progress; its dialectical method promoted synthesis; no fact was orphaned; all specific events were explicable within the logical development of history. At the same time, according to some of his supporters, Hegel desired to ground philosophy in experience, to emphasize that the particular and the general were one. Moreover, many American interpreters of Hegel found that his philosophy explained how the individual actively strove to realize an ideal end.[42]

Hegelian idealism, no less than Royce's Absolute Idealism, offered Americans a social explanation and a theistic view in an age when modern science occasionally seemed to undermine the scope of religion and cosmic order. Equally important, especially in America, Hegelian thought was quite favorable to the development of a centralized, powerful state. Hegelians viewed the state as an ideal expression of historical necessity; they further proclaimed that the state represented a higher stage of national unity. Despite this insistence on the value of the national state, American Hegelians did not believe that its development undermined the freedom of the individual. Hegelian dialectical logic promised, in the end, to resolve all apparent contradictions in a higher, more abstract synthesis.

The appeal of Hegelianism in America was widespread. Hegelian ideas took root in St. Louis, with its substantial German immigrant and intellectual community, immediately after the Civil War. From there Hegelianism spread eastward as remnants of the transcendentalist movement found in Hegel a kindred spirit. The curriculum of the Concord School of Philosophy between 1880 and 1887 attested to the continuing presence of Hegelian ideas in America. But this spirit was not confined to the lecture halls of the popular mind; it also spoke through the work of some of America's most influential thinkers.[43]

William Torrey Harris was the most famous and energetic promoter of Hegelian ideas in America. Harris received his Hegelian training in St. Louis. A philosopher remarkable neither for originality nor academic standing, Harris nonetheless occupied an important place in American intellectual life. He founded America's first professional journal of philosophy, the *Journal of Speculative Philosophy*, which he edited from 1867 until 1893 and which published important early essays by James, Hall, Dewey, and Peirce. He also served as superintendent of the St. Louis Public Schools from 1868 through 1880. He went east to organize the Concord School of Philosophy and later served as Federal Commissioner of Education from 1889 to 1906. In all of his endeavors, Harris approached practical and educational problems as a devoted Hegelian. For Harris and his legion of followers, who were librarians, judges, and politicians, Hegelian philosophy "came to mean with us . . . the most practical of all species of knowledge. We used it to solve all problems connected with school-teaching and school-management. We studied the 'dialectic' of politics and political parties and understood how measures and men might be combined by its light."[44]

In essence, Harris's Hegelianism exemplified the standard tenets of conservative social theory. In America, where individualism and social heterogeneity were supreme, Harris's Hegelianism stressed individualism and self-help. Capitalism was viewed in evolutionary terms, as promoting greater distribution of material wealth: "The age in which we now live is proclaimed to be an age of individualism and personal freedom." But Harris's Hegelian ideal of individuality was to be achieved best through the development of a unified community, further sanctified by a national state.[45] Differences of class (not understood in a Marxian sense) would be erased by the central role of the school system in elevating thinking to a higher, more general level through a uniform curriculum and school system. The school system, in Harris's view, functioned between the family and civil society, leading the individual toward a greater sense of community and social responsibility. In the end, the school was the motor of progress and unification.

Harris's educational philosophy was little more than a "static deduction" of familiar Kantian categories. It emphasized a standardized, traditional curriculum. In contrast, Dewey's developing views of the school and curriculum in *The School and Society* (1899) attempted to promote spontaneity, openness, and practical activity. Nonetheless, Harris did much to strengthen the American educational system through his Hegelian belief in centralized administration and planning. In the words of historian of education Lawrence Cremin, Harris was "the man who ultimately rationalized the institution of the public school."[46]

Other philosophers were proud Hegelians. George S. Morris was an unabashed idealist; his philosophy combined realism and romanticism. This allowed him to accept empirical science and the particularity of experience while also holding to the spiritual and ordered nature of ultimate reality.[47] Morris understood Hegel's *Logic* to prove that mind and nature were organically linked by their common grounding in spirit. Nature, comprehended in developmental terms, indicated nothing more than a "phase in the 'self-realization of Mind.'"[48]

Morris explicated Hegel's historical thought most fully in *Hegel's Philosophy of the State and of History* (1887). There Morris again posited that man, history, and the state were spiritual values unopposed to nature, since man, in Hegelian terms, realized himself and the Absolute Spirit in the world. The tortured drama of history would have a happy ending: the realization of freedom. The question of freedom, which had stymied idealists such as Royce, was explained in Morris's Hegelianism simply as action in accord with

46

greater ends. Individual acts of volition served ends not originally conceived by the individual. Hegelian philosophy, in Morris's eyes, not only demonstrated a deep appreciation for progress and individuality but also postulated the existence of God and order:

Philosophy is concerned only with the splendor of the Idea, which is mirrored in universal history. The fact that history is such a development . . . of freedom and of the consciousness of freedom, and so an actual and progressive realization of the spiritual nature of man,—"this is the true theodicy, the justification of God in history. The human spirit is capable of being reconciled with the course of the past and present history only when it sees that which has happened and which is daily happening has been and is, not only not without God, but in an essential sense the work of God himself."[49]

Other important philosophers cut their philosophical teeth on Hegel. G. Stanley Hall went through a youthful Hegelian period, although by the late 1870s he found Hegelianism "valueless as a method." Like many others in his generation, Hall initially viewed Hegel's ideas as a philosophical analogue of Darwin's notion of evolutionary development. Indeed, the reception of Darwinism in certain philosophical circles was eased by the earlier acceptance of Hegelian dialectical development. Hall probably dropped the Hegelian method because of its vagaries and the lack of respect it commanded in German academic circles. But he never ceased to accept its ultimate imperative: to place all development within a unified system. His Hegelian idealism was soon transformed into evolutionary naturalism.[50]

John Dewey's early thought, saturated by a Hegelian desire for synthesis, order, and theism in the 1880s, changed slowly under the influence of naturalism in the 1890s. Hegelian ideas learned from George S. Morris, his adviser at Johns Hopkins, did not prevent Dewey from pursuing work in psychology. However, in the opinion of some critics, Dewey's experimental psychology was undermined by his attempt to fit the data of consciousness into an overarching system. Nonetheless, as Dewey's essay "Psychology as Philosophic Method" (1886) made clear, Hegelian notions of consciousness promised to demonstrate "the reality of the spirit" as the "condition and end of all reality."[51] Dewey's ethical theory of Christian theism in the early 1890s also bore the important stamp of Hegelian ideas. He argued in "Christianity and Democracy" (1892) that "there is but one face—the more complete movement of man to his unity with his fellows through realizing the truth of life. . . . Democracy thus appears as the means by which the revelation of truth is carried on."[52] Although such Hegelian overtones would be absent from Dewey's work by the late 1890s, the essentials of his early system's emphasis on process, experience, and organicism all had their origins in the philosophical theories of Hegel.[53]

By the early 1900s the Hegelian view was in retreat, defeated in part by its dense and elastic language. The increasingly particularistic, rather than general, interpretive framework that was central to the practice of science and professional philosophy also inflicted damage on Hegelianism. In addition, the power of pragmatism's philosophy of science weakened the appeal of Hegelianism. By the time of the First World War, the Germanic bent of idealistic philosophy would ensure Hegel's demise, given the philosophical patriotism of the Allied powers. It should not be forgotten, however, that Hegel's ideas allowed many thinkers to accept the ubiquity of change, to acknowledge the centrality of experience, and to see mind and nature as part of a developmental process. In the midst of all this change and process, American Hegelians were able to defend traditional American values such as individualism, community, and religion.

Public Philosophy

Whether Hegelian or pragmatist, American philosophers between 1880 and 1900 took their public roles as intellectual leaders quite seriously. They were devoted to the presumption that philosophical rumination must never become a mere academic exercise. They were convinced that their theorizing about the nature of the world, the meaning of truth, the psychology of the mind, and the possibility of freedom had importance well beyond the confines of a meeting of professional peers at the American Philosophical Association. This expectation of a public role for philosophers was initially supported by the growth of the modern university, which understood its mission as supporting professional research with a view toward solving public problems and as a means of exerting moral authority in America.

Until the middle of the nineteenth century the minister had been the individual expected to exercise cultural authority and to interpret and soften the uncertainty of cultural change and social development. He was to place events of the moment into a larger, more comforting perspective. As the authority of the church declined and the credibility of the scientist increased, there arose a need for new cultural spokespersons who could address issues of public concern in philosophical or scientific terms. Philosophers became, as George Santayana remarked, "clergymen without a church . . . at once genuine philosophers and popular professors."[54]

Armed with their sophisticated knowledge of science and logic, philosophers regularly engaged cultural and social issues: the middle class's pessimistic view of life, the problematic relations between science and religion, the need for socially responsible leadership, the promise of education, the possibility of social reform. Between 1884 and 1894, while teaching at the University of Michigan, John Dewey not only laid the groundwork for his version of pragmatic philosophy but also collaborated with reformers in a variety of educational and social projects. What Dewey wanted in those years, and would continue to desire for another five decades, was "to show that philosophy has some use."[55] Similarly, Felix Adler balanced his academic commitments with a devotion to building up the Ethical Culture Society and to educating workers. Founder of the *International Journal of Ethics* in 1890 and, beginning in 1902, professor of political and social ethics at Columbia University, Adler was convinced that his philosophical investigations of ethical problems not only were valuable in solving public problems but also might be profitably communicated to workers throughout the country. Josiah Royce as well, despite the terribly abstract nature of his philosophical system, accepted his responsibility to explore public issues. He believed that his Absolute Idealism responded to cultural issues of the moment and that his insights might help to undermine the problem of pessimism that hounded the elite classes in the late nineteenth century. In many popular essays Royce called for Americans to adopt a higher ideal purpose, based on a community of values, that would be imbued with moral power.[56]

No philosopher played a larger role on the public stage in this era than William James. By 1890 James was immensely famous, thanks in part to his psychology textbook and his public lectures on pedagogy. His public renown was buoyed by his prestigious position as a Harvard philosopher. As discussed earlier, he believed that his philosophical perspective could resolve conflicts between freedom and determinism, between the individual and the environment. Moreover, he also maintained that a philosophical perspective could usefully intervene in political issues of the highest importance and controversy. In conflating the philosophical and the political, James was simply inhabiting the sphere of a public philosopher.

James used all the credibility he could muster to oppose American imperialism. He understood imperialism as more than a political quandary; it was also a philosophical problem. In a flurry of letters to editors of various newspapers and in speeches, he denounced American policy in the Philippines as a "national infamy." The implications of imperialism for the Filipino and for the American were ominous because the war threatened individuality. The sanctity of the individual occupied center stage in James's philosophy: "The impotence of the private individual, with imperialism under full headway as it is, is deplorable indeed. But every American has a voice or a pen, and may use it. So, impelled by my own sense of duty, I write these present words. One by one we shall creep from cover, and the opposition will organize itself."[57]

In the essay "On a Certain Blindness in Human Beings" (ca. 1898), composed while the cannons of imperialism sounded during the Spanish-American War, James attempted to allegorize imperialistic domination as the result of one person's perception crowding out another's reality. He did this by relating a personal experience. Traveling through the North Carolina mountains, James had come upon a squatter's hut. In the midst of astonishingly pure natural beauty, this individual had cut down trees "and left their charred stumps standing." Moreover, his cabin, "zigzag rail fence," and "irregularly planted Indian corn" represented to James's aesthetic of enjoyment only "a sort of ulcer, without a single element of artificial grace to make up for the loss of Nature's beauty." But, as he reflected upon his initial perception, James came to recognize the importance of perspectivism. He realized that there was no single abstract standard by which to judge architecture and beauty, as well as truth; in the mind of the squatter, what had been accomplished "sang a very paean of duty, struggle, and success."[58]

James's initial blindness to the reality of the squatter, one might say, was akin to the blindness of American imperialists to the rights and realities of the Filipinos. For James, Americans reduced the Filipinos to a mere "other," an abstract entity that existed to be controlled rather than understood. This idea was also expressed in his political polemics: "Surely any reflecting man must see that, far away as we are, doomed to invincible ignorance of the secrets of the Philippine soul (why, we cannot even understand one another's soul here at home) . . . our good will can only work disaster, and work the more disaster to the Filipinos the more conscious it gets of itself and the more *exalté* it grows over its 'responsibilities.'"[59]

Perhaps in his perspectivism James took his most modern stance. Yet in his desire to achieve a world of individual morality that was consonant with Victorian ideals of hardihood, belief, and individualism, James was a traditionalist. Whatever the ultimate worth of his nostrums, the point remains that James's public philosophy represented an active intervention in cultural and political issues, sometimes in the language of partisanship or in the form of philosophical speculation. In either case, James realized that philosophy had to be engaged in active intercourse with a world larger than the technical or professional sphere.

American philosophy, then, in attempting to adapt itself to its new academic home, did not abandon its public role. Just as the philosophizing of the New Psychology and pragmatism had led in the direction of a modern view dependent on experience, plurality, the instability of truth, and perspectivism, the emphasis of American philosophy stood strongly in favor of retaining the presence of God, individuality, and progress. In their "reluctant modernism," whether of a pragmatic or Hegelian bent, American philosophers did their best to be open to new knowledge and to recognize the important implications of science for the reinterpretation of religion and truth.

three

Anthropology, Progress, and Racism

The development of anthropology in America nicely paralleled in direction and concern the movement of philosophy. In each discipline the power of an evolutionary perspective promoted both liberation and imprisonment. Evolutionary theory, for philosophers and other intellectuals in the 1870s and 1880s, did more than promise a method and structure for explanation; it suggested that all phenomena might be unified into a framework of progressive development. But as a new generation of thinkers came of age in the 1880s, earlier evolutionary theory, which had once been so exciting, came to be viewed as confining, unscientific, and deterministic in many of its popular applications.

In anthropology (often referred to as ethnology) the transition from a hierarchical and evolutionary view of culture to a pluralistic and relativistic notion of cultures was hesitant. Between the late 1870s and 1900 America's greatest anthropologists—Lewis Henry Morgan, John Wesley Powell, and Franz Boas—battled to define the methodological premises for the analysis of culture. Although each of these men had a strong interpretive agenda, none of them was able to rid himself of assumptions about the superiority of American and European culture—assumptions that seemed to undermine the scientific value of their perspectives. Yet by the turn of the century a different perspective, based on ideas of particularism and pluralism associated with Boas and his students, became predominant.

Anthropological practice between 1880 and 1900 was marked by an uncertain modernism. To be sure, anthropologists exalted evolutionism, but like philosophers and religious thinkers, they were reluctant to drop ideas of progress when confronted by the inexorable demon of change. In the hands

51

of most anthropologists, the evolution of culture comfortably supported Victorian pride and progress. The era's anthropologists did, however, anticipate one of the central themes of modernist culture—a fascination with the primitive. But the allure of the primitive was never absolute. As much as anthropologists like Frank Hamilton Cushing gloried in the primitive, they also demonstrated their inability to shake off their most cherished cultural assumptions.

Racism and ethnocentrism stalked the field of anthropology as much as they did the American landscape in general during this period. The politics of cultural domination were never far removed from anthropological practice or American thought. Respectable academic anthropologists were all too ready to support racism and ethnocentrism through their work. The popular evolutionary ordering of culture and race invariably began with the "low" and ended with the "high," charting the progress from savagery to white civilization. At the 1893 World's Fair exposition in Chicago, the "best" research in professional anthropology, popularized for presentation to a wide audience, helped to rationalize racism and modern imperialism through its hierarchical descriptions of the races.

Cultural Evolution

American anthropologists in the 1880s fervently believed that a comparative approach to culture, combined with an evolutionary understanding of cultural development, promised to unlock all the fascinating riddles of culture and race. Method, more than anything else, seemed to define how anthropologists viewed the world. But their method, which sought to classify cultures on a hierarchical scale of development, was deeply influenced by a desire to discover an order and logic inherent in that process. Deeply troubled by the apparent chaos of the present, American anthropologists gained great satisfaction in uncovering a long train of progress leading up to modern civilization. Analysis of their data convinced them that the past was only a prelude to bigger and better things in the future.

Lewis Henry Morgan, the most famous American-born anthropologist of the nineteenth century, deplored the disorder that dogged his life and times. Tragically, he lost two daughters to scarlet fever and had a son who was born mentally retarded. His legal career began under the worst possible circumstances, coinciding with the depression of 1839. Living in the heat of religious revivalism in the "burned over" district of New York, Morgan was neither enthusiastic nor saved. Perhaps because of his personal misfortune and the dizzy pace of economic development and social change in his home town of Rochester, Morgan the anthropologist found progress and order in every nook and cranny of the long history of mankind.

Desire for comradeship, despite the dissolving bonds of traditional community, led Morgan to organize a fraternal order roughly based on Indian rituals and lore. His interest in the traditions and history of the Iroquois nation rapidly developed into an obsession. Morgan defended Seneca tribal claims in a controversial treaty dispute with the United States government; in recompense, he was initiated into the tribe in 1846. Access to the Iroquois nation proved to be a mixed blessing, however. Morgan too often generalized from the specifics of Iroquois social organization to explain the culture of other Indian groups.

In all of his anthropological work, Morgan employed a comparative and evolutionary approach. The massive *Systems of Consanguinity and Affinity in the Human Family* (1870), a theoretically weak book, was nonetheless important in laying the foundations for subsequent academic study of kinship relations, especially among British anthropologists. Its comparative method of analyzing various cultures promised to uncover parallel sets of ethnic relations through similarities in kinship arrangements. As a result of his research, Morgan concluded that America's Indians had originated in India.

Morgan's most important work, *Ancient Society* (1877), presented cultural development in an evolutionary and progressive framework. Contrary to the degenerationist school of anthropology, which interpreted "savage" cultures as remnants of earlier, higher civilizations that had declined, Morgan maintained that Greek and Roman institutions were "essentially identical" to those prevalent among American aborigines. Moreover, he theorized, the human race had originally been unified. Over the long course of development, fragmentation of culture had occurred as a result of "the unequal endowments of the continents." Despite divergences in cultural evolution, Morgan devised an essentially Lamarckian "ratio of human progress." Each "item of absolute knowledge gained became a further acquisition" for a given culture as a whole. Increments of technological innovation, piled upon other marks of cultural or social improvement, moved a culture in a progressive, ascendant direction.

Morgan's classification divided the evolution of culture into seven stages. Not all cultures would traverse the entire route leading to the attainment of civilization. Development began with a common stage of savagery, consisting of three distinct periods marked by certain technical achievements. For example, once a cultural group had mastered the art of pottery, Morgan contended, they had moved from savagery into the first stage of barbarian civilization. The ascendant culture next passed through an additional two stages of barbarism, defined by the domestication of animals in the Eastern Hemisphere and the cultivation of plants by irrigation or the use of certain building materials in the Western Hemisphere. If the culture mastered iron tools, then it was poised to move to the stage designated as civilization.[1]

Morgan's nomenclature and evolutionary classification of the stages of cultural growth were widely accepted and quickly became the defining set of assumptions under which the first significant generation of American anthropologists proceeded. In emphasizing that cultural development was intimately connected to technological innovation, Morgan's work gained the approval of Karl Marx and Friedrich Engels. Engels, in fact, borrowed many of Morgan's ideas for his own work, *The Origin of the Family, Private Property, and the State* (1884). Engels viewed Morgan's evolutionary anthropology as materialist in orientation; Morgan's theory of cultural development through stages of increasing technological innovation paralleled the Marxian historical theory of dialectical materialism.

Closer to home, John Wesley Powell respectfully borrowed from Morgan the essentials of his anthropology. A war hero, explorer, and scholar of prodigious energy and enterprise, Powell was director of the Bureau of American Ethnology (BAE). Thanks to chance and Powell's presence, the BAE was funded in 1879 as a separate entity of the Smithsonian Institution. Its initial budget allowed Powell to direct a major research project that culminated in the survey *Contributions to North American Ethnology*. Under Powell's leadership and influence, the BAE became the single most important source for the collection of ethnographic data in the United States.

An excellent administrator, Powell used his political connections and devotion to the study of the American Indian to win a place for the BAE within the governmental bureaucracy. According to historian Curtis Hinsley, although "Powell never intended to 'professionalize' anthropology, . . . he did hope to organize and systematize research." When Powell founded the BAE, no graduate programs existed in the United States to produce Ph.D.s in anthropology. Those who practiced anthropology came from diverse backgrounds—sometimes from the natural or physical sciences, sometimes from the humanities. Indeed, some contended that anyone willing to hone his powers of observation could contribute to ethnological fieldwork.[2] Powell imposed some degree of centralization, system, and standards on American anthropology. In an age marked by the centralization of function in government, business, and academe, Powell helped anthropology to take its initial steps into the modern era. Thanks to governmental support and institutional encouragement, fieldworkers systematically collected data from Indian tribes that were increasingly vulnerable to cultural extinction. The quality of the research and its interpretation may have been uneven, but its cumulative effects were not, as noted by both the British ethnologist E. B. Tylor in 1884 and the great French structuralist anthropologist Claude Lévi-Strauss in 1965.[3]

Powell turned a sequential notion of development into the chief theoretical tool employed by BAE ethnologists. He added an additional stage to Morgan's evolutionary sequence: civilization was to be followed by a new age of enlightenment. He rejected Darwinian strains of thought that reduced man to a prisoner of the environment, and argued instead that the development of man's brain represented the controlling factor in the evolution of culture. In arriving at this theory, Powell worked closely with Lester Frank Ward, who would eventually become the most famous American sociologist of the era.

Ward first met Powell while serving as a clerk and paleobiologist during a geological expedition to the American West. Ward's time was largely occupied, at government expense, in composing his manuscript *Dynamic Sociology* (1882). He dismissed all theories that drew an exact and continuous parallel between human and animal evolution. While conceding that natural selection did account for the initial development of species, he insisted that man and animal had forever parted company when the human brain had developed into its present form. Once the stage of intellect had been achieved, the course of evolution was transformed from a passive to a dynamic interplay between man and environment. Man became a positive factor directing the evolution of human civilization through mental exertion and institutional association.

Ward's sociology, like Powell's anthropology and the work of the New Psychologists, did more than simply promote an active role for consciousness in the course of evolution. Deep within the sinews of Ward's system was a natural order and a strong demonstration of evolutionary development in a sanguine direction. As he once phrased it, "The need of some inspiring progressive principle for mankind to lay hold of, for the satisfaction of that fundamental sentiment which aspires to a better condition, is as strongly felt now as it was in the days of Plato or of Paul."[4]

Powell, who shared this view, held that intellectual development was only partly due to heredity; it also resulted from the activity of individuals reacting to their environment. When pressed on the relative importance of these factors in human development, he preferred to see environmental influence as less significant than intelligence. He maintained that "human evolution is intellectual evolution, in which it greatly differs from animal evolution." In animals, the law of natural selection governed development; for instance, species with blubber were able to survive in arctic temperatures. But natural selection operated in an often inexact, slow, and not always progressive manner. In contrast, the Eskimo, blessed with the development of an inventive mind, was able to thrive by building houses out of ice blocks and by fashioning clothing from animal skins. Powell denigrated the work of physical anthropologists who focused on the study of physical attributes to the near exclusion of the interplay of cultural and environmental factors.

In much of his work Powell stressed that the proper method of scientific classification would organize, in a logical fashion, the development of diverse cultures. The particulars of history mattered less in evolutionary anthropology than did the necessity to discern order. Powell, no less than Morgan, reflected in his rage for classification the powerful Victorian desire for unity and order. This imperative may be quickly grasped by examining the neat, albeit simplistic, chart that Powell drew up to demonstrate that the tools and concepts of one cultural stage were internally consistent and that each stage evolved into a higher yet still unified cultural configuration:

Savage	*Barbarian*	*Civilized*
stone	clay	iron
canoe with paddles	boat with oars	sailing ships
maternal kinship	paternal kinship	nations
sentence words	phrase words	idea words
picture writing	hieroglyphics	alphabets
beast polytheism	nature polytheism	monotheism
men alone count	arithmetic	geometry[5]

William Henry Holmes and WJ McGee, along with other BAE scholars, applied this type of evolutionary classification scheme in their own research. Holmes was especially interested in the development of the arts. He believed that since savage culture had been greatly influenced by the immediate environment, its art necessarily reflected events of the natural world. According to Holmes, the aesthetic sense, properly cultivated and expressed, was the cultural consequence of true religious feelings, themselves indexes of a higher stage of civilization. In studying this aesthetic hierarchy, Holmes maintained that the status of the arts in a particular cultural grouping would be paralleled by the forms defining marriage, property, and governmental arrangements. All cultural expressions could be logically fitted together, like pieces of a jigsaw puzzle. "Investigations relating to the history of culture," he wrote, "proceed on the theory that from the simplest possible beginnings in the manual arts advance was made until the highest round of the ladder was reached and that a study of the entire series must reveal the steps, the processes, and the laws of advancement."[6] The passive voice employed by Holmes to describe the advance of culture indicated his confidence that the process was necessary and unalterable.

WJ McGee was a dominant figure in the field of anthropology from 1893 until 1903. Intimately involved in the rich intellectual life of Washington, D.C., he belonged to all of that city's scientific societies. Trained as a geologist, McGee was lauded for his ability to popularize scientific knowledge. With Powell's patronage, McGee undertook an expedition to the southwest in 1894, eventually wending his way into South and Central America to study the little-known Seri Indian tribe. The results of his fieldwork appeared in the form of a 300-page BAE report in 1896. McGee filled the tome with analysis and observation but did not question the categories he had carried with him on his trip to Seriland. Using Powell's methodology, McGee placed the Seri at the lowest stage of savagery. In every manner—in religion, tools, conceptualizations—McGee found the Seri to be animalistic. Their faith was "zootheistic," their art "zooesmatic," their technology "zoomimic," and their government, such as existed, "zoocratic."[7]

Progress

Throughout the texts of American anthropology a paean to progress was composed. Anthropological writing suggested that present civilization, especially white American culture, was distinctly different from other cultural formations—and also superior to them. Progress in cultural development, as discerned by anthropologists, comforted white, male American culture in a period of great industrial and cultural change. It allowed many to believe that their most cherished cultural institutions and practices were sanctified by historical development and would not soon be displaced.[8]

Marriage, when placed under the microscope of evolutionary ethnology, invariably revealed progressive development from the early consanguine family structure to the modern monogamous family of the Victorian era. For Morgan the advantages of the monogamous family were significant, representing "the graduated scale of human progress from the abyss of primitive savagery, through barbarism, to civilization." The family was "the richest legacy transmitted to us by ancient society, because it embodies and records the highest results of its varied and prolonged experience.[9]

In much of his work McGee vociferously contended that evolutionary anthropology placed American civilization at the top of the ladder of development. He was proud, like Morgan and Powell, that the power of the human mind distanced civilized man from the animal world. However, the enlightened mind of civilized man was rational and superior to the emotional and instinctual mind common to savage cultures.[10] Despite sorry vestiges of savagery in the modern world, McGee was confident for the future of human life. In "The Trend of Human Progress" (1899) McGee found that "Perfected man is overspreading the world." Even savage races would be improved over time by what McGee perceived as an increasing intermingling of different cultures, and through the white race's acceptance of its fatherly responsibility to care for those less able.[11] In fact, the future promised to achieve the unity of the human race because

when human experience concerning human blood and human culture is synthesized, and when the sum is analyzed into its simplest elements, a single trend is seen: The blood of the races is blending slowly, yet with steadily increasing rapidity, while the culture of the world is blending still more rapidly than the blood; the blood-blending

57

may be sometimes injurious, though it is more frequently beneficial, while the culture-blending is rarely followed by deterioration of the better, commonly attended by improvement of the worse; and human culture is becoming unified, not only though diffusion but through extinction of the lower grades as their representatives rise into higher grades.[12]

Victorian certitude and confidence, as expressed in the work of American anthropologists, was never absolute. Assertions of confidence were often nothing more than a veneer that concealed a foreboding about the consequences of change and uncertainty.[13] Probably the only thing that could be counted on was the ubiquity of change, of ceaseless formation. Recognition of this important reality of modernity was no less frightening to the American anthropologist than to his or her fellow citizens. Many intellectuals were not comforted by their observations of shifting social and cultural arrangements or by the suspicion that absolute certitude was illusory. Sometimes such perceptions led Americans to a greater fascination with cultures different from theirs, to a questioning of their own cultural assumptions. More commonly, however, fear of change led Victorian Americans to make grander and more impassioned assertions of cultural superiority in an almost shamanistic attempt to ward off the ardors of difficult transformations.

A functional and relativistic view of culture, later to become a mainstay of American anthropology, was at best only a minor, hidden theme in the period before 1900. A sometimes healthy, other times fearful optimism reigned; most anthropologists emphasized that culture was a developmental embryo that would evolve to ever-higher forms. James C. Welling, president of Columbian College, encapsulated this view when he wrote, "there is a limitless vista opened (though not an absolutely unlimited one) for the prospective working of better laws, purer justice, wiser economics, richer science, and higher morality."[14]

Morgan and Powell were not satisfied with the shape of the present, but they were confident of the future. Although they generally held firmly to the central thesis that modern civilization was the apogee of development, they never accepted it as a final statement of what had to be. Out of the chaos and unfairness of the past and present, they believed, would arise the order and beauty of a better, more humane world. In this vision of the future they combined the proprieties of Victorianism with the utopian vision of preindustrialism. Since there had been progress in the development of marriage and political institutions, a peaceful solution to the modern era's difficulties of labor unrest and capitalistic domination might also evolve. By following the modern logic of evolution, Morgan and Powell could take sustenance from the simple fact that all cultural and economic forms and institutions were subject to revision and would presumably progress toward a higher form.

This was the upshot of their anthropology—the other side of the coin of Victorian complacency that assured many that their civilization was the epitome of cultural development. Morgan made this clear in *Ancient Society*. In discussing marriage arrangements, he specified that throughout history, each type of marriage institution had been functional, reflecting the needs of its culture. Thus, further improvements could be expected, and greater equality of the sexes would be achieved as the economic and social environment changed. Both Morgan and Powell also anticipated a greater equality in the distribution of wealth. Powell concluded his essay "Competition as a Factor in Human Evolution" (1888) by noting that "The great problem in industrial society to-day is to preserve emulative competition and to destroy antagonistic competition." In Powell's glossary, emulative competition was undertaken in a "generous spirit"; its results were advantageous to all in the society. In certain respects, as Powell and Morgan made clear, their embrace of modern society was never total. When they looked at the economic arrangements of primitive societies, in which the group took priority over the individual, a certain wistfulness intruded on their thinking—a desire to return to a less economically destructive past.[15]

Boas and Cultural Relativism

The focus of anthropology in America in terms of both its theoretical underpinnings and its institutional identity had begun to shift by the turn of the century. The change resulted from the generalized professionalization of American life and culture and from the intellectual mastery and institutional activity of a German immigrant, Franz Boas. Rejecting many of the assumptions of Morgan and Powell's view of anthropology and their evolutionary classifications with parallel lines of development, Boas and his multitude of influential students slowly pushed anthropology away from grand generalizations and toward the intensive study of specific cultural groups through extensive fieldwork.

Born in Germany, Boas attained a Ph.D. with a dissertation on the color of seawater. His background was in the physical and natural sciences, but at an early age he had imbibed at the well of German romanticism and *naturphilosophie*. His fieldwork in anthropology began in 1883 when he journeyed to Baffinland and established contact with Eskimo culture. At that time he moved away from physics and toward ethnology, as evidenced by his publication of *The Central Eskimo* in 1888. By 1887 Boas settled in the United States, initially serving as geography editor for *Science*. He quickly established himself as a controversial and challenging presence in American anthropology.[16]

Boas staunchly came to oppose the "speculative anthropology" of Morgan and Powell. Throughout the late 1880s and into the early 1890s Boas's rejection of their views coexisted within his own work with his acceptance of the ruling conceptual framework of American anthropological science. In "The Aims of Ethnology," a lecture first delivered in 1888, Boas maintained that scientific laws for the study of cultural development might still be found. He noted that "the frequent occurrence of similar phenomena in cultural areas that have no historical contact suggests that . . . important results may be derived from their study, for it shows that the human mind develops everywhere according to the same laws."[17] Implicit in this observation was the assumption that the work of Morgan and Powell fell far short of the status of science. As he matured as an anthropologist, however, Boas increasingly indicated that the search for general evolutionary laws was a futile enterprise, given the proud particularity and confusing complexity of all cultures.

Boas publicly rejected formalistic anthropology in 1887, when he condemned the evolutionary and comparative classification in an exhibition of artifacts organized by Otis T. Mason of the U.S. National Museum and John Wesley Powell. Mason, the guiding intellectual force behind the exhibit, had organized artifacts such as cooking utensils, musical instruments, and farm-

Franz Boas posing for a Kwakiutl Indian ceremony for expelling cannibals, about 1895. *National Anthropological Archive. Smithsonian Institution Photo No. MNH 8304*

ing implements according to their presumed functional attributes. Artifacts from diverse tribes were grouped together for formal comparisons, without consideration of the possibility that the various tribes might use the instruments in different ways. An obvious evolutionary sequence of development based on a biological model of classification dominated this exhibit. Mason did not seek to discern how an individual instrument fit within the context of tribal cultural practices; he maintained that anthropological insight only followed from classifying an artifact within the larger interpretive schema of evolution.[18]

Opposition to Mason's assumptions would, by the turn of the century, come to form the essential outlines of the Boasian anthropological viewpoint: emphasis on the need for a contextual understanding of culture, along with a recognition that the interplay between race, culture, and language was complex and inexact. In contrast to Mason, Boas gave some sense of the complexity of understanding a single object when he analyzed an artifact that produced sounds. Of course, this implement might have been readily understood and typed as a musical instrument. Its formal classification allied it with other like inventions from diverse cultures. Yet in another culture this artifact might function not as a musical instrument but as a magical device. To Boas, a proper anthropological examination involved the formulation of a historical and contextual framework for understanding the experiences and artifacts of the group under analysis; this was accomplished through intensive fieldwork and hesitant generalizing. Modern science, as Boas understood it, "demand[ed] inductive methods" that respected particularity. Thus, he stated, "I cannot agree with Professor Mason's proposal of arranging the cases like a checker-board. *In ethnology, all is individuality.*"[19]

By 1895, when he published his monograph *The Social Organization and the Secret Societies of the Kwakiutl Indians,* Boas' break with the existing comparative evolutionary paradigm was powerfully apparent. Boas's analysis of Eskimo culture rejected the school of historical determinism, or "lock-step" anthropology. The imperative of anthropology must be the study of cultures within their historical contexts. In the view of George W. Stocking, Jr., by 1894 Boas had arrived at a firmly antievolutionary and antideterministic stance, the "implications [of] which tended to undercut any singular standard of cultural evaluation."[20] In "The Limitations of the Comparative Method of Anthropology" (1896) Boas found comparative analyses of "doubtful value, unless at the same time proof is given the same phenomena must always have had the same origin." Moreover, Boas's explicit methodological agenda promised to show, by "detailed study of customs in their relation to the total culture of the tribe practicing them, in connection with an investigation of their geographical distribution among neighboring tribes," the complex causation and interrelationship between psychological, material, and historical factors in the development of cultural formations.[21]

Boas's ideas gained predominance within the profession for a host of reasons. In part, Morgan and Powell's evolutionary approach was undermined by its generalities and by its inability to pigeonhole complex phenomena as neatly as their theory required. Their anthropological perspective was also hampered by its constant recourse to analogy and deduction as the primary tools of analysis. To Boas, the essentials of modern science were based on close observation of the phenomena under study, a willingness to use the inductive method, and a concern with the complexity of experience. In this manner, Boas followed a path similar to that taken by William James and John Dewey in psychology and Oliver Wendell Holmes, Jr., in law. All sought to discard categories of abstract and formal classification while retaining evolutionary thought's emphasis on historicity, process, and experience. Science remained the ideal vehicle for promoting inquiry, professional methods, and the establishment of a community of evaluators. No longer would science pretend, however, to encompass all thought under a single law. Boas and the others were engaged in "a revolt against formalism."[22] Boas's emphasis on experience, psychology, history, pluralism, and particularity, then, followed a path that was increasingly accepted in the social sciences.

Boas successfully gained converts to his methodology because he was particularly adept at building an institutional power base. When he came onto the scene, anthropology had not yet achieved professional status. Degree-granting programs were nonexistent, and training was lax for those who wanted to practice serious anthropological analysis. Although Boas himself had come to the study of anthropology from the physical and natural sciences, he was determined to carve out an independent niche for anthropology within the network of universities and museums then emerging in the United States. This institutional imperative, along with the strength of Boas' ideas, helped to insure victory in the battle of anthropology's conceptual systems.[23]

During the early years of anthropological study, the institutional framework was largely localistic, revolving around the core of a specific museum or scientific society. Boas and his allies helped to create a national consciousness and organization for anthropology. Professionalization became the new reality, with the emergence of national organizations, standardized qualifications for entry into the profession, and networks for the exchange of information and personnel. If earlier scholars had seen few dividends accrue from academic affiliation, anthropologists of Boas' generation made a university connection essential for professional success. When Boas was appointed to a position at Columbia University in the early 1890s he joined a handful of academic anthropologists; Daniel Brinton had been appointed a professor at the University of Pennsylvania in 1886, followed by F. W. Putnam at Harvard and Frederick Starr at the University of Chicago. None of these scholars had parlayed their university affiliations into a national academic power base.

Boas used his program at Columbia University to train the next generation of anthropologists, who assumed positions in the emerging university system and worked as museum administrators. From his positions at Columbia and the American Museum of Natural History, Boas successfully institutionalized and proselytized his conception of the methodology and scope of anthropological research. He further cemented close connections between the academy and the museum by placing university-trained specialists in important positions in America's museums.[24]

Anthropological Fieldwork

Boasian anthropology was distinguished by its requirement that students gain firsthand experience as field-workers; anthropologists must live inside the culture under examination. Fieldwork had always played a role, albeit limited, in nineteenth-century anthropological investigation. Morgan was an honorary member of the Iroquois nation and frequently visited with the tribe; Powell had spent long periods of time among the various Indian tribes of the West during his geological and mapping expeditions. Other anthropologists—Frank Cushing and Alice Fletcher, not to mention Boas himself—had by the 1880s already undertaken extended ethnological research among different Indian tribes. Yet British scholars such as E. B. Tylor and Herbert Spencer commanded wide influence despite their "armchair" method of anthropology. They relied on their well-turned theories of evolution and classification to transform travel reports on diverse cultures into the data base for their anthropological investigations.

The arrival of Frank Cushing signaled a change in the nature of fieldwork. He sought to experience Indian culture as an insider rather than as an outsider. In principle, this would give him a deeper understanding of the culture while satisfying a deep hunger on his part to become engaged with a "savage" culture. Cushing spent years living with the Zuni Indians of the Southwest, eventually becoming a member of the tribe. By shedding his American clothing and "going native," Cushing attempted to break down the division that continues to perplex anthropologists—the barrier that prevents an outsider from gaining a deeper understanding of an alien culture.

A creative and intelligent young man, at age 17 Cushing came to the attention of officials at the Smithsonian Institution when he submitted to them a brief report on his personal collection of arrowheads. After a desultory period at Cornell University, Cushing finally got his chance for adventure and anthropological research: he went west in 1879 with James Stevenson's party to collect artifacts. Thus Cushing, at age 22, escaped the tedium of the East for the excitement and mystery of the West. He would come to fully

Thomas Eakins. *Frank Hamilton Cushing*, ca. 1891. Oil on canvas. *The Thomas Gilcrease Institute of American History and Art, Tulsa, Oklahoma*

live out his fantasies as he transformed himself from Frank Cushing, sickly easterner, into Frank Cushing, anthropologist as hero.[25]

When the Stevenson party decided to leave the Zuni Indian region, Cushing made a momentous decision: he would stay and live among the Zunis. This, he assured officials of the expedition, was not a haphazard decision but one dedicated to the service of science, for it would allow him to examine Zuni tribal customs firsthand. He slowly gained the trust of the Zuni. In the end, Cushing was able to pronounce that "no Christmas dinners I have known have been filled or seasoned with so much badinage, repartee, and hearty laughter" as those dinners undertaken with his Zuni hosts. In sum, he wrote, "the Zuni are not such bad companions after all."[26]

Cushing worked hard to understand the Zuni Indians. He wanted to understand the Zuni language, and he showed an immense capacity to appreciate many of their customs and artifacts. In addition to being energetic, he was also insightful; he used his firsthand knowledge of the Zuni to question some of the assumptions of the evolutionary approach to anthropology. His study of Havasupi marriage patterns and the tribe's tracing of family descent through the father rather than the mother challenged Morgan's views on the development of the family.[27] Indeed, Cushing was one of the first to use the term *culture* in the plural, in the process diminishing the presumption that "civilized" culture was the embodiment of true culture. The Zuni had a religion and a culture that deserved, Cushing maintained, to be taken seriously as such, for they allowed the Zuni to adapt to their environment.

Yet Cushing could be highhanded and demeaning toward the Zuni. He wore the cloak of the intrepid scientific explorer proudly, threatening physical force against his Indian comrades when they did not allow him to sketch for scientific purposes their sacred rituals. At every turn in his story, Cushing made it clear not only that his presence was to be tolerated by the Indians but also that his imperative to gather information had priority over the Zuni's right to privacy. For all the respect he proclaimed for the cultural credibility of Zuni and Havasupi customs and religion, he never fully jettisoned his assumption that white civilization was ultimately superior. In letters to Spencer F. Baird, his superior at the Smithsonian, Cushing recounted with disgust the indignities he had to suffer by eating Zuni food and wearing Zuni clothing in order to be accepted as one of the tribe. In addition, Cushing judged the Havasupi grammatical structure, although regular, to be clearly inferior to that of the Zuni.[28]

Working closely with Indians, Cushing learned, could lead to political difficulties. For as much as Cushing liked to think of himself as a Zuni, he was viewed by the tribe, when necessary, as an intermediary for contact with white culture. The politics of anthropology never failed to confront Cushing. Sometimes he acted as a political partisan. Initial entry into the tribe was accomplished, in part, by his identification with one particular ruling stratum of the Zuni. Thus, during disputes between Zuni factions, Cushing came down on the side of his allies. Yet when the land-grabbing impulses of the son-in-law of an influential United States senator threatened Zuni property, Cushing did not hesitate to leap into the fray as protector of the Indian. Such interventions by a supposedly dispassionate scientist did not always sit well with Cushing's sponsors, who eventually cut off his funding for further study among the Zuni.[29]

Politics alone did not account for Cushing's mounting troubles with his BAE associates in the 1880s. Anthropological fieldwork, the collection and classification of artifacts, could be expensive. Cushing's work, when he returned to the Zuni pueblo again in 1886, was supported by the largess of Mrs. Mary Hemenway. Hemenway harbored dreams of creating an Indian museum in Salem, Massachusetts. But she wanted a quick return of her investment in Cushing's fieldwork. While his years among the Zuni had endowed him with a deeper, more empathetic understanding of their culture than anyone else in the profession possessed, Cushing had failed to produce a large number of professional studies. His work was often incomplete; his willingness and energy to undertake the painstaking labor of field supervision and archaeological digs were hardly apparent.

Wanting more publications and artifacts to enhance her museum's reputation, Hemenway replaced Cushing with Jesse Walter Fewkes. Fewkes had none of Cushing's panache or desire to become a "white Indian." He did have a thoroughly professional demeanor and an insider's understanding of the increasing professionalization of the anthropological establishment in the United States. And he was passionate in wanting to preserve Indian artifacts and to record rapidly vanishing cultural practices. Trained in the biological sciences, Fewkes was a keen observer and sketcher; he regularly produced ethnological reports and collected much information and artifacts. To everyone's mind, he was the ideal anthropologist; eventually, he became head of the BAE.

A number of women, especially Alice Fletcher and Matilda Coxe Stevenson, were highly respected field-workers. Fletcher, no less than Cushing, worked closely with Indian tribes and braved all kinds of opposition—environmental, political, and physical—in order to gain information and understanding. Fletcher was never able to separate the role of field-worker from that of political activist. At times she worked among the Omaha Indians as an agent of the United States government.

Fletcher, almost of necessity, became involved in the politics of Indian affairs. She played an important role in shaping the period's most significant piece of legislation affecting the Indian—the Dawes Severalty Act (1887). This bill, described by Fletcher as the "Magna Charta for the Indians of our Country," allotted land to Indians in parcels of 160 acres or less, depending on whether or not the recipient was head of a family. The act also granted citizenship to Indians who accepted the allotment, but did not allow them to sell the land for 25 years, lest speculators wheedle it away from them. Rather than function as a Magna Charta for the American Indians, as Fletcher had anticipated, the Dawes Act devastated the structures of the tribes affected and did nothing to prevent unfair lease agreements that stole land away from the Indians.[30]

Despite her political missteps, Fletcher was a trained observer of Indian rituals and a sympathetic and professional recorder of their religious beliefs. In part her success stemmed from her ability to recognize that she brought a great deal of cultural baggage to her study of Indian tribes. While reasonably free of "race prejudice," she recognized that her "eyes and ears were unconscious slaves of [her] previous training,—race training, if you will." She eventually shook off as many of her prejudices as she could and did excellent work, reporting fully on the Ghost Dance Religion that became a messianic cult among Indians in the late 1880s and also transcribing and performing Indian music.[31]

The success of male and female field-workers was greatly aided by native American anthropologists, whose support was crucial to the survival of "heroic" white anthropologists in Indian cultures. Francis La Flesche was perhaps the most famous Indian anthropologist of this period. An Omaha Indian, he became a trusted assistant and confidant of Alice Fletcher. Together they worked on studies of Omaha music and religion. They shared authorship of an important study, *The Omaha Tribe* (1911), under the auspices of the BAE. But if white anthropologists such as Cushing and Fletcher were frustrated in their attempts to penetrate the mind and cultures of native Americans, anthropologists such as La Flesche—born of a French father and an Indian mother—often found themselves marginalized. La Flesche was forced to endure the suspicion of the Indians and the racism of white society.[32]

Racism

More than two centuries of slavery had bequeathed a legacy of racism to America that remained virulent long after the guns of the Civil War had fallen silent. The era of Reconstruction, immediately following the war, brought forth expectations of equality and prosperity for recently freed slaves. But hope soon gave way to despair. In the South the Ku Klux Klan, using methods of intimidation and terror, and aided by the cunning and complicity of white politicians, circumvented constitutional guarantees for the right of black men to vote. Indeed, between 1896 and 1904, in the sovereign state of Louisiana, the number of black men registered to vote was decreased by "legal" means from 130,334 to 1,342. Hand in hand with political disfranchisement came the segregation of the races and destitution for blacks. This sad state of affairs became codified in the Jim Crow laws, which established segregated facilities and sanctioned other indignities designed to keep the black race under the foot of the white in the South. Northern goodwill for the black race was limited at best. Northern whites, moved in part by a spirit of reconciliation toward the South, were quite willing to bury the hatchet that had cut the nation in half during the war years—deep into the back of black rights. Finally, in 1895, the United States Supreme Court, in the case of *Plessy* v. *Ferguson*, approved in principle and practice the segregation of the races by a doctrine of "separate but equal." But as any black person could have told the esteemed justices, separate never meant equal for blacks in the south.[33]

A spiderweb of racism caught other groups in its deadly, sticky net in the period 1880–1900. As waves of white settlers moved to the western Plains region, hungry for land and satiated with ideals of civilization, confrontations with the native Indian population increased in frequency and intensity. Earlier, the white race's greed for land and control had been more easily accommodated because of the ample space for Indian resettlement in the West. In the 1830s, when white settlers, with the support of the state of Georgia, had encroached on the lands of the "Five Civilized Tribes" of the Southeast, President Andrew Jackson's solution had been to move the Indians west of the Mississippi River. This forced migration, now known as the Trail of Tears, banished the tribes from their ancestral lands, brought them into conflict with tribes to the west, and cost them many casualties.[34]

The situation had not improved by 1880. Government policy generally acceded to the demands of settlers, ranchers, and mining companies to remove the Plains Indians from the open land and to confine them to reservations. Through starvation, military defeat, or lack of other options, the Indians of the Great Plains were removed from blocking the path of white civilization. On the reservations the Indians' culture began to disintegrate, and their allotments of land and food were regularly raided by avaricious officials and speculators. The Plains Indians took to the Ghost Dance religion as a means of salvation, but it helped to contribute to armed conflict with the cavalry. In the grim Battle of Wounded Knee, the Indians suffered their final defeat of the era. In the racially tinged vision of white America, however, defeat for the Indians simply represented the success of civilization and justice; it was seen as the natural result of evolutionary processes.

Many white Americans, concerned about the plight of the Indians, believed that the only way of saving them from destruction was to instruct them in the ways of white civilization. In this view, the paternalistic white man knew what was best for the childlike Indian. "We must in a great measure," wrote Carl Schurz, secretary of the Department of the Interior in 1881, "do the necessary thinking for them to accept our conclusions."[35] Indian opposition to policies demanding their acculturation to white culture was invariably ignored. Many thousands of Indian children were removed, often kidnapped, from their tribal settings and transported to special schools, often run by Christian denominations whose mission was to "civilize" them. Indian boys were shorn of their long hair, forced to wear the white man's clothes, and forbidden to speak their native languages.

Asian immigrants, especially on the West Coast, had long been objects of white derision. Welcomed at first for their labor, they came to be seen as unfair competition with white workers when jobs were scarce, or as the cause of low wages or weak unions. Prejudice against Chinese immigrants was great, and it sometimes erupted into race riots. In the words of a Chinese scholar who observed the anti-Chinese animus in America, "If a single American was treated in China as were the victims of the anti-Chinese riots at Denver, the United States would send 100,000 missionaries to civilize the heathen."[36] By the late 1880s the United States Congress had banned further immigration of Chinese and prohibited states from allowing Chinese already in the country from gaining citizenship.[37]

Whites were vociferous in expressing their disdain for those races that seemed most different from their own. But even immigrants from southern and eastern Europe—Jews and Catholics especially—were greeted with jeers as they arrived at America's shores. Like other groups, they were perceived as willing to work for less, thereby cheapening the value of native American workers, and as practicing customs not consonant with Protestant values. To be sure, the intensity of racism against immigrants often seemed to rise or fall with shifts in the economy. The patrician Henry Adams, as he became more obsessed with his declining fortunes, increasingly came to blame "infernal Jewry" for not only America's problems but the entire world's. But the racist sentiments of the era cannot be connected solely to economic indicators, for even when the economy was on the rebound, antipathy toward immigrants remained.[38]

American anthropologists were born into a world heavily influenced by racist preconceptions. Not surprisingly, they often strengthened such perceptions by reinforcing them with an air of scientific authority. Thus, racism existed as much in the book-lined studies of academics and in museums of anthropology as it did in governmental policy directed toward blacks, Indians, immigrants, and foreigners in the period 1880–1900. Precious few anthropologists doubted for a moment that cultural groups were not only dissimilar but also unequal. Lewis Henry Morgan's schema indicated that certain cultures clearly lagged behind others in attaining a higher stage of civilization. Whether anthropologists had favorable motives in studying savage cultures or took a paternalistic attitude toward them, their findings conspired to fill white Americans with pride and certitude in their racial superiority. In an age marked by scientific classification, the self-serving theories of evolutionary sequences adopted by anthropologists of the era exiled the nonwhite cultures under study to a decidedly inferior status.[39]

The first university-based anthropologist, Daniel Brinton, proselytized for "evolutionary racialism." He claimed that "the black, the brown, and the red races differ anatomically so much from the white . . . that even with equal cerebral capacity, they could never rival its results by equal efforts."[40] In his *Races and Peoples: Lectures on the Science of Ethnology* (1890) Brinton presented a racial hierarchy in which the African stood lower than the American Indian, who in turn stood lower than the Asian: "the European or white race stands at the head of the list, the African at its foot." Brinton's volume listed the physical traits that marked a race as backward: "prominence of the jaws, recession of the chin, wide nasal aperture," to name only a few. He repeated this theme, illustrated by many racist stereotypes, in a pamphlet titled *Negroes* (1891) and in papers presented to his professional peers throughout the 1890s.[41] In a talk he gave as the retiring president of the American Association for the Advancement of Science in 1895, Brinton stated, "I must still deny that all races are equally endowed,—or that the position with reference to civilization which the various ethnic groups hold to-day, is one merely of opportunity and externalities."[42]

Evolutionary racism was hardly an aberration among professional anthropologists. WJ McGee, when president of the American Anthropological Association, used the evolutionary classification of cultures to defend the benefit and necessity of imperialism. Believing that the dark-skinned races were inferior to the lighter-skinned, he viewed the white race as having the paternalistic responsibility to control the destiny of the black race. McGee spoke of "the white-skinned man" as the world's leader, as a "burden-bearer" for those more backward.[43]

Frederick Starr, professor of anthropology at the University of Chicago from 1892 until 1923, proclaimed the reality of "Anglo-Saxon superiority." Analysis of the scale of human social and cultural evolution demonstrated conclusively, Starr maintained, that "ours [the white American culture] is the finest ever, all others fall short." Starr noted in 1895 that "in the march from savagery to civilization all peoples have not travelled at the same speed; some have hardly travelled at all."[44] Even John Wesley Powell, despite his years of trying to appreciate and understand the customs of Indian tribes, referred to their religion as little more than a conglomeration of "childish beliefs."[45]

Racism expressed itself as strongly in popular culture as it did in academic theory. Indeed, sometimes academic and popular racism intermingled. At World's Fairs, for example, the assumptions of evolutionary racism were built into the logic of the exhibitions. Familiar anthropological themes of progress, hierarchy, and race helped to rationalize the segregation of the races in the South and to support imperialistic practices both at home and abroad.

Draped in the bright and alluring colors of science and entertainment, these ideological premises were celebrated rather than questioned. The World's Fair served as a barometer of the accomplishments of white civilization and as a promise of future greatness. Said President McKinley, just before he was assassinated at the Buffalo Exposition of 1901, "Expositions are the time-keepers of progress. They record the world's advancement."[46]

Millions of fairgoers passed through the turnstiles into the Chicago World's Columbian Exposition of 1893 to encounter a conception of progress created by the nation's most respected scientists. Smithsonian Institution assistant secretary G. Brown Goode, who had studied under Agassiz at Harvard, worked out a system of classification for the exhibition that promised to demonstrate the backwardness of some races and the progress and accomplishments of white civilization. Other important anthropologists, such as John Wesley Powell and Frederic Ward Putnam, head of Harvard's Peabody Museum of American Archaeology and Ethnology, helped to organize the exhibition and to support these presumptions through the use of a "living ethnological display" and the exhibition of cultural artifacts. Fairgoers could see, and even touch, persons of other races and cultures—assembled to demonstrate, in the words of Putnam's assistant Harlan Ingersoll Smith, "the advancement of the evolution of man."[47]

The fair's midway, along which many popular exhibits were grouped, served as an ethnological museum in and of itself. Fairgoers passed Javanese, Samoan, and Dahomeyan villages. The primitive cultures represented, one guidebook conjectured, might be profitably contrasted with the apotheosis of modern civilization on display at the heralded and appropriately named "White City." American Indians were patronizingly depicted at the 1893 exposition as either savages or evolutionary throwbacks. The antipathy demonstrated toward the Indians was matched, if not exceeded, by that pervading the exhibits on the black race. One souvenir publication noted that compared with the Dahomeyan tribe of Africa, the Indians were "a thing of beauty and joy forever" [*sic*]. The institutional and popular ethnological racism of the fair has been summed up by historian Robert W. Rydell: "Anthropological attractions—consisting of cultural artifacts, lay-figure groupings of 'primitive types,' and selected nonwhites living in ethnological villages along the midways—charted a course of racial progress toward an image of utopia that was reflected in the main exposition buildings."[48]

Fairs, then, furnished at least limited proof for Powell and Morgan's belief in the parallel, uneven lines of cultural development and supported the notion that material progress was proof of the material and intellectual superiority of the white race. In this sense, the World's Fair expositions may be viewed as cultural expressions of racial and ethnological classification and domination, as well as reflections of the racism and elitism central to the white political culture of the era.

A Connecticut Yankee

First published in 1889, Mark Twain's popular novel *A Connecticut Yankee in King Arthur's Court* may be read as representing many of the popular themes and assumptions of the day regarding the superiority of modern civilization over savage cultures. What makes the novel more than a mere reflection of hierarchical views of culture is Twain's ironic and ambivalent attitude toward those views. At times he seems to support beliefs in the power and privilege of modern technology and in Victorian cultural assumptions; at other times he seems to demonstrate that modern men are no more civilized than their ancient forbears and that the blessings of modern technology are mixed at best.[49]

A Connecticut Yankee is a fantasy that revolves around a nineteenth-century Yankee, Hank Morgan, who awakens one day to find himself mysteriously dumped in King Arthur's England. A chronicle of his many adventures follows. By dint of his tremendous energy, scientific knowledge, entrepreneurial bent, and self-confidence, Morgan battles against the superstition, slavery, and backwardness of the Arthurian era. He intends to bring stupendous technical improvements to the lives of Arthurians. In the end, his attempt to change the ideals of the Arthurians fails; knights and religious leaders conspire against him. The novel concludes with Morgan and his technology for mass destruction arrayed against those who would banish him and his improvements from the kingdom. Morgan wins the bloody confrontation; his opponents' bodies are piled high, one atop another. But as he surveys the damage, a wounded knight thrusts his dagger into Morgan. So ends the experiment in cultural diffusion.

A Connecticut Yankee functions like an anthropological assessment of a savage culture, full of implications for Indian-white relations in the late nineteenth-century. Twain presents the Arthurians as savages. They are described in terms that anthropologists usually reserved for Indian subjects: "brawny men, with long, coarse, uncombed hair that hung down over their faces and made them look like animals." Hank Morgan cannot help but blush in the face of their wanton nakedness. In exasperation, he finally exclaims that "they are white Indians."[50]

Morgan manages in an intriguing way to gain the respect, if not the trust, of these "white Indians." He plays into their superstitions by "proving" that he can control a solar eclipse. Accompanied by his faithful native informant, Clarence, Hank Morgan learns much about the backwardness of the Arthurians, their strange rituals, silly religious beliefs, and unenlightened view of the efficacy of magic. Morgan attempts to bring them the ample benefits of civilization. Noting that the Arthurians know little of personal cleanliness, Morgan—with the Victorian ardor that placed cleanliness next to godliness—

not only begins a soap manufacturing plant but also hires individuals to advertise the value of soap.

A Connecticut Yankee is an extended commentary on the imperative that informs anthropology: the attempt to comprehend the "other." Inherent in that endeavor is an uncertain relationship between the "superior" culture of the observer and the "inferior" culture of the observed. Twain plays on such themes without resolving them. Are the Arthurians resistant to civilization? Must they go through a natural evolution (as the anthropologist Morgan had demonstrated in *Ancient Society*) before they can hope to become civilized? Can the anthropologist as reformer possibly succeed? Twain's novel may be interpreted as demonstrating the distinction between custom and culture. In this view, the customs of the Arthurians, their petty superstitions and beliefs, make them incapable of improving themselves under the beneficent direction of Hank Morgan. Yet the novel can also be read as a parable of the dangers of cultural imperialism, anthropological or otherwise; as a devastating indictment of the assumptions of the superiority of white culture, as posited by anthropologists; and as a warning of the dangerous implications of paternalistic policies toward Indians, blacks, and other groups. Indeed, the book might well indicate that human nature remains the same, no matter what clothes or technology accompany the Arthurians or the Hank Morgans. The progress of white culture and technology, the highest fruits of civilization, in the end only bring forth Morgan's horrific mechanized destruction of 25,000 Arthurians, whose dying cries "swelled out on the night with awful pathos."[51]

But all was not to be a saga of racism and evolutionary backwardness in the period 1880–1900, at least not within the profession of anthropology. Thanks to Franz Boas's institutional successes—as well as to his scientific work demonstrating that the physical characteristics of children born in the United States to immigrants might be appreciably changed by environmental factors such as better diet—anthropology would turn increasingly from the cultural hubris of the late nineteenth century toward the culturally relativistic position made famous by Boas's students in the initial decades of the twentieth century.[52]

four

Woman as Intellectual
and Artist

Few issues struck more sensitive nerves in the years 1880 to 1900 than "the Woman Question." Not confined to the political, economic, and social realms, this question touched powerfully on the issues of science, religion, sociology, and creativity. The only thing all sides in the dispute could agree on was that the pace of change and agitation was quickening. Women increasingly entered the public sphere to demand political and social equality. Changes in the social and economic structure of America helped to boost the number of women employed outside of the home. Tempers flared in the heat of what would be known by the turn of the century as the battle of the sexes. Traditionalists provokingly questioned whether women were capable of sustained thought or worth educating. Should women, they asked, be allowed a public presence, as demanded by suffragists? Many men feared, as did some women, the implications of a positive evaluation of women's independence.

The political and social successes of the women's rights movement were intimately connected to skirmishes on the intellectual front. In order to gain the vote, for example, women leaders had to confront an entrenched ideology that denied—on physiological, religious, and cultural grounds—the very notion that women could productively engage in a public life. At the same time that the conceptual foundations for women's rights were being laid, women increasingly pursued new intellectual and cultural interests. Education became a realistic alternative for women in a manner thus far unimagined in American history. Yet entry into the intellectual life was never absolute, assured, or easy for women. Overt gender discrimination greatly hampered the progress of women intellectuals and artists.

74

In formulating a philosophy of women's intellectual capacity and equality, domestic scientist Ellen Swallow Richards, theorist Charlotte Perkins Gilman, and novelist Kate Chopin often forcefully challenged the essential male-dominated structures of Victorian thought and culture. Nonetheless, for all of the modernism inherent in their emphasis on women's rights, women activists sometimes were reluctant to assault the nexus between women and the home, between natural endowment and environmental context. The domestic science movement, for example, sought to bring education and science into the daily routine of homebound women yet continued to emphasize rather than to question the cherished Victorian image of the woman as homemaker. In addition, while women intellectuals questioned all sorts of Victorian truisms confining women's intellectual capacity and public role, many still tended to couch their arguments in the logic and rhetoric of gender differentiation and complementarity—often embracing the very notions of a distinctive female nature that had kept them oppressed. Modern in their espousal of women's rights to freedom and equality, important leaders of the feminist movement remained entrenched within the familiar, gender-distinctive assumptions of Victorian society. They were excited to enter into a modern age of women's liberation but unable to drop their traditional intellectual and cultural baggage. In a world unkind to the notion of an intellectually powerful, independent woman, women thinkers would have been foolhardy to rush into the stream of modernism without any anchors.

The Danger of Thinking

By the closing decades of the nineteenth century, the educational system had finally begun to offer opportunities for women. Women's colleges dotted the educational landscape: Bryn Mawr (1885), Vassar (1861), Wellesley (1870), and Mount Holyoke (1837). In addition, major midwestern state universities began to offer coeducation for women students in the 1870s. By 1890 over 40 percent more women than men graduated from public and private secondary schools in America. Moreover, the number of women enrolled in colleges increased steadily, from about 11,000 students in 1870 to 56,000 in 1890. By 1900, 85,000 women were studying in colleges and universities; they represented just under half of all students enrolled in institutions of higher education.[1]

The statistical presence of women in institutions devoted to the intellectual life hardly dampened doubts about women's intellectual capacity. If anything, it elicited a host of worried opinions from a variety of sources fearful that sustained thought on the part of women would play havoc with the natural and necessary pursuits of childbearing and homemaking. Although most of the attacks came from male physicians and educators, some women also lent their voices in opposition to female intellectual and educational equality.

Opponents of women's rights and doubters of women's intellectual ability attacked under the cover of popular scientific ideas. In an age dominated by the claims of science, women often came up against a scientific establishment that firmly opposed female liberation. Historian Cynthia Eagle Russett argues that "science itself was androcentric and patriarchal. It did not go to the aid of opponents of social inequality; it was a key source of that opposition." In addition, familiar interpretations of Darwinian science powerfully supplemented existing scientific and social visions of the innate differentiation of the sexes.[2]

Darwinism was commonly used to defend a thesis of women's intellectual backwardness. Although Darwin had relatively little to say on the issue in his central text, *The Descent of Man* (1873), he did suggest that the struggle for existence, working through the law of natural selection, had selected for men the qualities of courage, strength, imagination, and intellect. In contrast, women had developed a quickness of perception and strength of intuition (to better anticipate the needs of husbands and children), as well as maternal tenderness. Darwin's thoughts on the differentiation of functions indicated that the nature of women was all but fixed in the sphere of their responsibilities for reproduction and mothering.

Scientific evidence "proved" in other ways that women could not and should not become intellectuals or creative thinkers. Using statistical evidence as well as a rudimentary Darwinian theory of heredity, the British statistician Francis Galton demonstrated that the annals of history revealed few women of genius. Many thinkers, pushing aside an environmental explanation for the discrepancy between male and female genius (although also stressing that women were less prone to idiocy), claimed that women's intellects were of a steadier, less volatile type than men's. Hence, women could never be expected to make impressive contributions to the worlds of literature, art, and science. Women's endowments, meant to conserve the race and selected for preservation over the ages, exempted them from the intellectual arena.

No work better, or more vehemently, used science to define the debits of women's education than Dr. Edward H. Clarke's *Sex in Education; or, A Fair Chance for the Girls* (1873). The book achieved instant notoriety and cast a long shadow over the future of women's education. As M. Carey Thomas, president of Bryn Mawr College, recalled nearly a half century later, she was "haunted . . . by the clanging chains of that gloomy little specter, Dr. Edward H. Clarke's *Sex in Education*."[3] Clarke's book presented a physiological perspective on women's education.[4] Women and men were endowed with significantly different physical organizations that necessitated separate schemes of development. Believing anatomy to be destiny, Clarke wished for women, no less than men, to achieve their "fullest development." Full development did not, however, bring equally beneficial consequences to each sex. Acknowledging that diet, fashion, and ignorance weakened women, Clarke emphasized that female physiology made women incapable of intellectual and physical exertion. The essential differentiation of the sexes, Clarke averred, resided in the nature of the female reproductive system.

Borrowing from scientific theories on the conservation of energy and from Herbert Spencer's ideas on the specialization and differentiation of function associated with evolutionary development, Clarke viewed the womb as the center of woman's energy. Too much energy devoted to thought—especially in the crucial adolescent period, when the reproductive system was not fully developed—undermined women's childbearing powers and caused a host of debilitating nervous ailments. In the Spencerian terms of the specialization of functions, Clarke found that "the physiological principle of doing only one thing at a time, if you would do it well, holds as truly of the growth of the organization as it does of the performance of any of its special functions." Hence, he maintained, women's attention should be directed to their highest function, motherhood, rather than to an education similar to that pursued by men. Clarke accepted that women might pursue education, but he advised that they limit their study time to a maximum of four to five hours a day, with time off every fourth week, lest they injure their health.

The luster of Clarke's argument lay not only in its scientific patina but also in how well it accorded with the traditionalist notion of separate spheres for men and women. According to that powerful ideology, women were consigned to labor in the private realm of domesticity, to have children and to pursue moral and religious devotion in a highly sentimental manner. The cult of "True Womanhood," which was central to the separate-spheres ideology, required a woman to remain at home, there to watch over the family with a pious and pure heart. Subservience to the wishes of her husband, rather than allegiance to the demands of original thinking or active engagement with public issues, represented the ideal life for a woman.[5] Concerns of public life were better left in the hands of men.

Article after article in the 1880s and 1890s presented evidence of women's intellectual inferiority and demonstrated the dangers of female education. Miss M. A. Hardaker wrote in *Popular Science Monthly* in 1882 that the science of craniology (the measurement of brain weight and capacity) demonstrated that women possessed smaller brains than men. Since bigger was better, in Hardaker's view, women could never hope for intellectual equality. Hardaker did not base her contention simply on difference in brain size, however. She surmised that the creation of energy required for serious thought depended on the amount of fuel the individual thinker consumed, and that since men ate more than women, they would forever be able to produce more thought. As Hardaker put it, "Of this smaller amount of food consumed by women some must always be spared for the continuance of the race; so that the sum total of food converted into thought by women can never equal the sum total of food converted into thought by men. It follows, therefore, that *men will always think more than women.*"[6]

Twenty years after Hardaker put forth her argument, respected psychologist G. Stanley Hall emphasized in his important study *Adolescence* (1903) that when adolescent girls subjected their nervous systems to vigorous thought, they endangered their reproductive and emotional powers. Women's education, Hall confidently proclaimed, with the backing of psychological science apparently behind him, must be "primarily and chiefly for motherhood."[7]

Psychological therapy was based on a presumption that women were harmed by too much thinking or creative activity. According to Dr. S. Weir Mitchell, under the strain of thinking, women succumbed to neurasthenia. This malady, which afflicted many women of the middle and upper classes, caused an individual to feel languid, to be incapable of facing her domestic responsibilities. In some cases, women with neurasthenia became deeply depressed, sometimes suicidal. In response, Mitchell developed his famous "rest cure," which required a woman to absolutely abstain from any exercises that might stimulate the brain. He administered this prescription to such intellectual women as Jane Addams, Charlotte Perkins Gilman, and Edith Wharton as their only hope for recovery from debility and depression.[8]

Disbelievers in women's intellectual capacity found evidence that their worst fears about educated women were being realized. In their minds, statistics indicated that women who attended college married less frequently than women without education; college-educated women who did marry produced fewer offspring than their less-educated sisters. Although the decline in the birthrate in the United States was a long-term phenomenon, many commentators chose to consider educated women responsible for it. Because they married later, and because excessive thought drained energy from their reproductive systems, these women were reproducing at unacceptably low rates. According to popular writer Grant Allen, by being offered the same education as men, women had been led away from their natural and necessary inclination toward motherhood. Allen advocated a gender-differentiated education that would train women to be better wives and mothers.[9]

Although supporting the notion of an "equal degree of breadth and thoroughness" in education for both men and women, David Starr Jordan, influential president of Stanford University, worried that women in the university diminished standards and threatened to undermine the significant contributions of science to modern education. Jordan found women naturally attracted to literature and language but prone to a kind of intellectual "dilettantism." Women lacked "originality" when it came to science; "they are not attracted by unsolved problems and in the inductive or 'inexact' sciences they seldom take the lead." In contrast, men worked for results; they sought to get behind the mere nature of appearances. Since Jordan believed that the modern university must be structured to facilitate scientific inquiry, he presented science in essentially male-oriented terms. Too much feminine influence in the university, Jordan feared, might reduce scientific study to sentimentalism and promote "a candy coated ethics of self-realization. There [would be] nothing ruggedly true, nothing masculine left in it."[10]

The Feminist Rebuttal

In the 1870s arguments against the scientific belief that women should not tax their brains too much were weak. By the 1880s, however, more women began to employ their own interpretations of science to refute arguments that women could not be intellectuals or should not have the right to vote. Most importantly, by 1900 significant numbers of women intellectuals became proudly visible, despite a bulwark of defenses erected to block their path. Success required first that women intellectuals refute the charges detailed most famously by Clarke, Spencer, Darwin, and Hardaker.

Protest was immediately heard against Dr. Clarke's pronouncements about the dangerous intimacy between female education and physical debility. Writers ranging from the feminist editor of the *Atlantic Monthly*, Thomas Wentworth Higginson, to the social-science reformer Caroline H. Dall, found Clarke's data suspect and incomplete. In contrast to Clarke's essential emphasis on the internal physiological limitations of women, these writers noted the importance of the environment in defining the question of women's education. Many of women's neurasthenic debilities might, some argued, be traced to fashion, diet, and lack of exercise rather than to excessive thinking or education. Julia Ward Howe maintained that different physical training for girls and boys helped to cause sexual differentiation in education. But for all the dismay over Clarke's volume, contributors such as Howe, Higginson, and Dall, in *Sex and Education: A Reply to Dr. E. H. Clarke's "Sex in Education"* (1874), willingly acknowledged the import of sexual differentiation. Women could and should be educated in a fuller manner, these thinkers declared— but despite their belief that women could thrive under a more rigorous educational regimen, they proved reluctant to drop the idea of differences in intelligence between the sexes. Such distinctions, they believed, were blessed by God or had developed naturally through the process of evolution.

Higginson found no essential commonalities between the sexes, only a welcome difference. Although he consistently supported education for women, he always viewed women as the repositories of truth, beauty, and sentiment. Dall also accepted Clarke's crucial notion that "the spiritual and intellectual functions of women" differed from those of men; she merely suggested that the formulation was incomplete. In a statistical sense, just as great a differentiation of capacities among a sample of men might be discovered as in a general comparison between men and women. Certain women, Dall contended, were more logical candidates for education than individual men. But even within the boundaries of coeducation, Dall hesitated to challenge the ruling ideology of separate spheres. While recognizing that college education represented a wonderful opportunity for young women to develop their natural capacities, Dall warned that "the social head of the college must be a woman who will exercise loving motherly care" while respecting "the natural differences of the sexes."[11]

By the 1880s feminist criticism increasingly employed a physiological and scientific perspective. After all, the antifeminist arguments of Miss Hardaker and a host of Darwinians and Spencerians had relied on the language of science. The stakes in this debate were high, for if Hardaker and others wrapped the banner of science around the ideology of separate spheres and women's intellectual inferiority, then the gains made by women on college campuses might easily vanish or be written off as a weakening of the college's standards.

Hardaker proved an easy target for attack. Nina Morais, writing in the *Popular Science Monthly*, criticized in scientific and logical terms Hardaker's argument for female intellectual weakness. Morais comprehended no necessary relationship between the amount of food consumed and any concomitant explosion of intellectual energy. After all, men of sickly or delicate temperament and physique—Newton, Napoleon, Comte, Shakespeare, Bacon, Heine, and Spinoza—had all been productive. Rejecting Hardaker's "grocer's scale" equating brain size with intellectual ability, Morais found the differences between male and female brains to be on the average rather insignificant. Moreover, she observed, a strict brain-size thesis implied that males with below-average brain weights should be barred from higher education, while women with larger brain weights should be admitted with full privileges. Yet Morais was forced to acknowledge that women, "because some of [their] time and energy must be devoted to motherhood," would never accomplish as much intellectual work as men. Rather than regret or question this reality, Morais simply requested that women as a group not be restricted to motherhood.[12]

The traditional vision of separate spheres was turned around to defend the idea of education for women. Alice B. Tweedy, in her essay "Is Education Opposed to Motherhood?" (1890), defended women's right to a college education in no uncertain terms while at the same time contending that education would not inflict undue damage on the essentials of "womanhood." By the turn of the century the image of the college woman had undergone a significant change. Many stories in popular magazines regaled readers with images of Gibson girls—healthy, vibrant young women who attended college to hone their social skills as a prelude to their assuming fulfilling and traditional roles as wives and mothers.[13]

As women entered the professional fields of social science and psychology, extended research was undertaken on the crucial question of sex differentiation. Helen Bradford Thompson's pioneering research sought to quantify degrees of sexual differentiation between men and women. Her experimental results proved a boon for those who maintained that male and female distinctions were more a function of environment than endowment. Thompson found that men possessed "better-developed motor ability and more ingenuity," while women had "somewhat keener senses and better memory." But she demonstrated that such distinctions were not necessarily biological, since these theories could support a variety of striking and contradictory traits. Biology could, in fact, be employed to explain women's superiority just as easily as it could be used to demonstrate her inferiority. In the end, Thompson promoted the significant role that environment played in explaining gender differentiation. She concluded, "The entire practical movement of sociology is based on the firm conviction that an individual is very vitally molded by his surroundings and that even slight modifications may produce important changes in character."[14]

Discussions of women's intellect and natural endowments were all part of a larger debate on women's suffrage. The essential tenets of the prosuffrage position sometimes relied more on a reluctant modernist framework than on a traditional argument for natural rights. Most women's rights advocates readily conceded their belief that men and women were naturally different. But they rejected the idea that such differences should prevent women from gaining the vote. Mary A. Livermore expressed this viewpoint most typically: "Each [sex] is endowed with aptitudes and capacities that the other, in some measure, lacks. Each is the complement and the supplement of the other."[15]

Before 1880 the argument for women's participation in voting had largely been erected upon the philosophy of natural rights—an ideal that Elizabeth Cady Stanton continued to uphold well into the 1880s. By the final decade of the nineteenth century an expediency argument for allowing women to vote became more common and compelling. Women supported their right to vote not by challenging Victorian assumptions about womanhood but by working within them and expanding their boundaries. For example, women needed the vote to protect themselves against the usurpations of devious men. In granting women the right to vote, home, motherhood, and children would all be better protected. The concept of women's moral and spiritual superiority to men also supported voting-rights arguments. Given the corruption of politics, women reasoned, how better to clean it up than to allow the moral voice of women to be heard and expressed at the polls? Despite the pervasive inequalities they faced in terms of education and career opportunities, women contended that voting rights would help to make them more equal and hence more responsible.

Women faced the biblical claim, especially as expressed in the gospels of St. Paul, that their gender must not have a public voice. This was a touchy point, since many of the male intellectuals who supported greater autonomy and suffrage for women were religious, and women suffragists did not want to alienate them. But men and women from a variety of religious backgrounds no longer swallowed unquestioningly the full range of biblical admonitions. Thus, suffragists rejected St. Paul's injunction that women within the church should be seen but not heard, claiming that its wording was an imprecise translation. In any case, they argued, the misogynistic view expressed was personal to St. Paul and therefore not to be confused with theological law.[16]

Women rarely attacked directly the historical role of religion and the church in supporting the oppression of women. Elizabeth Cady Stanton, however, at the close of her long and illustrious career as a suffrage advocate, edited and published in two volumes her highly controversial *The Woman's Bible* (1895). In this feminist reading of crucial biblical passages, Stanton and her associates drew upon a freethinking tradition to undermine the authority of the Bible as it related to women. Thundered Stanton, "The writers of the Bible are prone to make woman the standard for all kinds of abomination; and even motherhood, which should be held most sacred, is used to illustrate the most revolting crimes." In Stanton's view, "an expurgated version" of the Bible was needed "if we wish[ed] to inspire our children with proper love and respect for the Mothers of the race."[17]

Interestingly, the stronger Stanton's arguments against the Bible, the farther other women in the suffrage movement edged away from her. At the 1896 convention of the National American Women Suffrage Association (NAWSA), a resolution was passed to distance the association from the views expressed in Stanton's *The Woman's Bible*. By this act, NAWSA sought to prevent the taint of irreligion from harming the suffrage movement. Additionally, most of the suffragists remained comfortable working within the contours of traditional beliefs.

Expediency arguments for suffrage had an undercurrent of racism and xenophobia. America's electorate was changing because immigrants and black males had begun to exercise their right to vote. In the minds of many white middle- and upper-class individuals, this raised fears of political corruption, influence peddling, machine politics, and incompetence. Correction appeared to hinge on both limiting the franchise to those who were literate and increasing the franchise to include women. White women, it was assumed, would be able to meet voting requirements, thereby shifting the political balance of power back to the white elite. The NAWSA conference in 1893 "*resolved*, that without expressing any opinion on the proper qualifications for voting, we call attention to the significant facts that in every State there are more women who can read and write than all negro voters; more white women who can read and write than all negro voters; more American women who can read and write than all foreign voters; so that the enfranchisement of such women would settle the vexed question of rule by illiteracy, whether of home-grown or foreign-born production."[18] Thus, unfortunately, the important goal of women's suffrage was aided by recourse to arguments based on racial prejudice.

Women in the Professions

Women functioned as intellectuals, artists, and professionals in increasing numbers after 1880. Their accomplishments stood as the finest testament to the ability of women to participate fully in the intellectual life. Such participation, while increasing, was never absolute. Roadblocks and difficulties remained in the paths of women. The angry tones of Sarah Grand captured women's frustrations: "Man deprived us of all proper education, and then jeered at us because we had no knowledge. . . . He cramped our minds so that there was no room for reason in them, and then made merry at our want of logic. . . . Woman may be foolish, but her folly has never been greater than man's conceit, and the one is not more disastrous to the understanding than the other."[19]

Although gender discrimination and segregation were facts in America at the turn of the century, new opportunities and careers did help women to gain greater independence and confidence. Unable to attract qualified men with low wages and increasingly diminished status, certain vocations, such as public school teaching or librarianship, were opened to women in this period. In the process, the traditional segmentation of the labor force, which supremely favored male over female workers, was maintained. In the case of librarianship, for example, the traditional assumption that women were naturally inclined to serve and to be orderly became a rationale for easing the entrance of women into the profession. The presence of women in the library system also served educational purposes; libraries increasingly directed their attention toward childhood education. Likewise, in the arts and crafts movement, while women labored within the confines of gender-derived expectations, they used the opportunities before them to gain confidence, develop business skills, and increase their economic independence.[20] Women were slowly breaking out of the bonds of the Victorian home and beginning to be a more visible part of the public realm.[21]

The medical profession, despite opposition, slowly opened itself up to women doctors. The number of women physicians rose from 2,000 in 1880 to 7,000 in 1900. Some male physicians maintained that women could not be doctors because they would be squeamish at the sight of blood or unable to master the scientific knowledge necessary to practice medicine. Women and their supporters responded that women's natural sympathies were an endowment that male doctors lacked and one that was sorely needed within the medical profession. Mary Putnam Jacobi, an important physician, worked hard to integrate women into the male-dominated field. But she recognized that "opposition to women students and practitioners of medicine has been so bitter, so brutal" that progress had to be measured in spoonfuls. Her response to this situation was to counsel women to prove their mettle through grit and hard work. [22]

Female physicians were divided among themselves on the question of how they should approach the practice of medicine. Elizabeth Blackwell, a pioneer in the medical profession, considered medicine a sentimental endeavor, a form of moral education. Her philosophy of disease, as historian Regina Morantz Sanchez has insightfully demonstrated, was based on moderation and environmentalism. In contrast, Jacobi predicated medical science on laboratory and experimental research. She eschewed a moralistic approach to medical practice and held to the increasingly important germ, or bacteriological, theory of disease. Jacobi became a model of the professional physician, publishing nine books and over a hundred articles; she also gained a reputation as a first-rate laboratory scientist.

The newer a profession or mode of artistic expression, the better the chance that women could succeed at it. This was evident in the practice of photographic art. Invented in 1839, photography was a relative latecomer in the world of art. At first its appeal was largely confined to reproducing reality with great precision. Slowly, photographic artists began to convince the general public and art connoisseurs that photography was an art form with its own logic and structure—different from, but of equal aesthetic value to, painting. But photography's uncertain status in the nineteenth century— some saw it as nothing more than mechanical manipulation—allowed women to develop as artists in that medium. Because of its perceived limitations, the field of photographic art presented women with none of the barriers that had been erected to stymie them in pursuing careers as painters.

By the end of the nineteenth century, in an attempt to win a place for photography as an art form, photographers had increasingly adopted a pictorial style, attempting to use the camera to make images with a painterly quality or with mystical emotional content. Because of discrimination in art schools and the arts establishment in general (Mary Cassatt, after all, was an expatriate painter), women had often been discouraged from pursuing paint-

Frances Benjamin Johnston. *Self-portrait. Courtesy of the Library of Congress*

ing careers. Now many adapted their painterly skills to photography. In fact, larger numbers of women photographers than male were trained in art, and that background boded well for their success in photography.[23]

An observer noted in the late 1890s that "photography is becoming more and more recognized as a field of endeavor peculiarly suited to women." Women were thought to be graced with "inborn artistic feeling." Their proclivities and training in cleanliness and patience helped them to produce high-quality photographs. Furthermore, "the light, delicate touch of [women], the eye for light and shade," argued critic Richard Hines, Jr., "together with that artistic perception, render them peculiarly fitted to succeed in this work."[24]

In promoting a view of women as naturally suited for photographic art, critics implicitly touched on an important issue: Did women have a photographic or artistic vision significantly different from that of men? This question was also applied to other fields. M. Carey Thomas stated that women seeking careers as architects and mechanics must be given the same training as men. According to Thomas, women had no particularly feminine talent or vision within the professions. The proof of anyone's competence was simple: Would the architect's building stand? Could the mechanic repair the motor?[25] Women photographers consciously sought to avoid being pigeonholed because of their gender. Eva Lawrence Watson-Schultze, known for her sensitive portraits, proclaimed in 1900 that she did not want her work "represented as 'women's work.' I want it judged by one standard, irrespective of *sex*." Another portraitist, Amelia Van Buren, worked toward the lofty goal of "mak[ing] portraits to stand with [those of] Sargent and Watts and the other masters."[26]

Bohemian in her life-style yet also connected to powerful political figures, Frances Benjamin Johnston did important work in photodocumentation, depicting Theodore Roosevelt and his family, Alexander Graham Bell, Admiral Dewey and his fleet, and the Chicago World's Fair of 1893. Her best work was a series of photographs taken at the Hampton Institute in Virginia, a predominantly black school with some American Indian students. These photographs, which have a classical quality because of their compositions and the subjects' poses, successfully convey the dignity of the Institute's students, who strove for acceptance in the era of Jim Crow segregation. In perhaps her most moving and successful photograph from the Hampton album, "The Old Folks at Home," Johnston documented the reality of an older generation without hope, without possibility, yet clinging to pride. Her fine use of light, composition, and content resulted in a photograph of enduring interest.[27]

Gertrude Stanton Käsebier was the most important American woman photographer of this period and a great influence on other women photographers. Alice Austin credited Käsebier with opening her eyes to "the pos-

Frances Benjamin Johnston. *The Old Folks at Home. Hampton Album. Courtesy of the Library of Congress*

sibilities of art in photography." If Frances Benjamin Johnston worked in the realistic tradition, Käsebier preferred sentiment and romanticism. But she transcended the limitations of such expression through her excellence as a technician (she employed more printing processes than anyone else in the era, save Edward Steichen) and her uncompromising refusal to produce work of inferior quality or vision.[28]

Gertrude Stanton was a child of the frontier, born in a log cabin at Fort Des Moines in Iowa in 1852. She traveled westward with her father in search of gold, in the process braving Indian attacks on their wagon train. Later she was sent east for schooling at the Moravian Seminary for Young Ladies in Bethlehem, Pennsylvania. After college she married an ambitious German immigrant, Edward Käsebier, and quickly settled into a routine of domestic responsibilities, but the fires of artistic creativity smoldered within her. In 1889, when her three children were teenagers, Gertrude Käsebier enrolled at the Pratt Institute to study art in a sustained and serious fashion. She first approached photography as a diversion, especially since she had been warned by teachers that it was not a serious art form. By the 1890s, however, Kä-

Gertrude Käsebier. *Blessed Art Thou Among Women*, ca. 1900. Platinum print on Japanese tissue paper, 9⅜″ × 5½″. *Collection, The Museum of Modern Art, New York. Gift of Mrs. Hermine M. Turner*

sebier had become fascinated with the medium and determined to strike out on her own as a professional photographer.

Käsebier specialized in portraiture. She refused to retouch her photographs; she preferred to capture the veracity rather than the vanity of her subjects. The ideal photograph, she believed, did not reduce the subject to a single attribute but instead managed to capture his or her essential and intriguing nature: "From the first days of dawning individuality, I have longed unceasingly to make pictures of people, not maps of faces, but pictures of real men and women as they know themselves, to make likenesses that are biographies, to bring out in each photograph the essential personality that is variously called temperament, soul, humanity."[29]

Käsebier favored themes that fitted well with Victorian ideals of motherhood; she focused on women in a nurturing role. This emphasis is evident in her most famous photograph, "Blessed Art Thou Among Women." The intimate bond between a mother and daughter is stressed, yet at the same time the separateness of their generations is communicated by the sharp differences in both their poses and the color of their clothing. Although sentiment infused Käsebier's photographic images, her female subjects were always dignified, powerful in their own fashion, and even occasionally sensual, as demonstrated in her portrait of Evelyn Nesbitt, the well known actress and femme fatale. If Käsebier's subject matter, in contrast to Frances Benjamin Johnston's, tended toward the accustomed range of womanly emphases and emotions, the power of her artistic vision and the strength of her printing techniques gave her work a universal quality.[30]

Women photographers of this period reflected the mood of reluctant modernism in American thought and culture. Johnston, for example, portrayed modern subjects with a powerfully realistic eye. Yet she remained entrenched in a classical mode of expression; the essential flux of modernity did not influence her photographs in terms of pose and composition. For Käsebier, the modernist concern with the subjectivity of the self, along with the creative will of the artist, became the dominant themes of her artistic work. Yet Käsebier remained committed to an earlier Victorian ideal of sentimentality and romanticism in both the form and content of her photographs.

Women Writers

Women writers had long played an important, albeit highly controversial, role in America's cultural heritage. By the second half of the nineteenth century women were a large part of the reading public, and both men and women writers produced an avalanche of novels to satisfy their demands. Not surprisingly, given the religious and moral influences on the ideal of separate spheres for men and women, fiction invariably seemed to be highly sentimental in content, predictable in plot, and moralistic in conclusion. In the minds of some men who sought to establish American literature on firmer ground, the large-scale production and consumption of such novels threatened the future of serious art in America.

Literary women who produced novels dealing with domestic topics received little critical acclaim after the Civil War. Although large numbers of women continued to grace the best-seller lists, few of them commanded positions of power. The leading literary critics and custodians of taste—William Dean Howells, E. L. Godkin, George W. Curtis, and Thomas Wentworth Higginson—were all men. Male critics often considered the work of women writers to be of ephemeral or sentimental value. Female critics, such as Helen Gray Cone, also regretted the didactic and moral tone of much of women's fiction.[31] Women writers were commonly seen as limited by their domestic subject matter, imprecise characterizations, lack of a subtle or ironic voice, and unwillingness to veer from a moralistic or sentimental tone. Of course, many male writers of the era, from the immensely popular poet James Whitcomb Riley to the historical-fiction writer F. Marion Crawford, could be condemned in like manner.

Women faced the discouragement of forces that belittled their achievements and downplayed their intellects. Discrimination against women and lack of respect for their intellectual capabilities worked to make them conform to expectations. Moreover, the demands of the market for women authors to produce domestic and sentimental fiction further imprisoned them. For example, popular writer Mary Virginia Terhune longed to write an essay called "The Woman with the Suds" that would express "a plea for the class who make up three fourths of the women lunatics in the N.[ew] E.[ngland] insane asylums—the women whose intellects and finer tastes never have a chance."[32] But as Terhune made clear, to have pursued such subject matter from such a perspective would have been to skate on thin ice.

Did women writers in the period 1880–1900 produce work of enduring importance, fiction that has transcended its era? The answer depends on how "great work" is defined. Literary historian Jane Tompkins demonstrates that while women's fiction lacked the symbolic power of Melville or the moral nuances of Hawthorne, the work of women authors such as Harriet Beecher Stowe did have a power of its own—a "sentimental power." Women writers used the moral and political power of literature to address such public issues as slavery and temperance. In focusing on "internal dramas of sin and salvation" on both a personal and a national scale, they reorganized culture according to a woman's point of view.[33]

Important women writers were certainly to be found in the period 1880–1900. Sarah Orne Jewett, who later served as a role model for Willa Cather, was a talented writer of regional fiction. Focusing on the slowly vanishing world of isolated New England farms and fishing communities, Jewett fashioned a paean to the sturdy independence and quiet dignity of a life apart from the hubbub of modern urban and industrial life. Unlike Hamlin Garland, whose fiction about farm life was dominated by anguished cries about the villainy of the railroads and by political protests about the declining grain market, Jewett wrote timeless fiction with the power of remembrance. In her most successful work, *The Country of the Pointed Firs* (1896), Jewett presented her women characters as repositories of proud traditions—knowledgeable about folk arts and herbal remedies, appreciative of quiet pleasures, strong and capable in many ways. A sense of place is the essence of experience for these women of Dunnet Landing, a Maine seaport community. As the narrator of *Pointed Firs* says of her days among the people there, "the ease that belongs to simplicity is charming enough to make up for whatever a simple life may lack, and the gifts of peace are not for those who live in the thick of battle."[34]

The seaport or countryside communities so lovingly evoked by Jewett contrast with the country towns depicted by Mary Wilkins Freeman. In her novel *Pembroke* (1894) Wilkins Freeman focused on the deadening power of small-town social proprieties and the powerful effects of wills that cannot be bent. In contrast to Jewett, Wilkins Freeman worried about the dangerous inability of the farmers and their wives to drop custom, to opt for love over propriety. Other dangers lurked at every turn; for an unmarried woman, the risk was less to face loneliness than to flirt with financial insecurity. In this bleak landscape, sometimes littered with poorly drawn characters, Wilkins Freeman presented a sentimentalized version of naturalistic fiction. Here, no less than in the works of Frank Norris or Theodore Dreiser, the force of circumstance and the strength of inherited will define the action. Yet in keeping with the moralism and sentimentalism that Wilkins Freeman's readers expected, the characters that populate *Pembroke* somehow manage, in the end, to head in the direction of restitution for earlier stubbornness and to have some chance of finding love.[35]

Kate Chopin's *The Awakening* (1899) is a compelling novel that transcends its domestic setting and its regional appeal; it addresses issues central to women. Marked by subtle nuance and a distanced narrative style, *The Awakening* follows the fortunes of Edna Pontellier without the moralism that characterizes other novels of the period structured around the themes of adultery and sexuality. The novel may be read as a cri de coeur of nineteenth-century feminism. To be sure, in her personal life, Chopin assiduously avoided any public pretense to a feminist position. But in the early pages of *The Awakening* she writes in no uncertain terms that Edna's husband regards her "as one looks at a valuable piece of personal property." The novel chronicles in rich, sensual images the awakening of Edna's sexual desires, need for independence, and creativity. Yet Chopin does not present Edna as a hero. Edna is flanked by a host of other women, each in her own fashion a certain character type. One woman, Mademoiselle Reisz, who may be seen as representative of artistic creativity, lacks the love of family. Another woman, Madame Ratignolle captures the ideal of Victorian motherhood and evidences little dismay over her fate and routine.

Edna's essential problem lies in confronting the gap between desire and reality. Although she is able to break free from many of the expectations of her class and caste, the words of her friend Mademoiselle Reisz echo throughout the novel: "The bird that would soar above the level plain of tradition and prejudice must have strong wings. It is a sad spectacle to see the weaklings bruised, exhausted, fluttering back to earth." Edna engages in a passionate love affair and even moves into a house of her own and works successfully as an artist. Throughout these glimpses of freedom, however, remains the prophecy of failure. Faced with a life of desire—perhaps having tasted too strongly of freedom in a world that does not allow it for women— Edna strips off her clothes and wades into the sea in a final scene that speaks as much of the freedom of death as it does of the horror of suicide.

Yet Chopin does not ask the reader to feel moral indignation over Edna's adultery or her unwillingness to accede to the role of good mother and wife. Instead, Chopin presents Edna as a woman who has tried to soar, attempted to follow her inner passions. Her failure in this endeavor, as Mademoiselle Reisz points out, may be due as much to Edna's character as to the power of the forces arrayed against her. In any case, the attempt at freedom and sexual awakening is not condemned. By the end of the novel Edna has grown as a person, and her eventual surrender to fate is not so much a defeat as it is an overcoming. The nonjudgmental tone of the book did not sit well with contemporary critics accustomed to women's novels that left little to the powers of the moral imagination. According to the St. Louis *Daily Globe-Democrat*, *The Awakening* was "not a healthy book."[36] Healthy or not, Chopin's novel captured the reality of suicide as a passionate and perhaps even reasonable response for women faced with the confining burden of life in a patriarchal society.

In Edith Wharton's classic *The House of Mirth* (1905), Lily Bart appears to have only one option available to her—to find an eligible, wealthy husband. "What a miserable thing it is to be a woman," sighs Lily. "We are expected to be pretty and well-dressed till we drop—and if we can't keep it up alone, we have to go into partnership." The quest proves too hard for Lily's body and spirit, and she seeks solace in a fatal dose of sedatives. Art in this period often imitated life, and vice versa. Marian "Clover" Adams, wife of Henry Adams, demoralized by personal tragedies—the death of her father, her inability to have children, the frustration of having few avenues for the expression of her intellectual and creative impulses—poisoned herself with the chemicals that she used in her photography.[37]

Chopin's *Awakening* deserves a place alongside other major works of fiction produced in this period, including Theodore Dreiser's *Sister Carrie* (1900), Stephen Crane's *Maggie: A Girl of the Streets* (1896), and Frank Norris's *McTeague* (1899). Interestingly, all deal with the theme of the fall of a woman. For the male writers, the environment or the iron will of a man is to blame for the woman's decline. Although sympathetic to the plight of the fallen woman, these male writers made her emotional needs secondary to the overwhelming demands of heredity or social circumstance. In contrast, although Chopin makes clear that Edna is confined by an environment marked by restrictive expectations and requirements, she mines the depths of Edna's own needs in a female voice that eludes the male authors. Unlike Sister Carrie or Maggie, Edna chooses to follow her emotions; she has free will. She accepts the consequences of her acts within her own moral universe. Hence, her suicide recalls her earlier assertion that "I would give up my life for my children; but I wouldn't give myself."

Domestic Science

For most late-nineteenth-century women, freedom was limited; they occupied a circumscribed reality and strove to meet rigid expectations. Living in an age of science and increasing professionalization, many women of the period 1880–1900 continued to celebrate the home-centered values of "True Womanhood" or the cult of domesticity represented by Madame Ratignolle—but with a new twist. Seeking a professional niche and firmly believing that the benefits of modern science should extend to the home, women intellectuals turned to colleges for training and support in an attempt to make the traditional sphere of woman into a scientific environment. In developing the new field of domestic science, these women began to build the ideal of an independent, new woman.

Catharine Beecher was in many ways instrumental in originating the field of domestic science. Never an advocate of feminism, Beecher maintained that women required an education in order to be more efficient and enlightened housekeepers. Hewing closely to the traditional ideology of separate spheres, Beecher's writings kept women in their domestic cubbyhole. Yet ironically, these same writings paved the way for women to escape the confines of the kitchen through education. The generation of women academics that followed Beecher's wanted to professionalize the study of domestic science by building upon many of her insights. At the same time, the new domestic scientists desired to connect education and research to a more feminist and reformist agenda that touched on issues of nutrition and architecture.

The field of domestic science at first helped to open new career opportunities for women college professors while only gently challenging the presumptions of male-dominated academe. No less than any other bastion of male power, the university was resistant to the inclusion of women. In 1890 only 4 colleges in the United States had domestic science programs; the number rose to 21 by 1899 and 195 by 1916. But the road to academic success was not always a smooth one. Initially, the Massachusetts Institute of Technology would not accept Ellen Swallow Richards as a student because of her sex. She persisted, however, and became the first woman to earn a Bachelor of Science at MIT. The university then hired her as an assistant professor of chemistry. By 1882, when MIT decided to admit women students on a regular basis, Richards had become the first female instructor of sanitary chemistry and one of the founders of the field of sanitary engineering.

From her academic perch, and with her solid scientific training, Richards sought to make domestic science into an intellectually respectable and socially important enterprise. When she examined the American home, especially its kitchen, Richards uncovered problems aplenty. She sought to enlarge the function and design of the home to make it more beautiful and efficient. She wanted to bring the value of modern science into the Victorian domestic sphere. By training women to become better shoppers and cooks of balanced, nutritious meals, Richards intended to enable the new professional homemaker to produce a healthier and happier American family. Firmly believing in the value of careers for college-educated women in domestic science, Richards helped to professionalize the field. The initial organization of women domestic scientists began in the late 1890s with meetings in Lake Placid, New York. By 1908 the American Home Economics Association had been organized.[38]

Richards' work was not narrowly confined to an academic setting. She continued an earlier tradition of feminism that emphasized the connection between education and reform.[39] In the 1890s Richards and Mary H. Abel attempted to give domestic science a public presence—without challenging notions of women's responsibility to nurture and to dominate food production—by organizing in Boston the New England Kitchen, a public restaurant that served slowly cooked foods (to maintain the food's nutritional value) for at-home consumption. The public kitchen, a precursor in some ways to later lunch programs in schools, was an efficient and inexpensive means of addressing public health needs in increasingly immigrant-populated urban areas. Richards and Abel's enterprise failed, however, not because its nutritional theory was problematic, but because they refused to acknowledge that their idea of what food should taste like—bland and simple—did not jibe with the traditions and culinary expectations of the public they sought to serve.[40]

Marion Talbot and Helen Campbell were influential domestic scientists who combined science with reform. Talbot joined the faculty at the University of Chicago in 1892 as an assistant professor of sanitary science connected with the Department of Social Sciences and Anthropology. Talbot's presence in that prestigious department supported her deeply held belief "that a very close relationship exists between sanitary conditions and social progress. Sanitation and sociology must go hand in hand in their efforts to improve the race." Talbot was tireless in the pursuit of this lofty ideal. She fostered good relations between her academic students and Hull House, created by Jane Addams to serve the needs of the urban poor in Chicago. Talbot published widely on sanitary reform and served as dean of women at the University of Chicago for three decades. In her course "The Citizen as Householder" she emphasized—in the manner of the emerging Chicago school of sociology—an interdependency model, which revealed as a dangerous conceit the individualistic ideal of the home as a castle removed from interaction with other homes and with public problems. In Talbot's view, public health legislation and low-cost housing promised not only greater social unity and legitimacy but also salvation for the American family.[41]

Helen Campbell stressed that home economics would make the world a more ideal place as well. She maintained that architecture must adhere to an aesthetic of advanced thinking in which useless ornamentation was replaced by practical design. Social considerations broader than the whims of the individual owner were to become the guiding lights for home construction. In *Household Economics* (1896) Campbell proposed abandonment of the "isolated, individual system" of housing based on "organized waste and destruction." Better planning, which for Campbell meant scientific organization, became the key to a more rational domestic architecture and to the production of happier, better-adjusted children.[42]

Richards and Talbot believed that domestic science would connect the study of home and sanitary issues to a menu of science and public reform. In this manner, they hoped, their enterprise would extend beyond the boundaries of the female sphere to become a field of national significance. Along with the social reformer Jane Addams, Richards and Talbot recognized that family life was in need of reform and that the best way to achieve change was through the intervention of professionals sympathetic to the problems and scientific in devising solutions. But as Talbot painfully recognized, sanitary science was too often deemed limited to the realm of the home; its wider ramifications were not taken seriously. Male-dominated colleges and universities perceived domestic science in gender-based terms and consigned it to a peripheral status in their curricula. Thus, the success of domestic science, which had seemed to promise a breaking down of gender-based segregation, had had the opposite effect. Women were now expected to study domestic science; traditional views about their abilities and inclinations still closed off other avenues to them.[43]

Nonetheless, the work of Talbot, Richards, and Campbell in reforming the architecture of both the mind and the home gathered a wide audience in the 1890s. The popular press published articles about how to make house-keeping a more scientific and efficient endeavor. In 1898 *Cosmopolitan* magazine sponsored a contest in which a prize of $500 was offered for the best essay on how to organize a home. The winning essay, by Mrs. Edith Elmer Wood, stressed that behind successful housekeeping, "as in everything else, brain counts. It makes itself felt, above all, in method and organization." Intelligent cooks, wrote Mrs. Wood, were more economical. Perfect house-keepers combined science and intellect with womanly emotional qualities; they were stoic amidst calamity, helping others by "maintaining a perpetual external cheerfulness." Other contestants' essays extolled the moral function and scientific organization of the home, seeing in the efficient and contented housewife the possibility of a happier race. On the one hand, these essays captured women's desire to take the problems of the household seriously and to apply science to their solution. On the other hand, they revealed the tremendous power of the Victorian ideal of womanhood to domesticate scientific ideas for application in the acceptable domain of the kitchen and home.[44]

Charlotte Perkins Gilman

No one wrote more impressively or fully on the themes of science and home, evolution and feminist liberation, than did Charlotte Perkins Gilman. Gilman was an important feminist theorist because she combined in her work many of the themes central to American thought between 1880 and 1900. A confirmed believer in social evolutionism, a follower of Lewis Henry Morgan and Herbert Spencer, Gilman was also intimately connected with the domestic science movement, although she gave it her own particular slant. In addition, she addressed the most burning issues connected to the "woman question"—the proper role for women and the nature of the family. In her career as a thinker and activist, she questioned Dr. Clarke's earlier conclusion that women must shun the intellectual life.

The arguments that had been offered by intellectuals and doctors against women pursuing the life of the mind echoed strongly in Charlotte Perkins Gilman's ears. A descendant of the Beecher family, Charlotte had from a young age shown a streak of independence and intellect. Marriage to Walter Stetson, however, did little to foster those qualities. Indeed, marriage and motherhood only seemed to exacerbate Gilman's anxieties; she eventually became a full-fledged neurasthenic. When Gilman looked back on her ailments of the 1880s, she was convinced that they were linked to the conflict between her traditional domestic responsibilities and her burning need to have a life outside of the home. Socially defined expectations threatened, in her life, to negate individual desire. The initial cure for her neurasthenia had proved to be just as bad as the ailment. Concerned about her languid condition, Gilman's husband had borrowed funds to have her treated in Philadelphia by the leading expert on neurasthenia, Dr. S. Weir Mitchell. As noted earlier, Mitchell believed in the "rest cure" for his patients. Accordingly, Gilman recalled, Mitchell told her to "live as domestic a life as possible. . . . Have but two hours' intellectual life a day. And never touch pen, brush or pencil as long as you live." This was a prescription for disaster, given Gilman's artistic and intellectual desires. As a good patient, she acceded to her doctor's wishes, only to find herself burdened with "just mental torment, and so heavy in its nightmare gloom that it seemed real enough to dodge."[45]

Gilman captured the nightmare of her "rest cure" in "The Yellow Wallpaper," composed in 1890 and first published in 1892. In this gripping and frightening tale, she detailed her own experience of painful imprisonment in the sphere of the home. Rather than celebrating the home as woman's natural place, "The Yellow Wallpaper" presents the home as conspiring to strip away the protagonist's mental stability and creative power. The wallpaper takes on a life of its own, representing not only the pattern of Gilman's imprisonment but also the horrors and allures of the writer's life. Escape from such confinement is gained only through madness.[46]

A real-life solution for Gilman arrived when she decided to leave her husband, and therapy, to escape to California. This was a radical and dangerous endeavor for a middle-class woman of the era, but Gilman felt that she had no choice if she were to avoid succumbing, body and soul, to the imprisonment and unhappiness of domestic life. The times that followed this break from her past and from social expectations were terribly difficult. Like Emerson before her, Gilman sought to become the independent intellectual, living by her mind and her varied talents. She sought out commissions for articles, produced poems, composed fiction, worked in graphic design, and gave lectures in order to remain fiercely independent and self-supporting.

Gilman established her reputation in 1898 with the publication of *Women and Economics*, a work that contained the seeds of nearly all her later work.[47] Structured around an evolutionary viewpoint, the book exudes the authority of science. Gilman condemned as antievolutionary those social arrangements that she found wanting and praised certain social forces as being in step with the process of evolution. The work was a brilliant and passionately argued defense of motherhood and women, as well as a stirring feminist critique of antiquated and inefficient modes of organization and thought. This essential tension between the two gave the work its power. Praising on the one hand the changes in social organization that would finally free women, she remained committed to Victorian perceptions of women that were being undermined by the very forces of change that she so powerfully enunciated and supported.

In *Women and Economics* Gilman proposed that a new age was dawning for women. "Specialization and organization are the laws of human progress, the organic methods of social life," she wrote. In Gilman's evolutionary saga, women were the conservators of the species, the elemental racial type. Women were endowed with the powers of caring and support required for motherhood and for the success of the rapidly emerging interdependent society of the twentieth century. These values, however, had been pushed to the side, trampled on by the combativeness and assertiveness of men. Gilman did not regret this, however; in her evolutionary schema, what has been must eventually be for the good. Although male aggression had helped the social organism to grow, the time was now ripe for change. Why? "Principally, because we are changing" was Gilman's evolutionary, deterministic response. Civilization required less combativeness than cooperation, more nurturing and efficiency than individualism and assertiveness. The patience of women through a long era of pain and sorrow would be rewarded.

But evolutionary change could be hastened by the actions of men and women. Men needed to recognize that sex differentiation had been taken to the extreme. Using analogies of behavior in animal species, Gilman consistently sought to demonstrate that no creature emphasized differentiation of the sexes to the degree that humans did. Indeed, such distinction was dangerous not only because it weakened women, but also because it ultimately undermined the race. Refusing to accept that women were naturally weak, Gilman presented a strong environmental explanation for their dependence on men. She believed that women could be stronger and more capable. The key to their freedom would be their rejection of the constraining and inefficient definition of their lives by the cult of domesticity and the concept of female weakness.

Gilman tried to make it clear that she had no desire to weaken motherhood or marriage as abstract and natural ideals. At the same time, she held, marriage—rather than being based, as it should, on love and mutual sharing—was too often nothing more than a form of servitude little different from prostitution. In highly traditionalist terms, Gilman firmly stated that "motherhood is not a remote contingency, but the common duty and the common glory of womanhood." The necessary path of social evolution had, however, through excessive distinctions between the sexes, undermined that most natural of functions. Women of the Victorian era were incapable of producing and raising healthy children; domestic arrangements presumed to be natural were both artificial and dangerous. Gilman promoted a feminist vision of a domestic culture that would encourage women to partake of life both inside and outside the home.

Victorian women were a sad lot, in Gilman's view. Confined to their homes, they were, like the woman in "The Yellow Wallpaper," prone to maladies such as neurasthenia. Forced to exaggerate secondary sex characteristics in order to attract and hold a man, women were economically dependent and physically weak. Considering that many upper-class women got inadequate exercise, subsisted on unhealthful diets, and wore clothing that was often painfully restricting, one need not look far to comprehend why infant mortality rates were high and childbirth risky. But the problems of motherhood were not limited to these. Gilman attacked the cherished idea that women were somehow magically blessed with a knowledge of child care and education. She found that women were often ignorant of the interrelated needs of children and society. Gilman's discussion of such issues, tied to her extended critique of the home as the center of the family, made *Women and Economics* a startling analysis of the problems inherent in the sacred ideals of motherhood and home.

Gilman wanted to prove that the home and motherhood could be transformed into modern, efficient enterprises that would benefit not only mothers but children as well.[48] Society was moving in the direction of greater specialization and interdependency. Why should this movement not be mirrored in the practice of motherhood? Perhaps generalizing from her own experiences as a mother, Gilman noted that not all women were sufficiently educated or inclined to be good mothers. Their natural maternal instincts could be profitably expanded and supplemented by trained experts. Gilman also roundly condemned the organization of the home, with its emphasis on privatization. Most women were inefficient cooks, she held, because they lacked the resources and knowledge to produce meals of high nutritional value. She suggested that the solution might be a division of labor in housekeeping.

Gilman proposed that cooking should be done by professionals, as Richards and Abel were attempting to demonstrate through their New England Kitchen experiments. In her designs for feminist apartment houses, Gilman omitted kitchens from all apartments. In their stead she included community kitchens, where bulk buying and production would not only make meal preparation less costly and more efficient but also would provide a more varied menu than the individual homemaker ever could. Gilman declared that "eating is an individual function. Cooking is a social function. Neither is in the faintest degree a family function." Moreover, she criticized housework as onerous and inefficient. Domestic servants could do the job, but at the expense of the residents' privacy. Banishing kitchens, Gilman maintained, would appreciably lessen the need for cleaning.

Gilman's vision of feminist apartment buildings offered other advantages as well. Each building would be provided with a day nursery and kindergarten staffed by trained professionals. Children would thus be aided in developing necessary social skills of cooperation at an early age and educated in a proper, efficient, and inexpensive manner. Advantages would also accrue to the mother. Freed from domestic supervision and drudgery, she might enter the work force and escape the narrow and maddening confines of the home. In painting such a scenario, Gilman in one stroke vanquished the logic of domestic servitude responsible for the insanity depicted in "The Yellow Wall-paper" and demonstrated that her momentous restructuring of home life would serve to support the ideal of motherhood. As she emphasized in her concluding words to *Women and Economics*, "When the mother of the race is free, we shall have a better world, by the easy right of birth and by the calm, slow, friendly forces of social evolution."

By 1900, however, freedom for women had not yet arrived. Suffrage was still nearly two decades away. For women intellectuals the picture was brighter but not yet sufficiently illuminated. Gender-based assumptions exiled women to fields that were deemed appropriate arenas for their natural inclinations and abilities. Nevertheless, despite their problems, the generation of women intellectuals in the period 1880–1900 had accomplished much. They had refuted arguments for women's inherent intellectual deficiencies, produced enduring works of fiction and art, developed domestic science as a serious discipline, and begun to make a mark in the social sciences. Yet because of the power of the ideal of separate spheres, women were not able to jump fully into the modernity that inspired hopes of freedom for women. If not reluctant to advocate changes that would allow them to pursue their career and personal goals more freely, women were forced to challenge traditional ideals largely in the language, and through the assumptions, of the past.

five

Consuming Culture

The concluding decades of the nineteenth century were defined by the frightening specters of political and social disintegration. Political corruption and major convulsions of labor protest had dominated the 1870s. The decade of the 1880s began with a severe and prolonged depression that returned to plague Americans by the early years of the 1890s. Labor disputes became even more commonplace in the 1890s, and the rhetoric of class warfare entered into the vocabulary of Americans rich and poor. Labor issues, the protests of women against their inferior status, the nature of the developing monopoly system, and the decline of the family farm were all matters that demanded public attention.

Many intellectuals raised strident and shrill voices to register the fears of their class about the social dislocation and anomie that shook the foundations of polite culture and society. An equal, and possibly greater, number of thinkers, however, preferred to see the problems as challenges to be met. They did not want to dismantle their culture any more than they wanted to effect major shifts in the bedrock of the political economy. To deal better with the disintegration of society, which they understood to be a consequence of modernity, they established cultural and intellectual institutions designed to ease the transition from the Victorian into the modern world. By so doing, they hoped to retain the essential flavor of the earlier era while erecting a system of culture that would synthesize the increasingly diverse and antagonistic parts of American society.

Culture has many definitions. British critic Matthew Arnold's statement that culture is "the most widespread effort which the human race has yet made after perfection" perhaps best captured the meaning of the term in the late nineteenth century. Culture was equated with civilization as expressed through works of high literature and art; it was expected to elevate, to fill the individual with higher aspirations and awe for ideal values. In this definition culture represented not only an encyclopedic array of knowledge but also a state of being, a life-style of cultivation and refined manners. The individual who possessed culture, it was thought, had a more sophisticated, humanistic, and expansive view of the world.

Culture also represents, especially in anthropological parlance, the worldview of a distinct group—the way in which the group understands and adjusts to its environment. Thus, according to this definition, there are many cultures in America, and no single culture has any abstract superiority to another. In this sense of the word, one might speak of the culture of the working class and black culture as distinct entities. Each human being is, in the well-known words of Clifford Geertz, "suspended in webs of significance he himself has spun." Those webs represent culture, which simultaneously allows the individual to survive and keeps the individual unable or unwilling to escape its grasp.[1]

Culture as the possession of an elite group and culture as a general way of approaching the world were often engaged in a spirited interplay in the period 1880–1900. The cultural assumptions, values, and accomplishments of the elite classes in America were communicated to workers and immigrant groups through the efforts of well-to-do men and women known as cultural custodians. To a degree, these cultural assumptions were indeed assimilated by large numbers of individuals from different cultural formations. But the endeavor was never totally successful; those from the working class, for example, could never escape the web of their cultural and class assumptions. Instead, individuals from the working class adopted many elite values that coexisted, sometimes uneasily, with the essentials of their own cultural worldview.

Mixed motives lurked behind the desire of cultural custodians to inculcate their values in a wide audience. On the one hand, they acted out of confidence and sincere belief that the values they upheld were abstractly, positively good. The elite viewed it as their noble duty to share their culture with those from different backgrounds. At the same time—especially when faced with increasing signs of class and cultural conflicts, as well as general social instability—these custodians became convinced that workers and immigrants might forget the realities of class and power struggles by accepting the assumptions of elite culture. Worker and capitalist, immigrant and native-born might all join hands in celebration of a unified, ideal culture. In the end this ideal of a shared culture based on the values and assumptions of the elite proved to be unattainable.

Ironically, a cultural synthesis of sorts did occur through the birth of a society organized around the ideal of consumerism. With the rise of the modern corporation, as the producer ethos gave way to the consumer ethic, America slowly began to transform itself from a culture of scarcity into one of abundance. As mass consumption started to exercise its mesmerizing power over Americans, the earlier idea that high culture might be shared between the elite and the masses slowly began to unravel at the edges. Although the cultural custodians of the 1880s and 1890s might not have foreseen or approved of the bonds that consumerism would begin to forge, the result was not necessarily dissimilar to the original intent behind the dissemination of high culture—to pave over class, racial, ethnic, and sexual distinctions with a roadway that would produce some degree of stability in a world increasingly marked by social conflict and instability. The value of consumerism might be questionable, but it did help to unify the American population through desire and consumption—two mainstays of the modern world.

Cultural Custodians

Cultural custodians tended to live in the northeastern United States, although by the 1880s, thanks to the diffusion of ideas and the proliferation of literary magazines, their ideals of genteel culture were widespread throughout much of the country.[2] Self-appointed and self-conscious arbiters of taste such as E. L. Godkin, editor of the *Nation*, Richard Watson Gilder of *Century*, and George William Curtis of *Harper's* all attempted, through editorials, fiction, poetry, and criticism, to shape the reading tastes of the American public. They believed that art was and should be elevating and beautiful. An idealistic literature based on their own values of the good and true, they believed, would be a palliative for the narrow materialism associated with American capitalists and workers; a healthy dose of idealism might be the antidote for the divided loyalties that threatened America.

Barrett Wendell, professor of literature at Harvard, was a typical cultural custodian. Wendell sensed that "he was born too late in a world too old; and he could not find his way back to the earlier Boston." If he could not easily return to a world lost, then he was determined, even if less than confident about his chances of succeeding, to battle for the values of an old world of literary culture. Wendell viewed himself as a proud defender of the American tradition against philosophies of European democracy, which he viewed as tinged with the excesses of anarchy and socialism. American reading tastes would be well satisfied with a main course of the classics and a rich dessert of English and American works that stressed excellence and idealistic human aspiration. Try as he did to warm to the experimental and energetic prose of Walt Whitman—Wendell acknowledged its daring cadences and its power to evoke the experience of the common man—he condemned Whitman's *Leaves of Grass* poems for their excesses, as well as for their "perverse rudeness of style" and "decadent eccentricity." In his attempt to form a canon of literary study and to proclaim the strength of American literature, Wendell maintained in his important *A Literary History of America* (1900) that while democracy was necessary, it had to be tempered by elite and enlightened leadership in both the political and literary realms. He longed for the good old days of the American literary renaissance, when Emerson, Hawthorne, and others had reconciled an ideal of democracy with a striving for excellence. In those times "the saving grace of American democracy ha[d] been a tacit recognition that excellence is admirable."[3]

In similar fashion, influential editors and writers such as Richard Watson Gilder, William Cray Brownell, and Charles Eliot Norton sought to create a genteel and powerfully American literary culture. Along with Wendell, they did not attack American democracy and individualism as dangerous in and of themselves; instead they focused on the anarchy and extremism in which these traits often took root. In their view, tradition, taste, and excellence needed to triumph over the common and vulgar. Wendell and Norton found value in English culture and Renaissance art, respectively; Brownell pronounced himself a devotee of French culture. In France, wrote Brownell approvingly, society was more important than the individual. And in France a public culture exuded energy, while in America the chaos of the urban environment mirrored the chaotic state of American national culture.[4]

The cultural custodians who dominated the American scene between 1880 and 1900 were not of one mind about what constituted good literature; their tastes ranged from the tepid and sentimental to developing forms of the realistic novel. For all, however, the avocation of literature was the highest calling imaginable, and they believed in the power of custodial guidance to elevate even the most degenerate of souls. Julia Ward Howe maintained that Oscar Wilde, a poet and wit of savage temperament, could be "saved" from his rather self-conscious bohemianism and daring sexual tastes: "To cut off even an offensive member of society from its best influences and most humanizing resources is scarcely Christian in any sense."[5] Culture, then, could redeem the degenerate and, in the process, cleanse the world of evil.

The politics of the cultural custodians were varied, but consensus was to be found in the belief that America's future hopes must be placed in their cultivated and intelligent hands. They longed for the days when the masses would be deferential and would have the good sense to elect their betters to high offices. As they scanned the political landscape, cultural custodians saw nothing but the diminishment of the virtues of the earlier republic. Most of the custodians hooked their hopes to the Mugwump movement, designed to uncover fraud in government, to support Civil Service reform, and to reform the monetary system. Their political successes were few and fleeting, however, for in the hardball world of electoral politics, these reformers were simply outmaneuvered and outmanned. But frustrations with electoral politics often served to further convince them that their views were noble in contrast to the materialistic and crass values of the rest of the population. If power could not be exercised through elections, they reasoned, then influence must be exerted through culture.

The successes of these arbiters of culture, whether they took Britain or France as their model, or whether they hewed to a liberal or conservative politics, were often quite impressive. Their ideals spread to the drawing rooms and salons of middle America. William Dean Howells, growing up in rural Ohio, took his talents and ambitions, neither of which knew any bounds, on a pilgrimage to Boston, there to make his fortune as a literary man and to celebrate the values of high culture. The bigwigs of established culture welcomed him with patrician grace into the fold, and Howells reciprocated by respecting and extending their contributions to American culture. Similarly, Edward Bok, born in Denmark, found that well-known cultural authorities were quite willing to accept him. Through a combination of grit and belief in culture, he eventually became editor of the *Ladies Home Journal.* From that perch, he attempted to disseminate the values of culture that had excited him.[6] And for Henry Seidel Canby, growing up in small-town Delaware in this period, the siren song of genteel cultural ideals swayed his imagination and filled him with longing. Pushing aside the commercialism that he deemed unsavory, he became a major arbiter of culture, eventually serving as the guiding light behind the Book of the Month Club. For Canby, literature was defined by its moral values and idealistic sentiments.[7]

In the Midwest the power of genteel culture remained unchallenged throughout the decades of the 1880s and 1890s. Perhaps Hoosier poet James Whitcomb Riley was the strongest exemplar of this culture of idealism and confidence. Blessed with a fine ear for regional dialect and a boundless sympathy for the sentimental, Riley composed uplifting poems that won him great acclaim and ready imitation. Along with Richard Henry Stoddard, Edmund Clarence Stedman, and Thomas Bailey Aldrich, Riley was one of the band of "little sonnet men" whose work was found in the more popular literary magazines and who could be counted on to commemorate occasions large and small with a bit of public verse. In honor of the passing of President Ulysses S. Grant in 1885, Riley wrote, "But O the sobs of his country's heart / And the driving rain of a nation's tears!"[8] To make the nation's heart beat according to ideal, cultivated, and shared assumptions represented a goal of the cultural custodians. It also necessitated the formation of cultural institutions to widely disseminate such ideals.

Public Culture

In major urban areas around the country in the 1880s and 1890s the diffusion of culture became a significant possibility. This period witnessed the creation of a self-conscious business elite concerned with the lack of cultural institutions and with the ever-widening gap between the rich and the immigrant poor in burgeoning cities. Armed with pride, a sense of civic responsibility to create a cultural revolution, and resources of both the will and the pocketbook, the wealthy began to bring culture to their communities on a host of fronts.

Philanthropists organized cultural institutions to heighten their own status, to improve society at large, and to transform an idealistic notion of culture into reality. Underlying the grandiose plans of these cultural custodians for the production of museums, symphony orchestras, public parks, and libraries were motives that bespoke their insecurities as much as their hopes. These individuals never considered that their institutions of culture and the assumptions that those institutions reflected might in any way be biased or classbound. Indeed, they held their ideals to be abstractly valuable. In that spirit, cultural leaders accepted their civic responsibility to communicate their values to the masses. Confronted by city governments increasingly marked by corruption, cultural custodians set up their own institutions as largely private ventures in the paternalistic hope that they would bring sweetness and light, culture and authority to their cities.[9]

The successes were apparent. New public libraries were built not only to house rare books and manuscripts but also to loan books to the public. Opera houses and art museums became signs of civic responsibility and pride, and promised to make the fruits of high civilization available to all. Public parks became increasingly important. These ample green spaces brought the country into a city and served as common, public settings in which the city's diverse population could come together in harmony.

Influential citizens in New York supported a campaign of commissioning public sculpture. Such sculpture would serve valuable purposes: it would give artists an outlet for their creativity, and it would allow for the development and communication of shared national values. In the capable hands of architect Stanford White and sculptor Augustus Saint-Gaudens, public projects such as the monument to Civil War naval hero David Farragut, dedicated in 1881, presented the public with heroic presences that symbolized not only the strength of the nation but also the necessity of a shared national identity.

The power of public sculpture to elicit expressions of social solidarity was evident in Boston in 1897, at the dedication of Augustus Saint-Gaudens's monument honoring Robert Gould Shaw and the black troops who had been killed in the heroically futile attack on Fort Wagner during the Civil War. The spirit of the event was not such as to rekindle animosities between the North and the South; not even for Booker T. Washington, the leading black figure in the country and a speaker at the ceremony, did it raise troubling questions about race relations. Washington brought the audience to tears with a sentimental oration extolling the flag, loyalty, and the courage of the black troops. The other featured speaker at the event, philosopher William James—one of whose younger brothers had participated in the attack on Fort Wagner—used the forum to combine exuberant praise for the national spirit and unity of the commemorated soldiers with a plea for civic courage in the present era. James appealed for a combination of idealism and practical action focused on the achievement of American unity and the preservation of enlightened democracy.[10]

At times cultural diffusion had ironic consequences. Successful institutionalization sometimes led to the sacralization of culture—that is, the veneration of cultural institutions and ideals—which often distanced them from the very public they were intended to inspire. Arbiters of culture worked mightily to erect standards of conduct that would apply to all classes of potential art consumers. The first time the Metropolitan Museum of Art in New York City opened its doors on a Sunday, the museum staff carefully monitored the behavior of the visiting public. Canes had to be checked, lest people use them to poke holes in offensive canvases; dogs had to be kept out; and unkempt individuals who might threaten the cleanliness of the museum or offend other patrons had to be prevented from entering that citadel of culture. There arose an etiquette for the appreciation of art that actually diminished the appeal and accessibility of art. By the 1880s and 1890s the once-raucous level of audience participation in the theater and opera was also coming under scrutiny. Chatting and cigar smoking during performances was prohibited. Even the wives of captains of industry were warned not to wear their monumental hats, so that all opera lovers might better view the stage.[11]

The Function of the Library

Nothing better illustrated the assumptions guiding the custodians of culture, and the ironic impossibilities of imposing a totalistic view of culture, than did the development of the public library system. Public libraries, as Andrew Carnegie often emphasized, were intended to fulfill the democratic ethos of an educated populace, to create in America a class of upwardly mobile and intellectually voracious workers. To achieve this end, Carnegie endowed libraries across the country. Starting in the 1890s, he began contributing what would amount eventually to over $41 million toward the construction of 1,600 library buildings.[12]

A desire for social control and moral education were the bricks that built the public library system in the final years of the nineteenth century. Faced with a bewilderingly diverse and increasingly hostile working class, many believed that social harmony and uplift might be appreciably aided through public libraries. In this equation workers and immigrants would use the resources of libraries not only to gain a sense of what Arnold had called "sweetness and light" but also to learn skills that would allow them to be upwardly mobile. Armed with both high and practical ideals, workers would achieve moral, spiritual, and occupational betterment. Carnegie contended that the knowledge accrued by workers in these repositories of wisdom would help to make them "not violent revolutionaries, but cautious evolutionists; not destroyers, but careful improvers."[13]

Crucial to the social-control aspect of the public libraries was the care and prudence exercised by trained librarians in the selection of reading materials for the masses. Strong debates raged within the developing circle of professional librarians about whether libraries should stock fiction that was deemed more sensational than moral in content. In 1881 the American Library Association Cooperation Committee sent out a questionnaire to 70 major public libraries to ascertain which works might be excluded from libraries because of their "sensational or immoral qualities." No uproar over censorship ensued; instead, librarians listed 16 highly popular works of fiction as likely candidates for exclusion. These books, most by women novelists, questioned Victorian ideals about the family and the role of women.[14]

Although librarians worried about the inclusion of certain works of fiction in their collections, their qualms were vitiated by the recognition that popular fiction attracted patrons. While fiction reading was considered an acceptable form of recreation, the hope remained that readers of sensational stories might be nurtured toward an appreciation for better, more ideal literature. Censorship was not unusual; professional librarians regularly distinguished between "good" and "bad" works of both fiction and nonfiction. Librarian Melvil Dewey stated that it was "unwise to give sharp tools and powerful weapons to the masses without some assistance of how they are to be used." Moreover, Dewey, the inventor of the library cataloging system that bears his name, viewed his categories as not only offering easier access to a library's holdings but also imposing order on chaos. Libraries were to serve, then, as citadels that would both uplift the masses and quell the disorder of the age.[15]

Did libraries succeed at their calling? Certainly, public libraries did serve for some working-class people as places of escape from the tedium of everyday life and sources of inspiration and betterment. Mary Antin waxed eloquent in recalling her impressions of a public library as a child only recently arrived from Russia: "It was my habit to go very slowly up the low, broad steps to the palace entrance, pleasing my eyes with the majestic lines of the building, and lingering to read again the carved inscriptions: *Public Library—Built by the People—Free to All.*" Antin remembered spending "rapt hours" devouring the prints on the walls of this "palace," reading, and memorizing lines from Tennyson.[16]

But the confrontation between reader and text is not a predictable experience. The reader does not necessarily imbibe in any singular, certain fashion the pure meaning of a given text. Librarians attempted to stock books that would exercise a conservative influence over workers and immigrants, but their best-laid plans often went awry. Books that might have been read by some as conservative in tone were interpreted by others as radical works. Consider the many books by philosopher Herbert Spencer, which were staples in public libraries in the 1880s and 1890s. Although his books were controversial because of their apparent diminution of God's power, they seemed to support many aspects of a conservative social philosophy by presenting an orderly and progressive universe, along with a political agenda that stressed evolution over revolution, laissez-faire capitalism over state socialism, and individualism over collectivism. Nonetheless, another reading of Spencer was possible. At the public library in Oakland, California, future novelist and radical Jack London, then an impoverished worker, encountered Spencer. Speaking through his fictional alter ego Martin Eden, London wrote of feeling awed and "humbled" by "the high, bulging shelves of heavy tomes." After a feverish all-night encounter with Spencer's *First Principles*, London emerged with a belief that the universe was unified; "there was no caprice, no chance." This was proof to him of the order and logic of socialism. For London, the next necessary step in social evolution must be revolution.[17]

Thus, libraries achieved mixed results in attempting to educate and to shape the values of a working-class audience. To be sure, many workers and immigrants, such as Mary Antin, found the library to be a shrine to elite cultural values. Yet libraries failed to impose a culture, for they were often forced to stock a variety of works that the public demanded. Moreover, workers and immigrants did not enter these citadels of knowledge as tabulae rasae; they came full of assumptions and perceptions honed by the realities of class, race, and ethnicity.

Looking Backward

A dualistic reading of the cultural commonplaces of the era appears in works of fiction and autobiography from the pens of important figures of the period. Although the culture and ideas of the powerful could be transformed into doctrines of protest by those outside the pale of respectability and influence, the dominant culture continued to exercise immense control. The power of elite culture may be discerned by examining the lives and thoughts of Edward Bellamy, the socialist author of *Looking Backward* (1888); Samuel Gompers, cigar maker and leader of the American Federation of Labor; and Booker T. Washington, influential black leader. The values of elite culture influenced all of them deeply and constrained their radicalism. At the same time, they were able to use the perceptions and assumptions of the elite to do battle in the name of alternative assumptions.

Born a minister's son in Chicopee Falls, Massachusetts, Edward Bellamy was suspended between two worlds: a preindustrial world marked by cultural and social unity, and an increasingly industrialized and fragmented world. In his monumental bestseller *Looking Backward* (1888) Bellamy embraced the modern as little more than a sanitized vision of the past. The future—as it had been comprehended by reluctant modernist evolutionists in science, anthropology, and philosophy—was to be celebrated only to the degree that it augured the continuation of the earlier assumptions and realities of genteel culture.

Nonetheless, *Looking Backward* was one of the strongest critiques of American capitalism ever penned. In a marvelous metaphor early in the novel, Bellamy describes the capitalist society of the 1880s as "a prodigious coach which the masses of humanity were harnessed to and dragged toilsomely along a very hilly and sandy road. The driver was hunger." Even those occupying the plush seats on this slow-moving coach lived in mortal terror that they might fall to the ground and thereby relinquish their privileged status. Everyone groaned under a "constant cloud" of unhappiness.[18]

Bellamy projects the protagonist of *Looking Backward*, Julian West, into the new and better, yet calmly familiar, world of the year 2000. In a paean to evolution rather than revolution, Bellamy paints in sentimental hues the progression of society to a utopian future in which everyone is cared for and in which the distribution of products and the organization of work are both logical and humane. The new world that Bellamy outlines contrasts markedly with the earlier world of the coach. When the incredulous West questions how human nature could have changed so dramatically, his kindly tour guide, Doctor Leete, advises him that by rationalizing the productive forces and banishing the greed that scarcity had engendered, the new society changed human nature in a beneficial manner. At first skeptical, West eventually embraces the order, rationality, and abundance that characterize the twenty-first century.

The strengths of Bellamy's novel were apparent and far-reaching. By 1890, only two years after its publication, over 325,000 copies had been sold. Enthusiastic followers of Bellamy organized the Nationalist movement and founded a newspaper, *The Nationalist*, designed to serve the campaign and to further Bellamy's ideas. Bellamy and the Nationalists argued that evolution was not only leading the country progressively and inexorably toward becoming a socialist utopia but also that its ends might be achieved more rapidly through human intervention. No problem was insoluble if approached through rationality, science, and community spirit. Many read *Looking Backward* as a religious text, finding their lives forever transformed by its vision and hope. A reader from California wrote that *Looking Backward* "is the full and complete realization of the hope . . . that some 'Apostle of Humanity' would arise, capable of showing the people the way and of making the righteous path plain. When the Golden Century arrives . . . [Bellamy's] name will receive the homage of the human race of that period as being the only writer of the 19th Century capable of seeing, feeling, and portraying the 'better way.'"[19]

Yet Bellamy's *Looking Backward* was ultimately not a radical work, because it failed to question the cultural proprieties of Victorianism. To be sure, Bellamy perceived unbridled capitalist competition as the chief villain in the drama of modernity, the force that threatened to undermine the cultural commonplaces that he idealized. Capitalism, in Bellamy's analysis, threatened the community, social solidarity, and neighborliness that he associated with the preindustrial days of Chicopee. Meanwhile, Bellamy's analysis of women's issues was sorely lacking in vision. He was conversant with, and supportive of, late-nineteenth-century feminist ideology. In contrast with the utopian feminist works that would be composed after 1900, *Looking Backward* does little to upset the traditional view of women. Although women in Bellamy's utopia are educated, they remain responsible for the genteel pleasures and busy themselves (albeit more rationally than ever before) with the consumption of goods of both material and cultural quality. In addition, difficult questions of race and class are pushed under the rug in *Looking Backward*. The refined drawing-room culture of sentiment and confidence, individualism and ideality, reappears in the noncapitalist environment of the year 2000. Bellamy's critique of capitalism is thus contained by its inability to extend to the arena of cultural control. Authority, rather than freedom, is the key ingredient in the utopian experiment in *Looking Backward*.

Cultural Assimilation

American authors who might have been expected to have little allegiance to the dominant culture of white Anglo-Saxon Protestant America often revealed, in autobiographical works, a deep and abiding respect for the very culture that excluded them. In his rich work *The Souls of Black Folk* (1903) W. E. B. Du Bois stressed the concept of a "double consciousness." The American Negro, he averred, suffered from a "sense of always looking at one's self through the eyes of others. . . . One ever feels his twoness,—an American, a Negro; two souls, two thoughts, two unreconciled strivings; two warring ideals in one dark body, whose dogged strength alone keeps it from being torn asunder." In his evocative essays—sometimes punctuated with the scientific jargon of the era, other times bordering on the novelistic— he powerfully rendered the realities of Negro life in the South, the promises unfulfilled, and the racism dominant in America.

Du Bois knew what he was talking about. Despite his sympathy for the oppressed, he too was a victim of this double consciousness. He celebrated the values of higher culture yet waxed enthusiastic about black folk culture. This dualism was a signature of the modernist synthesis of diverse cultural spheres. But Du Bois, for all of his identification with the problems of the black masses, remained an elitist; he placed hope for the Negro race in the leadership of the "talented tenth," his own version of a class of cultural custodians.[20]

Experiences similar to Du Bois's development of a double consciousness appear in the autobiographies of Samuel Gompers and Booker T. Washington. Quite different in their respective backgrounds—Gompers a Jewish immigrant and trade unionist, Washington a black educator who had been born into slavery—they represented their lives (sometimes, unwittingly, to the point of parody) as fitting comfortably within the genteel assumptions of the dominant culture. In the American tradition of spiritual and material betterment, both Gompers and Washington had worked hard as young men to overcome their poverty and to establish themselves as bona fide members of the bourgeoisie.

Over and over again in their autobiographies, Gompers and Washington emphasize how important cleanliness was to them. Echoing the Victorian ideal that cleanliness is next to Godliness, Gompers positively exults about how clean his mother kept his family's home. Washington nearly makes a fetish of cleanliness, going so far as to announce that "I sometimes feel that almost the most valuable lesson I got at the Hampton Institute was in the use and value of the bath." Moreover, he writes, "In all my teaching I have watched carefully the influence of the tooth-brush, and I am convinced that there are few single agencies of civilization that are more far-reaching."[21]

Gompers imagines himself as the good bourgeois in the coarse clothes of a workman. His life is one of discipline and hard work, thrift and sobriety. He expects to be treated with a respect that is earned by the quality of his enterprise. His "manhood" is a quality never to be surrendered "to any living person—whether he were boss or President of the United States." In the same vein, Washington creates for himself the image of a selfless individual devoted solely to the advancement of his race, within the guidelines that he had marked out in his famous Atlanta Compromise Address of 1895: blacks were to eschew agitation for social and political rights and to work for economic benefits while relying upon the established white power structure for beneficent guidance and support. Washington believed that a sober, thrifty, and industrious black working class would slowly prosper and win the respect of the white world.

Gompers and Washington were always careful not to appear too cozy with the civilization and circumstances of white culture and power. Intriguingly, each of them demurred when it came time to dine at the table of the powerful. Gompers worried about what he should wear to formal gatherings, lest his etiquette and garments alienate his hosts and reduce him to foolishness.

Thus, he accepted conventions, noting that "non-conformity" would not serve the cause of labor respectability. Nonetheless, Gompers tried to distance himself from bourgeois respectability and expectations. At a massive dinner given by the National Civic Federation, he refrained from the repast, fearful that he might "arouse suspicion or doubt" about his working-class credentials (he did not, however, exercise the same restraint when it came to the quality after-dinner cigars offered him). Booker T. Washington describes a similar dinner in his autobiography, *Up from Slavery* (1901). Washington partakes of the dinner, but his thoughts harked back to the humbler days of his enslavement, when the taste of simple molasses enticed him. For Washington, this memory served not to unconsciously celebrate the institution of slavery, as some analysts contend, but to emphasize that his roots remained one with those of his followers who were still impoverished and prevented from hobnobbing with the wealthy and elite.[22]

Both Gompers and Washington sought to create an image of themselves as respectable members of bourgeois culture, while also holding steady to their respective constituencies. They believed that no contradiction existed between their espousal of bourgeois ideals and their fighting for the rights of workers and blacks. Of course, their opponents thought that close association with the powerful corrupted the ability of Gompers and Washington to be strong voices of protest. In contrast, both maintained that their relationships with the wealthy and their careful cultivation of elite manners and habits made them more efficient, harder working, and more successful representatives of the downtrodden. In any case, the lives of both men serve as examples of the immense allure of bourgeois values, despite its uncertain implications, for those born into quite different cultures.

The Ideal of Success

Cultural ideals can serve to unite a populace, whether or not those ideals have any relationship to "real" experience. From 1880 to 1900 the success ideal, based on the individual working hard and striving for success, functioned as a unifying cultural myth. Its origins in America can be traced back to the Puritan's idea of a calling or to Benjamin Franklin's homilies about work and thrift. By the end of the nineteenth century the ideal of success had become a cultural commonplace undermining radical critiques of American society and uniting the wealthy with the impoverished in a shared vision of America as a land of uncompromised opportunity for all.

Andrew Carnegie, an immensely successful industrialist, exemplified the myth of the self-made man. He rarely let anyone forget his humble origins. Through hard work and imagination, he had progressed from the furnace of sweated labor to the comforting hearth of wealth. In all of his paeans to the work ethic, Carnegie celebrated wealth as a means rather than as an end, and he envisioned competition as directed toward increased quality and lower cost for manufactured goods. Carnegie emphasized the social aspects of wealth and upward mobility for their bounteous contributions to the social unit and to the ideal of progress. In his doctrine of a gospel of wealth, Carnegie proclaimed the millionaire a heroic steward whose "surplus wealth should be considered as a sacred trust to be administered by those into whose hands it falls, during their lives, for the good of the community."[23]

Others shared these views with Carnegie and worked hard to promote the ideal of success. The popular novels of Horatio Alger, with their intriguing characters, including Mark the Match Boy and Ragged Dick, drove home the traditional message that hard work and good, clean Christian living were the keys to success in both business and life. In almost all of the stories, Alger presents an urban child whose life is marked by petty crime, bad habits, and lack of positive direction. Luckily, through events at once predictable and unlikely, the lad comes into contact with a wealthy benefactor. The street child demonstrates his essential honesty and is rewarded by the wealthy friend with advice and support. Before too long the wayward urchin absorbs the proper values of Victorian culture—hard work, sobriety, and thrift—and in the process becomes assured of a successful life. By luck and pluck, goes the message of Alger's novels, any young man can make it in America.

In the early twentieth century Russell Conwell, in his highly popular lecture "Acres of Diamonds," preached that anyone in America could become wealthy, given a little ingenuity and desire. Wealth need not be pursued in faraway Western gold-mining camps; it may be uncovered in one's own backyard if one simply reflects on society's needs and how an individual might service them. Conwell envisioned a community of interests common to both labor and capital: "Let the man who loves his flag and believes in American principles endeavor with all his soul to bring the capitalist and the laboring man together until they stand side by side, and arm in arm, and work for the common good of humanity."[24]

Were these ideals internalized by the public at large? Certainly Alger's books sold consistently throughout the period, and Conwell's message was delivered over 6,000 times to an audience of tens of thousands. The power of the culture of success is evident in how easily working-class immigrant Samuel Gompers and impoverished black Booker T. Washington accepted many of the bourgeois assumptions popularized in books on the success ideal. Other joined them. Morris R. Cohen, a well-known philosopher and teacher, had been born in 1880 into an impoverished immigrant Jewish family. He was deeply influenced by Franklin's *Autobiography* and the writings of the Victorian self-help apostle Samuel Smiles. Cohen's commitment to the ideals of upward mobility, hard work, and discipline, suggests historian David A.

Hollinger, transformed his early allegiance to Marxism into nothing more than a "romantic venture."[25] Even those with firmer links to socialist beliefs than Cohen's were seduced by the song of success. How else to explain the expenditure of advertisers who placed the following advertisements in the radical socialist journal *International Socialist Review?* One advertisement "guaranteed" a "$5,000 a Year Income" if the reader purchased a ten-acre farm in rural Florida. Another urged workers to "USE YOUR MONEY" to establish a profitable business and achieve the American ideal of becoming *"your own boss."*[26]

Works of fiction directed explicitly at a working-class audience further disseminated the success ideal with similar moralistic overtones. In the early 1880s Frederick Whitaker wrote "dime novels," with titles such as *John Armstrong, Mechanic; or, From the Bottom to the Top of the Ladder. A Story of How a Man Can Rise in America*—or, no less impressively, *A Knight of Labor; or, Job Manley's Rise in Life. A Story of a Young Man from the Country*—that focus on honorable workers who gain respect and wealth in life. Class lines seemingly dissolve in the face of each energetic, resolute, and virtuous young worker. If in Alger's formula success came by a combination of luck and pluck, for Whitaker the imperative to succeed was usually a function of pluck and love, with the love directed toward a woman graced with higher social status. Despite labor strikes and jealous competitors, the heroes of Whitaker's books slowly rise upward through their devotion to hard work and high ideals. Although these stories might in some aspects fit into the category of the sensational, their moral certitude was worn forthrightly, and they invariably concluded on a note of confidence in American ideals not unlike those promoted in any work of Victorian sentimental fiction. John Armstrong's story closes triumphantly with his election as mayor of New York City. The final refrain of the novel is this: "Look up, then, workman of the land, man with the muscle hardened by labor, brain trained in the struggle of life." Remember, finishes Whitaker, "In America everything is possible for the workingman."[27]

The success ideal, whether in the hands of Carnegie, Alger, Conwell, or Whitaker, was predicated on an image of American society as open to change yet dependent on fixed moral values. These merchants of success literature might be seen as having pandered to a crass materialism that some cultural custodians found at the root of American cultural decay. But actually, these authors stressed the social utility of wealth. Their beliefs were firmly rooted in the ethos of the producer. It was the responsibility of both the capitalist and the worker, they maintained, to give fair value for the money invested in either products or labor. Pride came from production; production was the source of pleasure and wealth. Success did not come overnight; it was a result of carefully cultivated habits, along with a dose of luck. But these ideals, rooted in the producer ethic, were already under siege by the late 1880s as a new ethic, based on consumerism, gained popularity and became a cultural force of immense proportions.

The Department Store and the Culture of Desire

No institution better heralded the onset of a consumer ethic than the modern department store. Emphasis was less on production than consumption; organization centered on desire rather than denial. The rise of the department store represented more than an important shift in the marketing and centralization of commercial capitalism; it intimately connected to the rise of urban, industrial America. These stores, which offered a diversified and impressive sampling of consumer goods under one roof, were major industrial enterprises. Two of the more famous emporiums, Marshall Field's and Macy's, each had over a million feet of floor space. In 1898 Macy's employed over 3,000 workers, and Jordan L. Marsh represented the fourth-largest employer in New England.

These pleasure palaces offered a cornucopia of goods in often sumptuous surroundings, albeit with a wink in the direction of polite taste. Fashioned along the eclectic but often classical lines that informed elite cultural standards in the era, the department stores had immense rotundas with upper floors that were visible from below. Skylights and windows combined with Greek columns in these stores to add to the effect of a fantasyland at once utopian and familiar.

Omnipresent sales personnel, ready to service the slightest need of the customer, signified a new era in which shopping became a pleasure and an end in itself for many women. With the decline of household production and the development of a new middle class still caught in the throes of an ideology that denied employment opportunities to women, wealthy women's leisure activities began increasingly to focus on the department store as a place where desire and identity, self-worth and possibility were interconnected. Intent on not only selling goods but also projecting an image, department store owners wanted to make their palaces as comfortable and compelling as possible in an effort to attract women shoppers on a regular basis. One store advertised its "ladies' waiting room" as "the most luxurious and beautiful department devoted to the comfort of ladies . . . the style is Louis XV, and no expense has been spared in the adornment and furnishing of this room." The results were impressive. Women from the well-to-do and middle classes flocked to these emporiums. The department store thus combined the cultivation of pleasure with the merchandising of products.[28]

Department stores sought to expand their clientele beyond the elite classes in American society; after all, they were interested in turning a hefty profit by attracting as many customers as possible. At first the tremendous expenditures that went into making these stores into outrageous pleasure palaces seemed to have a debilitating effect on workers and lower-middle-class shoppers, who felt out of place and unwanted in urban shopping centers, even when they had sufficient funds to buy certain items. But the allure of the culture of consumption cut across class lines. After all, the consumer ideal was predicated on desire and fantasy as much as on reality. One dreamed of goods to be possessed. If the funds were available or made possible through credit, then one could purchase desired items, in the process confirming one's worth as an individual. In its headiest moments, the culture of consumption manufactured desires that would become the common property of all Americans.

Perhaps the power of the consumer ideal was best captured in Theodore Dreiser's 1900 novel *Sister Carrie*. Carrie is a young woman swept along by the power of objects and the insatiable hunger of desire. In making transitions from country to city and from a stable self to an actress who occupies different selves, Carrie becomes the modern consumer, defining herself by the objects she can obtain. She is mesmerized by the riches of consumer society: "She realized in a dim way how much the city held—wealth, fashion, ease—every adornment for women, and she longed for dress and beauty with a whole and fulsome heart." Carrie encounters the city as a department store, and she seeks employment as one of the army of clerks. But the power of the object is what drives Carrie to distraction. In the department store,

Carrie passed along the busy aisles, much affected by the remarkable displays of trinkets, dress goods, shoes, stationery, jewelry. Each separate counter was a show place of dazzling interest and attraction. She could not help feeling the claim of each trinket and valuable upon her personality and yet she did not stop. There was nothing there which she could not have used—nothing which she did not long to own. The dainty slippers and stockings, the delicately frilled skirts and petticoats, the laces, ribbons, hair-combs, purses, all touched her with individual desire, and she felt keenly the fact that not any of these things were in the range of her purchase.[29]

For immigrant Mary Antin the department store served no less than the public library as a means of access to the riches of American culture. Mary and her friends would press their "noses and fingers on plate glass windows ablaze with electric lights and alluring with display." Life in America became for Mary a "fairy story" in which she happily exchanged her "hateful home-made European costumes . . . for real American machine-made garments." All of this was made possible by the cultural power of the "dazzlingly beautiful palace called a 'department store.'"[30]

The culture of consumption had important implications for Americans at the turn of the century. The rise of a consumer culture represented a new mechanism of control. With old proprieties and traditions breaking down as

117

the nation became increasingly diversified and divided, consumerism promoted social reconciliation: Americans from all class, racial, and economic backgrounds could share in the desire for consumer merchandise. Moreover, a consumer culture helped to create a market for the durable items that were being produced by industrial capitalists in ever-increasing quantities. The formation of a particular kind of identity was fostered by consumerism. Individual worth increasingly became less a function of what one produced than a function of what one was able to consume. Even when one did not have enough money to buy certain luxuries, one could still look into the windows of the shops and imagine the pleasures of possessing those items. In sum, the department store and the modern advertising industry not only created but also exemplified a shift in American culture from scarcity to abundance, from a producer ethos to a consumer ethos.[31]

Control and conformity were not the only ideals promoted by this mania for consumption. The department store also gave direction and vision to utopian reformers. Edward Bellamy may have been repelled by the sumptuous excesses of the department store culture, but he marveled at the goods it offered. In Bellamy's *Looking Backward*, the "central warehouse" of the twenty-first century exemplifies the apogee of centralization and organizational efficiency. This modern department store is organized less for pleasure than for practicality. Gone are the middlemen who gouged profits; banished is the army of clerks trying to convince the customer to purchase unnecessary goods. Standardized, quality goods are readily available, and the educated shopper has no problem picking the proper and practical garment or product. To be sure, Bellamy's vision is somewhat antiseptic, but in rationalizing the nature of the department store, he attempted to direct its allure toward his socialist agenda. Others saw in the department store a different image of liberation. For certain feminists, the department store helped them to push aside the repression and control of Victorian culture. In turn, they began to explore an ethos of freedom and possibility that helped to impel women into a secular and public posture.[32]

The consumer ideal was perfectly elucidated as the mark of the modern age by L. Frank Baum, who made it one of the key themes of his classic work *The Wonderful Wizard of Oz* (1900). Baum lived in two worlds. For a number of years he was a newspaper editor in rural Aberdeen, North Dakota. This gave him an appreciation of the farmers' plight during the horrible years of depression in the early 1890s and made him an enthusiast of the Populist movement among the nation's farmers. Yet by the mid-1890s Baum had relocated to Chicago, where he became a spokesman for National Association of Window Dressers, edited their trade journal, *The Show Window*, and composed a book, *The Art of Decorating Dry Goods Windows*. Perched between rural ideals and a cosmopolitan career, between a producer ethos and a consumer ethos, in the midst of a society that longed for the strength of tradition yet had enthusiasm for the ideal of desire, Baum was able to capture these oppositions in *The Wizard*. Most significantly, he managed to combine a nostalgia for the rural past of the producer ethos with a recognition of the desires of consumerism that only urban areas might offer.[33]

At first glance *The Wizard* is a paean to traditional values, as Dorothy illustrates when she exclaims that "there's no place like home." Home may only be a poor, dilapidated farmhouse on the barren Kansas plain, but it represents to Dorothy the love of family, a comforting sense of place, and the possibility of satisfaction. But Baum is less than convinced about the joys of life on the farm. While he is clearly drawn to the rural ideal, he also recognizes that it is often clouded by mythology. Thus, the Scarecrow (who, it is supposed, has no brain) responds with irony to Dorothy's celebration of her Kansas homestead. Speaking of this dry, "gray place you call Kansas," the Scarecrow says that "if your heads were stuffed with straw, like mine, you would probably all live in the beautiful places, and then Kansas would have no people at all. It is fortunate for Kansas that you have brains."[34]

As the Scarecrow indicates, the land of Oz is very much about the allure of objects, the possibility of desire. All of the central characters are compelled to travel along the yellow brick road in a quest for something they want or believe they must have: the Scarecrow is in search of a brain, the Tin Woodman wants a heart, the Lion is in need of courage, and Dorothy seeks the means to return to her beloved Kansas. In a real sense, however, the characters already possess what they crave. This irony may be seen as Baum's rejection of the ideal of desire, expressed by the Wizard when he tells each of his supplicants that they already have what they need; they simply have failed to realize it.

The powers of illusion and desire are at the center of the landscape that is Oz and within the control of the Wizard. The Wizard thrives on trickery and congenial deceit. His Emerald land of Oz is no greener than any other land; he had simply "put green spectacles on all the people, so that everything they saw was green." Illusion had become reality over time as the inhabitants of Oz had become familiar with the imagery; the people of the Emerald City had been fooled for so long that they ceased to question the illusion. The Wizard is a self-professed "humbug" and ventriloquist, able to present fantasy as fact and to create illusions that prove satisfying. In the deployment of these skills he comes to represent the power of desire that Baum so well comprehended as an expert on the decoration of department store windows. As the wizard exclaims, "How can I help being a humbug when all these people make me do things they know are impossible."[35] How, indeed?

Coney Island of the Mind

The emerging consumer ideals of the 1890s expressed themselves in many ways. In the birth of Coney Island and the Chicago Fair of 1893, and even in the rise of urban nightclubs, a shift to consumerism was evident. Of course, the transformation did not occur overnight; the proprieties of Victorianism still reigned in many quarters. But unquestioned allegiance to those values faded as the American populace rushed to enjoy the excitement and power of new forms of entertainment. The cultural custodians had anticipated that their ideal of culture, based on ideal attainments and assumptions, would unite the populace. The American population would slowly grow more united as lines of division were blurred by the homogenizing power of culture. But the rise of mass culture achieved unification in a way never imagined or desired by the cultural custodians.

The split between the private and public realms had been essential to Victorian culture. The home was not only a "haven in a heartless world"; it was also the place where culture was to be enshrined, either through the collection of books and prints that elaborated the cultivation of the individual or through the decoration of rooms with bibelots, or bric-a-brac, that exuded prosperity and eclecticism. In any event, the home (and perhaps the church)

Daniel Chester French's *The Republic* at the Chicago World's Columbian Exposition of 1893. *Avery Architectural and Fine Arts Library. Columbia University in the City of New York*

120

seemed to many middle-class Americans to be a holy place where culture and inspiration dwelled. In contrast, the cities appeared to offer an ever-widening array of public sources of entertainment, often comprehended by traditionalists as closely connected with sin. The saloons, theaters, and public spaces of cities were crowded with possibilities, and there the power of objects seemed to shine most brightly. By the 1890s urban entertainments would become more acceptable to middle-class tastes. This process was appreciably aided by certain styles of entertainment popularized at the Chicago Fair of 1893 and permanently institutionalized at Coney Island.

The Chicago Fair celebrated Victorian confidence and values. The White City section of the fair, so called because of the solid white exteriors of its neoclassical buildings, was described by journalist and reformer Henry Demarest Lloyd as demonstrating "to the people, possibilities of social beauty, utility, and harmony of which they had not been able even to dream." These visions, noted Lloyd, contrasted sharply with the "prosaic drudgery" of most peoples' lives. Even the most refined of the cultural custodians could

Dreamland at Twilight, Coney Island, 1905. Photo by Detroit Publishing Co. *Courtesy of the Library of Congress*

121

find proper culture at the Fair: Charles Eliot Norton marveled that "the general design of the grounds and the arrangement of the buildings was in every respect noble, original, and satisfactory, a work of fine art."[36]

In the mind of its master builder, Daniel Burnham, the White City was to be a vision of order and unity, carefully shaped along classical lines. It also served—not unlike Oz—as a fantasy world. Behind the marble facades, the magnificent whiteness, and the imposing nature of the buildings was staff, "a compound of plaster and fibrous binding, clothing wood and steel."[37] The green glasses that exemplified the falseness of the Emerald City were replaced by the blinding glare of Chicago's White City. The Fair became at once a monument to the Victorian ideal of order and culture and a form of mass culture, an entertainment not to be missed. "*Everyone* says one ought to sell all one has and mortgage one's soul to go there," wrote William James of the Chicago Fair, because "it is esteemed such a revelation of beauty. People cast away all sin and baseness, burst into tears and grow religious, etc. under the influence!!"[38]

The Midway Plaisance at the 1893 World's Columbian Exposition in Chicago was both more and less than met the eye. If the White City was marked by buildings "essentially dignified in style," admitted Daniel Burnham, then one found in the Midway Plaisance "no distinct order . . . it being instead a most unusual collection of almost every type of architecture known to man— oriental villages, Chinese bazaars, tropical settlements, ice railways, the ponderous Ferris wheel, and reproductions of ancient cities. All these are combined to form the lighter and more fantastic side of the Fair."[39] Architect Louis Sullivan considered the buildings of the Midway to be retrograde, without any intrinsic relationship to anything in the American tradition or environment. Nevertheless, the Chicago World's Columbian Exposition actually served as a prototype for the mass culture of the twentieth century. In its wake, traveling carnivals with Ferris wheels of various dimensions became popular attractions around the country. New amusements such as Coney Island became "a harbinger of modernity . . . a symbol not only of fun and frolic but also of major changes in American manners and morals." Coney Island came to define the contours of modern entertainment.[40]

Coney Island amusement park, like the Midway at the Chicago World's Columbian Exposition, heralded the development of a new urban reality marked by an increasingly heterogeneous population, a new audience made up of white-collar and skilled blue-collar workers with increasing leisure time and spending power. Since these urban masses craved new sensory experiences and releases from the routines of modern industrial life, entrepreneurs of entertainment sought to develop forms of enjoyment that might be satisfying to their patrons and remunerative to themselves. Places like Coney Island were never intended to lead an outright revolt against genteel culture; they only sought to challenge the lines of Victorian morality without giving undue offense.

As it developed in the mid-1890s, Coney Island offered visitors a fantasy world, a place of escape and excitement. At Coney Island, with the Atlantic Ocean and a wide variety of entertainments ~~always close~~ at hand, the urbanite could find release and relaxation. The proprieties that fueled polite society were erased; class and ethnic lines did not seem quite so divisive. Even the standards of Victorian public morality, never known for their looseness, appeared to relax in response to the demand for pleasure. In place of the ideals of sobriety and thrift, Coney Island supported abandon and spending. The development of urban mass entertainments like Coney Island reflected what sociologist Simon N. Patten called the "new basis of civilization," defined by a shift from a producer culture to a consumer culture, from the elitism of the cultural custodians to the popular culture of modernity.[41]

With Coney Island, urban nightclubs and restaurants also proliferated in the 1890s. Once the domain of the underclasses, nightclubs became an acceptable forum for the entertainment of middle- and upper-class urbanites. As Lewis Erenberg has demonstrated, nightclubs supported a new culture of enjoyment—one not so closely connected to the confines of the Victorian home. Nightclubs offered their patrons a smattering of spontaneity and daring in contrast to the controlled existence of bourgeois life. Urban nightclubs highlighted a new vision of sexuality, in both jazz music and new styles of dancing, and allowed the individual to escape temporarily from everyday routine. Elite and popular culture, black and white traditions, all intermingled during the infancy of the urban nightclub.[42]

The Cult of Heroism

During the 1890s a "reorientation of American culture" (to borrow historian John Higham's term) was clearly under way. The genteel culture of the Victorian era was being replaced by a more energetic and pleasure-oriented culture associated with the modern age of consumerism. This transformation from gentility to exuberance, from a producer ethos to a consumer ethos, came to define modern American civilization by the second decade of the twentieth century. The development of a cultural system based on the powers of desire, excitement, and self-expression was not accomplished immediately. Victorian propriety coexisted in the 1890s with cosmopolitan daring. Nonetheless, the changes in American culture were momentous.

For many intellectuals Victorian culture by the 1880s had come to be confining, narrowly encased within the bounds of the home and church, restraint and sensibility. They believed that their era was tepid, pallid, lacking in excitement. Too much comfort and control had led to weakness and lethargy. William James, after some time spent at the Chautauqua campground—where middle-class families reveled in the homilies and comforts of polite Victorian culture—called out for release: "I long to escape from tepidity.

123

Even an Armenian massacre, whether to be killer or killed would seem an agreeable change from the blamelessness of Chautauqua. . . . Man wants to be *stretched* to his utmost, if not in one way then in another!"[43]

To be "stretched" became a desirable goal for many Americans in the 1890s. They craved a chance to experience life to the fullest. Images of exuberant and active middle-class Americans became increasingly familiar. Bicycling became a major fad, more for the enjoyment that it promised than for its utility as a means of transportation. Professional and collegiate football and baseball offered their participants a new and heady sense of vigor and courage while also promising their fans a vicarious escape from the increasingly bureaucratic and rational everyday world. Americans rushed to purchase muscle-man Bernarr McFadden's home cures and exercise books, which promoted the possibilities of a strenuous self.[44]

Strenuosity was celebrated in the 1880s and 1890s through the development of a cult of heroism. Americans voraciously digested tales of heroic action in novels, chronicles of battles, and works on medieval history.[45] One of the most popular books of the era, General Lew Wallace's novel *Ben Hur* (1880), captured the nation's desire for excitement by presenting Hur as a man of action. He was committed to ideals, unwilling to bend to injustice and tyranny. No cloistered intellectual or neurasthenic idler, Ben Hur teemed with strength and daring. But the power of his heroism was not an end; it was a means to higher ideals. By the end of the novel, Hur's individualistic rebellion had been channeled into an acceptance of Christianity. Heroism and heaven had become united.

Others found heroic possibilities in the more familiar lives and activities of many Americans. Painter Thomas Eakins, in some of his more powerful portraits, depicted businessmen and physicians as modern exemplars of action and strength. In both *The Gross Clinic* (1875) and *The Agnew Clinic* (1889) he represented the physician as a lifesaving hero, using his scalpel as deftly as any ancient swordsman wielded his blade. Just as the canvases of the French impressionists captured the rhythms of the bourgeois life-style, Eakins's works chronicled the heroic accomplishments of Americans. Indeed, Eakins found heroic acts everywhere. In his at once contemplative and strenuous evocations of rowers along the Schuylkill River, Eakins depicted the confident heroism that he saw in the everyday lives and pleasures of Americans. Even William James agreed with Eakins that heroism might be found in unexpected places. Although James had not encountered it at the Chautauqua, he discovered heroism in the exploits of workers "on freight-trains, on the decks of vessels, in cattle-yards and mines, . . . among the firemen and the policemen, the demand for courage is incessant; and the supply never fails. There, every day of the year somewhere, is human nature *in extremis* for you."[46]

No one in the era better captured the essentials of the cult of heroism and activism than did Theodore Roosevelt. Roosevelt had been weak as a child, but through a regimen of strenuous exercise and iron resolve had built himself into a fine athlete. Never one to sit on the sidelines when a good fight was being waged, Roosevelt organized the Rough Rider brigade to fight in the Spanish-American War. Even in his rhetoric, Roosevelt transformed speech from a complex, genteel mode of expression into a manly way of communicating through powerful, jabbing phrases. In his oratory he depicted himself as being "as strong as a bull moose" and noted that one should "speak softly and carry a big stick," while celebrating the very ideal of a "strenuous life."[47]

Although Roosevelt condemned the weak tea of vague idealism and cultured comforts that dominated the Victorian era, he refused to reject the essential ideals of Victorian cultural and political conservatism—elite leadership, capitalist development, and cultural unity. Like so many of his contemporaries, Roosevelt experimented with new forms of activism without severing his attachment to familiar values and ideals. He wanted, in essence, to reinvigorate Victorian culture, and he viewed his ideal of the strenuous life as the means to achieve that end. The heroic or strenuous individual, by acts of courage and commitment, served the community. Reform became a heroic undertaking.

Yet Roosevelt's cult of heroism had deep implications. The difference between strenuosity in reform and in foreign policy, as Roosevelt demonstrated, was often uncertain. By promoting an image of the heroic individual, Roosevelt helped to whip up nationalism; he created a new image of the American that promised to unify the population through either reform or military battles. The restoration of America's "moral health" in the Spanish-American War of 1898 had a variety of consequences for nations such as Cuba and the Philippines, which experienced this cult of heroism as the objects of a foreign policy of political domination.[48]

The Upshot of Culture

Culture produces and defines, creates and expresses values. In the decade of the 1890s changes in public morality and technology slowly began to create a culture of modernity based on pleasure and consumption, experience and possibility. This culture was driven by an engine of desire. Change came slowly. For example, one of the key technologies of the culture of modernity was only just beginning in the 1890s. The kinetoscope, a precursor of the modern motion picture projector, had been popular at the Chicago Fair in 1893, but in the following years its novelty weakened and its presence was confined to the urban netherworld of vaudeville houses. By 1900 motion pictures found their greatest audiences among the new urban immigrant pop-

Thomas Eakins, *Salutat*, 1898. Oil on canvas. 1930.18. Gift of anonymous donor.

Thomas Eakins, *Professor Henry A. Rowland*, 1897. Oil on canvas. 1931.5. Gift of Stephen C. Clark. ©*Addison Gallery of American Art, Phillips Academy, Andover, Massachusetts. All Rights Reserved*

ulation. But Victorian Americans proved reluctant to embrace the medium of film, often perceiving it as tied to a rise in urban immorality and as a dangerous corrupter of the nation's youth. By the second decade of the twentieth century, however, the motion picture would achieve the kind of cross-class appeal of Coney Island. Once that had occurred, its power to express and define culture would be immense. By the 1920s Americans would identify themselves not only by the commodities they purchased in department stores but also by their longings to be just like their favorite stars on the silver screen—at times heroic, at once sensual and cultivated. The possibilities, all manufactured, would be endless.[49]

Yet this was still in the future. American culture between 1880 and 1900 was informed by tremendous fears about the effects of disintegration as well as by great hopes of integration. The cultural custodians attempted to initiate, through institutions of high culture and education, the communication of an ideal of culture to the populace. Such cultural consumption, directed by those best able to appreciate the ideal aspects of culture, served a variety of purposes, not the least of which was to unify the nation in spite of increasingly apparent and troubling divisions along ethnic and class lines. For some Americans the promise of this culture was both charming and problematic. Identification with the dominant high culture brought to individuals like Samuel Gompers a sense of belonging, a pedigree that might otherwise be lacking. But it did not, as W. E. B. Du Bois's "double consciousness" made clear, necessarily result in complete obeisance to the political and economic realities that high culture often obscured.

The dream of cultural unity began to become more of a reality in this period, but not in the fashion originally envisioned by the custodians of culture. The reorientation of American culture that occurred in the 1890s was directed as much from below as from above; it questioned many of the ideals of Victorianism, replacing a culture of control and restraint with a culture increasingly defined by freedom, heroism, and possibility. But such parameters were also highly limiting, defined as they were by the production of desire and the frenzy for consumption. In the 1880s Americans, in ever-greater numbers, began to define themselves according to their mass-produced desires. In this momentous cultural shift, the values of a producer ethic would come to be replaced by a consumer ethic. The Victorian ideal of character, based on a notion of the self as controlled and inner-directed, would come to be questioned by the ideal of personality, whereby the individual created a self in keeping with the images and desires manufactured outside of the traditional community.

Not all Americans approved of these changes. Certainly, the cultural custodians of an earlier generation greeted the new culture with derision, finding its unity to be based on false notions and plastic ideals. The increasing comfort and confidence that seemed to enthuse many Americans were met with a questioning glance by a handful of intellectuals who exemplified the spirit of the American fin de siècle. For Henry Adams, Louis Sullivan, Thorstein Veblen, Edgar Saltus, and Stephen Crane the pious musings of the Victorian cultural custodians and the heady promises of the apostles of consumer culture seemed equally hollow. It is true that in their rush to embrace a modernist ideal, these intellectuals savagely quarrelled with the assumptions of Victorian culture. Yet for all the modernity of their adversarial stance and biting irony, most American intellectuals continued to believe in order and to posit progress.

six

The American Fin de Siècle

The waning years of the nineteenth century saw a tremendous burst of artistic and intellectual creativity in Europe. These years were the seedtime for much of modernist culture. In England the aesthetic movement led by Walter Pater and Oscar Wilde wrapped itself in a holy shroud of art as an end in itself; the ideal of art became enshrined as a new god to contrast with the Victorian worship of science. At the same time, English aesthetes distanced themselves from the grit of modern industrial society through their ideals of art and artifice. In Vienna artists and thinkers confronted the powers of the irrational, faced the magnetism of desire, and explored the depths of the unconscious. In the process, artists as dissimilar as Gustav Klimt, Sigmund Freud (the artist of the psyche), and Hugo von Hofmannsthal grappled with understanding the modern self in a period marked by political and intellectual disintegration. In France the fin de siècle brought forth not only wails of ennui from the gloomy comfort of decadence but also a rediscovery of the creative power of childhood, of play, in art. There, in the work of belle epoque artists such as Alfred Jarry, Erik Satie, and Henri Rousseau, the power of primitivism explosively combined with explorations into the nature of perception to form the most modern of art forms.

The modernism that arrived hand in hand with the fin de siècle has often been defined as a sensibility that fiercely rejected the past and celebrated the new. An adversarial culture with anarchistic and bohemian tendencies, modernism was founded on an unwillingness to rest satisfied with traditional ideals of art and taste. In their adversarial posture, modernists raged against the pallid assumptions that they viewed as central to Victorianism in social theory, manners, and morals, no less than in art. Modernists proclaimed their belief in the progress of their artistic and creative visions but waxed less eloquent about the possibility of progress in society. They worshiped culture as much as the cultural custodians had, but their understanding of art and literature was more rebellious, less based on "sweetness and light" than on relentless questioning and experimentation.

But despite its spirit of rebellion and experimentation, the American fin de siècle was also marked by an attempt to maintain many assumptions essential to Victorianism. While American intellectuals such as Henry Adams, Thorstein Veblen, and Louis Sullivan pushed aside the tired nostrums of evolutionary progress and genteel culture, American modernist intellectuals continued to cling to an almost spiritual belief in the creative possibilities of the individual and in science as forces that would conquer everything in their paths. American fin de siècle modernism found that irony coexisted with faith, antagonism with celebration, reason with unreason. This creative tension between opposites helps to account for continuing appeal of American fin de siècle thought.

Writers Stephen Crane and Edgar Saltus were exceptional thinkers in the period 1880–1900 because they refused to compromise, to make peace, or to rest secure with either Victorian certitude or reluctant modernist synthesis. Thus, the contradictory rhythms of Adams, Veblen, and Sullivan, as well as the strident drum roll of Crane and Saltus, were the opening bars of modernism in America. Its music may not always have been soothing; in fact, it was often atonal and harsh. Nevertheless, the American fin de siècle had a birth that was as strikingly dependent on American conditions and concerns as it was on the imitation of trends then predominant in European culture and thought.

The power and coherence of a fin de siècle spirit in America prior to 1900 is blurred somewhat because of the diffuse geography of American intellectual life. Because Boston is generally viewed as the hub of American thought and culture from 1880–1900, with some nodding glances thrown to New York and Chicago, the relative dearth of modernist communities of thought in those urban centers during that period is taken by some to attest to the failure of modernism to take root in American soil until it finally crossed the Atlantic after 1900. Yet the fin de siècle movement had indeed found expression before that time, in a host of minds scattered around the country. Henry Adams is an exemplar of the American citizen embracing an ideal of modernity. Although his roots were planted firmly in New England culture, he lived much of his life in Washington, D.C., and abroad. Thorstein Veblen, an American of Norwegian parentage and rural Wisconsin birth, possessed a remarkably modernist sensibility. In Chicago the modernist imperative was most fully developed in the architecture of Louis Sullivan. In literature, the stark and powerful cadences of a modernist Calvinism are found in the works of Stephen Crane, who haunted the streets of New York City, traveled to

Cuba to cover a war, and died in poverty in England. Geographically diverse, often unaware of each others' attempts to grapple with challenging ideas, literature, and art, these American originals all contributed to the American fin de siècle.

Henry Adams

Swimming in despair, reared on disappointment, his pen dripping with irony—Henry Adams, unwilling to settle for the polite assumptions of his age, was without doubt an apostle of modernism. Yet despite his adversarial posture, he refused to give up a quest for spiritual or scientific truth. Even though his conclusions differed violently from the optimistic evolutionism of Henry Ward Beecher or Joseph LeConte, Adams found it necessary to drink from the waters of science to satisfy his thirst for absolute knowledge in the frightening face of apparent chaos and contradiction—conditions that are perhaps the benchmarks of modernity.

Henry Adams could never escape tradition or a nagging sense that he had failed to live up to expectations. He inherited the weight of two presidential forebears and an influential father. Adams had spent the Civil War years as a diplomatic attaché in London. Having returned to America's shores in search of career and influence, he dabbled in politics, journalism, and history. He was active in reform politics, fighting corruption from his position as editor of the *North American Review*, an influential journal of opinion. But, he admitted, his political power was limited. By the 1880s his interest in reform was nothing more than an unhappy memory. Adams composed an impressive nine-volume work, *A History of the United States during the Administrations of Jefferson and Madison* (1889–91), but took little apparent pleasure in the fruits of this labor. Following the suicide of his beloved wife, Clover, in 1885, Adams took flight from the mundane world of politics and history to seek salvation, or at least surcease, by turns in the South Sea Islands and in the study of medieval art and architecture. In his monumental work of autobiography, *The Education of Henry Adams*, he attempted to represent his life as an exercise in failure. His failure, as he saw it, was not only a consequence of an inability to rise to the heights of his powerful ancestors but also a consequence of his failure to rest content with a world marked by essential contradictions, forces that seemed to be careening in different directions.

Henry Adams's thought was defined by its fervent disdain and pessimism. The influx of immigrants, the corruption of business and politics, and the general demise of standards that the Adams family had always rigorously upheld only seemed to confirm the righteousness of his pessimism. Those who promoted the progressive nature of evolutionary science, Adams maintained, were starry-eyed and ignorant. Indeed, as Adams phrased it, simply by studying presidential succession from George Washington to U. S. Grant, one would be forced to discover "evidence enough to upset Darwin" and any other theorist of progressive evolution.[1] Adams refused to rest comfortably until he had demonstrated that the decline in the presidency was little more than a single part of a larger frame of reference—the unrelenting and general degradation of human thought and progress.

Adams turned to science to prove the ubiquity of decline. In a presidential letter to the American Historical Association, "The Tendency of History" (1894), Adams announced his desire to uncover a science of history that would "be absolute, like other sciences, and must fix with mathematical certainty the path which human society has got to follow."[2] With tremendous enthusiasm, Adams threw himself into the maelstrom of modern scientific theory. What he found there, not surprisingly, satisfied his already well-developed pessimistic appetite. The hope that science might provide unity was proven to be a sham; all that science revealed was the prevalence of multiplicity, of chaos, of disorder: "In plain words, Chaos was the law of nature; Order was the dream of man."[3] History pointed only "to the final and fundamental necessity of Degradation."[4]

Yet the recognition of chaos and degradation could also fascinate, and even enthuse, Adams. For Adams, nothing seemed to express better the raw power and chaotic energy of the modern age than the dynamo. He was awed by the power that exuded from a 40-foot engine. This apotheosis of industrial technology came to represent for Adams a dizzying force, a motor of change propelling America from a society marked by tradition and community into a baffling and frightening cacophony of cultures. Movement to and fro now characterized the American experiment, without bequeathing to the nation significant improvement or cause for hope—at least not according to the rigorous, and often narrow, standards of Henry Adams. The power of the dynamo, the exemplification of modernity, only hid the ultimate lesson that Adams drew from history: that progress was an illusion, that America would not reign forever youthful, and that morality was largely a matter of force.

But force and power, unity and order could still be found in the realm of the spiritual. In contrast to the energy of the dynamo, Adams discovered, there was transcendence and calm in the power of the cult of the Virgin of the Middle Ages. Adams was driven to study the Middle Ages because that period represented the youth of the present era; in order to experience it, one must "grow prematurely young." In his monumental work *Mont-Saint-Michel and Chartres* (1905), Adams often presents himself in the guise of a modern pilgrim, searching for salvation. The Virgin represents womanly power, marked by a spirit of nurturing and faith. As depicted in the glass murals of the Chartres Cathedral, the Virgin provides a sense of comfort and respite. In the Middle Ages, Adams writes, the Virgin contentedly waited "to receive the secrets and the prayers of suppliants . . . there she bent down to our level, resumed her humanity, and felt our griefs and passions."[5] Additionally, in the twelfth century, Adams found a unified culture, an organic society held together by the mortar of faith and tradition. The great architectural accomplishments of this period evidenced the ecstatic possibilities of belief.

As with almost everything he considered, Adams's relationship to the Middle Ages and the spiritual was tinged with irony. Much as he might have wished to ignore it, Adams could never forget that the power of the spiritual, as depicted in the architectonic unity of medieval architecture, society, and religion, was consigned to the past—possible to study but impossible to replicate. The spiritual power of the Virgin could only be experienced vicariously; Adams was imprisoned by the chains of modernity, with its stance of scientific scrutiny and staunch agnosticism, and its tortured sense of the uncertainty of selfhood. After all, Adams never ventured into the gothic churches that graced the skylines of New York City or of Washington, D.C. Perhaps they lacked the aura of Chartres; perhaps faith for Adams was more easily apprehended in books and fanciful journeys than in real life. In typically ironic fashion, Adams was an agnostic drawn to the spiritual; he was a self-professed follower of modern science, absolutely in love with the ideal of religious devotion.

In sum, Adams was a man beset by two selves. One was highly skeptical and ironic, excited by his discovery of a law that captured the tendency of history, a tendency that Adams found to be degenerative and irreversible, contrary to the theories of his self-satisfied contemporaries. The other self was childlike, seeking out the maternal embrace of the image of the Virgin, hungering after the succor of the unified belief system of the medieval age. In part, this ambivalence was a blessing for Adams. It prevented him from settling comfortably into any particular frame of reference. It allowed him to always have a fresh, if not a refreshing, perspective—one that embraced much that was modern and adversarial while refusing to let go of the past and the spiritual.

Thorstein Veblen

Adams's sense of alienation from his historical era was equaled, and perhaps surpassed, by the fierce distance that divided Thorstein Veblen from many of the assumptions of Victorian culture. Veblen's was an ironic and scathing perspective loaded with criticism of his society. Yet he expressed his condemnation in the language, and with the faith, of science. Despite a strongly adversarial stance, Veblen was not without hope; he invested faith in the progressive power of the evolution of the machine process to make things right.

Veblen came by his ironic demeanor quite naturally. As a young man he was graced or damned, depending on one's opinion, with a particularly biting wit. All of his teachers recognized the brilliance that lurked behind his laconic speech and lazy nature. Veblen was always a square peg in a round hole, whether in the insular Norwegian farming communities of his youth in Wisconsin and Minnesota, during his peripatetic higher education (undergraduate studies at Carleton College, followed by graduate work at Yale, Johns Hopkins, and Cornell), and throughout his checkered and spectacularly unsuccessful teaching career at the University of Chicago, Stanford, the University of Missouri, and the New School for Social Research in New York City. In his written works, Veblen confused some, instructed many, and always challenged—armed with a wealth of knowledge drawn from anthropological literature, the latest in economic theory, and government statistics; a penchant for the coining of phrases and the use of scientific jargon; and a proclaimed stance of objective neutrality. Indeed, Veblen wielded the scalpel of irony so deftly that readers were often uncertain whether its target had been harmed or healed.[6]

Veblen was a strong Darwinian. He discovered in the laws of evolutionary science a methodology that stressed process over teleology, fact over concept, experience over abstraction. His interest in anthropology led him to discover the links that brought together ancient and modern customs, less as a means of demonstrating progress than as a mode of indicating continuity and the tortuously slow and conservative nature of change. From the New Psychology being developed by James and Dewey in the 1880s and 1890s, Veblen borrowed an emphasis on instinct and habit, not as absolutes but as pointers to help determine how psychical factors affected the individual's interaction with a given environment and, in turn, how the environment was transformed in the process.

In his most famous book, *The Theory of the Leisure Class*, first published in 1899, Veblen joined his evolutionary perspective with his powerful wit.[7] Dense and heavily weighted with economic and anthropologic analysis, the volume wears its learning proudly. Written in a detached style, Veblen builds a barbed-wire fence of argument with his prose. He excoriates the leisure-class subjects of his book, despite his claims that he intended not to pass judgment on them but only to evaluate them in the value-neutral terms of modern science. Let the reader be wary of Veblen's claim. He opens the introduction to this work with the famous line, "The institution of a leisure class is found in its best developed stages at the higher stages of the barbarian culture." By the end of the volume, Veblen has devastatingly shown how the modern leisure class exhibits a barbarian style of behavior. Indeed, he finds it to be evolutionarily backward.

In many ways, a mythical structure predominates, and lends force to, this argument in *The Theory of the Leisure Class*. Once upon a time, suggests Veblen, there existed primitive cultures marked by peace, tranquility, and a strong sense of community responsibility. But a devil lurked in the primitive Garden of Eden. The accumulation of wealth fostered the predatory culture of the barbarian stage of civilization, when warriors began to raid other communities as a means of gaining not only food but also honor and glory. In the process, as Veblen paints the picture, the values of predatory culture became hardened; labor came to be viewed as a lowly undertaking, something better left to slaves and women. This "invidious distinction" between "exploit and drudgery" remains an unfortunate staple of modern civilization.

In the advanced industrial societies of Veblen's era, a leisure class had developed that was dedicated to nonproductive activities. Status and leisure, social standing and nonproductive labor become the paired opposites that inform Veblen's analysis of the leisure class. In fact, the less closely members of this class were related to the nitty-gritty of productive enterprise, the greater the honor and glory that would accrue to them. In this view, war and sport figure as acceptable endeavors for males of the leisure class: "government and war are, at least in part, carried on for the pecuniary gain of those who engage in them; but it is gain obtained by the honorable method of seizure and conversion. These occupations are of the nature of predatory, not of productive, employment." Veblen penned these words as America became a colonial power during the Spanish-American War.

Veblen's work may be seen as an early and sustained assault against the developing assumptions of a consumer culture marked by what Veblen called "conspicuous consumption." This coinage signified for Veblen the modern tendency for individuals to define themselves and their status, worth, and identity through their ability to surround themselves with lavish and often unnecessary objects of consumption. Most intriguingly, Veblen understood that women would be at the forefront of this consumerism: their lives and values would be defined by what they could buy; their sense of identity would be contained in a spiral of never-ending desire about how to transform themselves into status objects.

Veblen argued that modern American women functioned largely as ornaments. Women and children, as indexes of their husbands' and fathers' status, became prime examples of the power of conspicuous consumption. The desire and expression of status was barbarian in origin, according to Veblen. The plumage that ancient chieftains wore as a symbol of their exalted status was paralleled in Veblen's culture by the immense hats that graced the heads of women from the wealthy class. The ancient principle of adornment translated into a "display of wasteful expenditure" in modern society.[8] Veblen found that "the high heel, the skirt, the impracticable bonnet, the corset, and the general disregard of the wearer's comfort which is an obvious feature of all civilized women's apparel, are so many items of evidence to the effect that in the modern civilized scheme of life the woman is still, in theory, the economic dependent of man—that, perhaps in a highly idealized sense, she is still the man's chattel . . . delegated the office of putting in evidence [her] master's ability to pay."

Veblen ranged widely in his critique of the backwardness, waste, inefficiency, and dangers of a culture based on various forms of conspicuous consumption. He wrote at a critical juncture when American society was dominated by labor strife, periodic depressions, and massive social dislocation. He also wrote at the time when new business organizations, the trust and the monopoly, were being formed. Everywhere he looked, Veblen uncovered the evil hand of a "pecuniary culture" that defined business practices. In the end, whether in the university, the halls of government, sporting events, or industrial enterprise, the logic of the profit motive and of wastefulness appeared to be predominant. Although Veblen's critique of capitalism was strident and sustained, he refused to place himself in the socialist camp. He heartily disavowed certain staples of Marxist belief, including the theory of the progressive nature of the class struggle and the theory of surplus labor.

Veblen, despite the almost numbing power of his criticisms of the modern culture of pecuniary emulation and waste, was not without hope. His evolutionary schema had set the stage for a new cast of possibilities. The logic of modernity, as exemplified in the development of a machine culture, along with the continuing presence of an instinct of workmanship deep in the marrow of man, represented for Veblen the possibility of salvation. Veblen's faith was not of a piece with nostalgia for the days of preindustrial workmanship, associated with the utopian idealism of Edward Bellamy's *Looking Backward* and with the ideals of William Morris and his American followers. To be sure, Veblen found much that was of interest in the rise of the arts and crafts movement around the turn of the century: he admired the heartfelt emphasis on the value of skilled labor and the notions that work must be a delight and that craftsmanship and workmanship were ideals that needed to be reintroduced into society. Veblen realized that the arts and crafts movement was confined largely to the elite classes. The goods they produced were quite expensive, which made their production not only an acceptable leisure activity for the leisure class but also, ironically, a new example of conspicuous consumption.

Hope, in Veblen's opinion, lay in falling into line behind the development of modern machinery.[9] If Veblen had had a fuller understanding of that machinery and of factory life, then perhaps his praise for them would have been more restrained. But he, as well as certain socialist theorists and efficiency experts, was convinced that the evolutionary development of modern machinery had arrived at a fork in the road. One path pointed in the direction of continued control of the process of production by those interested in the profit motive. There inefficiency and waste, profit, and market forces predominated. At the end of this path, suggested Veblen, were economic calamities and labor struggles of apocalyptic proportions. Another road seemed to promise that the process of production would, by its own internal evolution, achieve an impressive state of efficiency. The ultimate logic of the machine process demanded greater productivity and quality rather than the pecuniary rationale of business ethics. Only the trained engineer and the skilled worker comprehended the possibilities of the emergent machine culture and the concomitant possibility of bringing rationalization and order into the system of production and consumption. Toward the engineer, then, Veblen cast his most optimistic glance.

In *The Theory of Business Enterprise* (1904) Veblen most fully described the machine process and its immense implications. Although industrial evolution had reached a higher stage of development, cultural evolution—the understanding of the logic of production and distribution of goods—remained mired in an essentially highly barbarian, predatory, and pecuniary mode. In his most prophetic cadences, Veblen predicted that out of the "natural decay of the business enterprise" would arise new forms of organization, run by engineers who would revolutionize, in accordance with the evolutionary development of production methods, the economic system of the United States.[10]

Despair, or at least powerful skepticism, eventually replaced Veblen's confidence in the engineer as the motor of progress. Although the machine process developed steadily, its growth was rivaled by the continuing strength of a pecuniary culture that celebrated profit over quality. By the final years of his life, in the 1920s, gloom became increasingly predominant in Veblen's work. The engineer and the scientist, no less than the skilled worker, had become too deeply enmeshed within the web of pecuniary culture. Thus, major changes in the functioning of the industrial enterprise seemed terribly unlikely in the near future. The engineers, the onetime saviors of society, were now "consistently loyal, with something more than a hired man's loyalty, to the established order of commercial profit and absentee ownership."[11]

Veblen, like Adams, used the language of modern science to wage an unrelenting battle against the powers that be. He threw himself into the stream of modernity, finding in its heady waters a power that might turn the wheels of industrial development and that would eventually move the lagging cultural configuration so as to better reflect the new and necessary premises of the machine process. Fiercely agnostic in his religious beliefs, Veblen retained a spiritual sensitivity, reflected in his condemnation of waste and inefficiency, in his fervent belief in the value of workmanship, and in his faith in the ultimate power of the machine culture to liberate human beings. Yet both Thorstein Veblen and Henry Adams were fascinated by the machine age and condemned the assumptions that comforted many of their compatriots. They remained reluctant modernists, men who believed in the liberating potential of modernity but also maintained hope in the progressive nature of evolution (Veblen), the transformative nature of faith, and the potential of an individualistic aesthetic (Adams)—assumptions that had rested comfortably within a Victorian hierarchy of values.

Louis Sullivan

Louis Sullivan was another American modernist attempting to combine the ideals of an earlier age with a sensitivity to new ideas and realities. In some ways he was a throwback to the Emersonian tradition, as enunciated in "The American Scholar" address of 1837. In that speech Emerson had called for American cultural independence from the cumbersome ideals of British culture: "Each age, it is found, must write its own books; or rather, each generation for the next succeeding. The books of an older period will not fit this."[12] In the spirit of Emerson, but with more anger, Sullivan fired diatribes against cultural constraints and demanded a style of thought and architecture that would better represent American realities, that would be in keeping with the spirituality and character of the American experiment as it entered into a new century. If the years and experience worked on Emerson to lead him into a less belligerent relation to tradition, years of failure and unhappiness further isolated Sullivan from traditional presumptions and helped to transform him into an angry and lonely prophet for an American style of architectural modernity.

Sullivan was vague in defining precisely what ideals American architecture should embrace. Sometimes good architecture seemed to exist in nothing more than its ability to reproduce or approximate the spiritual truth contained in the book of nature. In nature, Sullivan maintained, the architect found inspiration. Successful architecture, he posited, was the result of the interaction between the creative spirit of the architect—"Poet," "Prophet," "MAN THE CREATOR"—with the demands of a particular site and the needs of a specific building's functions. In the end the great architect adhered to spiritual principles and democratic ideals that celebrated the creativity of the individual and that expressed the organic unity of nature and society. To Sullivan's mind, for modern scholarship, no less than architecture, "to be true it must bear a genuine relation to the vital, aspiring thought of our day and generation."[13]

When Sullivan examined the architecture of the two greatest metropolises of his era, New York City and Chicago, he found little to praise. Sounding like Veblen, Sullivan described New York City's architecture, in his *Kindergarten Chats* (1901–2), as "one barbarism heaped upon another until the incongruous mass reaches the limit of its idiocy in height and culminates, perchance, in a Greek temple." New York architecture lacked heart and artistic value; it was tired and traditional. Like Adams before the dynamo, Sullivan stood awed by the power that the city projected, but that power was not apparent in the architecture. Urban architecture was simply "gigantic energy gone wrong." In Chicago, where many of Sullivan's own commissions were located, the verdict, although less forceful, remained unfavorable. If New York was stuck in the mud of the old, then Chicago was "young [and] clumsy." Its architecture captured "vacant, sullen materialism, brooding and morose . . . the spectacle of Man's abject spiritual beggary."[14]

In this criticism, Sullivan failed to confront a dilemma that arose out of his own presuppositions based on an Emersonian-influenced doctrine of the organic, of the infinitude of the private man exemplifying the spirit of the age. But Sullivan avoided the fact that the architects of Chicago, whose buildings exemplified the commercial spirit, were doing nothing more than expressing in grand form the underlying assumptions of the era. In this sense, the architects that he condemned were guilty only of the crime of listening to their own heart strings and those of their patrons. The falsity in this equation is not directly condemned by Sullivan except in the most general terms. In the end Sullivan, no less than his fellow architects, was determined to work hand in hand with the emerging elite of the industrial world.

Sullivan's embrace of the spirit of modernity was most apparent in his espousal of the skyscraper. Sullivan was not alone in believing that the skyscraper was a predominant metaphor for modernity. Philosopher George Santayana wrote that "The American Will inhabits the sky-scraper; the American Intellect inhabits the colonial mansion. . . . The one is all aggressive enterprise; the other is all genteel tradition.[15] Sullivan, in his most programmatic statement on the skyscraper as architectural form and problem, "The Tall Office Building Artistically Considered" (1896), spoke in similar, if more measured, tones. The evolution of technique and materials used in building had allowed for the possibility of the skyscraper, but it was incumbent upon the architect to realize the greatness of this particular form. Rather than strictly emphasizing the creative aspects of this new type of building, Sullivan approached it first from a practical angle: how should a skyscraper function? In general, he wanted to divide the building into its essential parts: below-ground area for boilers; ground floor for bank and shops; additional stories for offices, divided according to the needs of the particular businesses; and a top floor devoted to the mechanisms for air circulation and elevator service. Once these practical design problems had been met, then the artistic aspects of the skyscraper had to be considered fully. Otherwise the skyscraper would be nothing more than a "sterile pile." Sullivan sought to "proclaim from the dizzy height of this strange, weird, modern housetop the peaceful evangel of sentiment, of beauty, the cult of a higher life."

This "cult of a higher life" was achieved in the skyscraper through the resolution of technical problems and the incorporation of "the imperative voice of emotion" in the design. The tall building must stand with nature, not against it. Sullivan's most famous architectural principle was that form must follow function. Despite the harshness of this formula, Sullivan did not mean to suggest that function obliterated the need for artistic creativity or that the architect was little more than a draftsman. The artistic spirit of the individual architect entered into the solution to any design problem. The heroic interaction between form and function, Sullivan believed, would make the skyscraper into a living art form, an organic monument as valid in its own time as the Greek temple or Gothic church had been in earlier eras.[16]

The Wainwright Building in St. Louis, constructed in 1890–91, may be the closest Sullivan came to realizing his ideal of the skyscraper. The Wainwright structure responds to the demands of its function, with ground-floor stores and succeeding stories devoted to office space. The building is not a mishmash of styles; it is marked by a simplicity of design and execution that contrasts markedly with the eclectic style then in vogue. Yet for all of the functional qualities of its design, what is most striking about the building is the impressiveness of its ornate decoration. Sullivan's "Ornament in Architecture," written in 1892, just after the completion of the Wainwright Building, suggests that ornament as an afterthought, ornament as mere decoration, is without architectural value. But ornament can, Sullivan maintained, represent an addition of equal worth to the functional attributes of a building. In this sense it represented the artistic spirit of the architect, a harmonizing of nature and building through the agency of the architect. Rather than detracting from the loftiness of the Wainwright, the ornamentation that Sullivan provided for it added luster. To Frank Lloyd Wright, the great architect of the twentieth century and a self-professed disciple of Sullivan, the Wainwright Building had a "virtue, individuality, beauty all its own"; it represented "height triumphant."[17]

The optimism of "height triumphant" was often evident in Sullivan's theorizing about art and architecture. Sullivan saw himself as a prophet. He desperately wanted his assumptions to be shared by other architects. Indeed, he wanted his ideals to bring forth an artistic renaissance in America, a movement that would not be beholden to the past. He associated his optimistic spirit with the springtime, when the natural world casts off the gloom and stasis of winter with new buds and possibilities. "I have in my heart," wrote Sullivan, "a profound reverence . . . for the inexhaustible activity and imaginative flexibility of . . . the American heart, mind, and spirit."[18]

But Sullivan's optimism was strongly compromised by his pessimism as a prophet who found himself without influence or sufficient numbers of followers. Sullivan faced the abyss of pessimism at a number of points. In surveying the architectural monuments that grace the Chicago skyline, the architect / seer was moved to despair, and "in danger of arriving at conclusions deepening into a hopeless pessimism."[19] Likewise, in New York City, he

Exterior view of Louis Sullivan's Wainwright Building, St. Louis, Missouri. ©1991 *The Art Institute of Chicago. All Rights Reserved*

found only degeneracy and a lack of creative spirit. The root of Sullivan's problem was that he fancied himself an apostle of modernity (for example, in espousing the skyscraper as an art form). If the cities had come to represent for Sullivan places of pessimism and degeneracy, then he was clearly situating himself outside of the apparent and obvious direction of American development. Sullivan did not present an alternative, nor was he naive or nostalgic in promoting a vision of a utopian agrarian middle ground. The city was the site of modernity, the place where Sullivan's architectural work was domiciled, but it also represented the ironic culmination of degeneracy intermingled with optimism, of decline walking hand in hand with possibility.

There is a long prose poem in *Kindergarten Chats* entitled "Pessimism." It has a relentless cadence that almost anticipates the dirge style that predominates in T. S. Eliot's *The Waste Land*, a monument to the modernist mentality. In "Pessimism" Sullivan notes:

> For them, all life is cruel; and Death, Man's only friend.
> For them, all men are cruel; and no man has a friend.
> For them, the best in the heart is the worst, because it is a deception.
> For them the best in the mind is worthless, because powerless.
> For them, the soul is a sorrow which intensifies our sorrow.

On and on "Pessimism" grinds in this spirit. In the original version of the poem, Sullivan had included many passages that seemed to argue against the pessimistic temper. Intriguingly, in the version revised in 1918, Sullivan removed many of these retorts and replaced them with the following sentence, which may be seen as indicative of the temper of his life at the time: "For pessimism is the winter of the mind, the winter of the heart, the winter of the World."[20]

There is a degree of the heroic in Sullivan's thought. He was flush up against the modernist notion of a world bereft of ultimate meaning. His adversarial stance against the mainstream of American architecture was as vehement and unrelenting as Veblen's thrusts at the pretensions of the leisure class or Adams's barbs against the soothsayers of gentle and complacent progress. Despite all of his venom, Sullivan maintained a sense of hope, a belief that in the power of American democracy resided a force capable of casting off the dead cloak of tradition. Sullivan, no less than Adams, recognized the possibility that "Man surely is alone" or that "Man's little life [is] but a tinkle that is muffled quickly in the eternal night." Although drained by the despair of a prophet without disciples, Sullivan, in Emersonian fashion, continued to demand individual perseverance and creativity. This optimistic message was the foundation of Sullivan's program; whether it remains sufficiently solid to support the structure of his thought is open to interpretation.

Decadence

A fin de siècle spirit of deep pessimism afflicted many American intellectuals and artists. They faced the present with disgust and felt only despair in the face of the future. Faith in progressive evolution, confidence in the liberating power of technology, and even belief in God struck these individuals as nothing more than cruel illusions. For these thinkers, a properly modern perspective demanded a cold and clinical glare at the world and immense amounts of either resignation or courage to persevere.

The dim fires of pessimism were fueled by a number of sources. By the 1880s the dizzying pace of change had ushered in a "megaphonic" age marked by constant movement and sensory stimulation. The new and frenzied urban industrial age represented excitement incarnate for some and jarred the nerves of others. In the analysis of Dr. George Beard, neurasthenia, or American nervousness, had become the defining affliction of modern times, with its common symptoms of ennui, languidness, and depression. Neurasthenia, it appeared, led to a nightmare view of life in this era.

Doubts about God and progress, the twin pillars of nineteenth-century confidence, also contributed to the pessimism common around the turn of the century. Certainly, religious doubt already had a long history. But in this period historical evaluations of the Bible and the implications of Darwinism increasingly undermined theological faith. Armed with an Enlightenment confidence in reason and science, popular lecturer Robert Ingersoll presented himself to audiences across America as an atheistic Daniel in a lion's den of Christians. In an age of science, many American lions seemed to have lost their roar. They puzzled over what Ingersoll had to say and, even when not converted to atheism or agnosticism, seemed willing to entertain greater doubts about the validity of the Bible or the presence of God than had their ancestors. Watered-down religious beliefs translated into a less confident response to the world. This stance was well depicted in Harold Frederic's novel *The Damnation of Theron Ware* (1896), in which the protagonist, a minister, suffers a crisis of faith; his doubt is manifested in neurasthenia and depression. The sustaining power of religion, in a modern age of doubt, proves to be a weak antidote for the spiritual and intellectual problems that ail Theron Ware.

Those no longer able to take refuge in religion often turned for sustenance to a hearty belief in secular progress. Progress was raised almost to the level of a theology in the nineteenth century, and it could function to prop up religious confidence that eventual salvation, or at least improvement, was the necessary next step in a natural process of social and ethical evolution. By the 1890s, however, thinkers like Henry Adams, with a perverse faith in chaos and decline, became more common. Darwinism and theories from the physical sciences, once the props for doctrines of progress, now appeared to lead to opposite conclusions. Order seemed to be an illusion. The logic of science pointed only in the direction of chaos and degeneration. Even America's greatest storyteller and humorist, Mark Twain, fell victim to these dark sentiments. He hid them from public view, lest his image and his book sales drop as a result. The sense of being alone in an inhospitable universe became a major theme of his late, posthumously published work. He ended the novel *The Mysterious Stranger* with the scary lines:

"It is true, that which I have revealed to you; there is no God, no universe, no human race, no earthly life, no heaven, no hell. It is all a dream—a grotesque and foolish dream. Nothing exists but you . . . a vagrant thought, useless thought, a homeless thought, wandering forlorn among the empty eternities!"

He vanished, and left me appalled; for I knew, and realized, that all he had said was true.[21]

Twain was not alone in this bleak world. Many thinkers ceased to pay lip service to idealized notions about the regal nature of humanity. The dividing line between the human and the animal, between vaunted reason and vicious instincts, had become too thin to discern. The power of the naturalist model of fiction brought the ideality of man down to the level of animal instincts. In Frank Norris's *McTeague* (1899), the character McTeague is an unlicensed dentist; he works hard, but he is not successful or even particularly respectable. Through a series of events outside of his own control, McTeague suffers reversals in business and finds himself unable to control the animality in his nature, which breaks through the thin walls of his shabby bourgeois respectability like a volcanic eruption. He reverts to an animal self, a welter of instincts and insatiable appetites. Drawing on the popular notion of atavism (which also figures in Jack London's novels of this period), Norris demonstrates that the instinctual desires, the animal past, in each and every human being remain powerful and dangerous. As McTeague's animal nature comes to the fore, he craves desperately after wealth and love, and proves himself quite capable of murder when his demands are unmet. The climax of the novel finds McTeague and his enemy fighting to the death in the desert. McTeague vanquishes his opponent, only to perish of thirst with his dead prey handcuffed to him. So much for the nobility of man.

Religious doubt, rejection of progress, neurasthenia, and naturalism all contributed, then, to what German physician Max Nordau labeled a form of "moral sea-sickness." Nordau popularized this notion of a fin de siècle degeneracy in his widely read book *Degeneration* (1895). His ideas struck a resonant chord in America. Moral sea-sickness, Nordau sadly maintained, was the disease of modernity. The ability of men and women to function in a useful, wholesome, and idealistic manner had become corroded by the acid of modernity. In turning his glare to the world of literature, Nordau uncovered among a group of diverse literary giants—Tolstoy, Zola, Ibsen, and Baudelaire—the defining characteristics of the modernist temperament: a dangerous pessimism and a passive acceptance—sometimes a celebration—of a sense of decline. In the kindly fashion of the Enlightenment rationalist, Nordau was not without hope. Diagnosis of the disease might lead to its cure and control: "Characterization of the leading degenerates as mentally diseased; unmasking and stigmatizing of their imitators as enemies to society; cautioning the public against the lies of these parasites."[22] But Nordau's worst fears would only be realized by the work of Stephen Crane, America's most talented novelist, and in the popular philosophy and fiction produced by Edgar Saltus.

The Red Badge of Disappointment

Pessimism and degeneracy, whatever their social or moral implications, could sometimes give rise to powerful art and to searching philosophical interrogations into the meaning of life. In America, writers Stephen Crane and Edgar Saltus threw their intellectual hats into the ring of pessimism and decline. They faced the present and the future without faith in God, progress, or science. Their modernism consisted in their willingness to confront the world on its own terms. If salvation was to be found—and they were not convinced of its presence or even its utility—it consisted only in the harsh rigor and personal satisfactions of their respective contributions to art.

Both were born into wealth and quickly made names for themselves as brilliant writers, although Crane's reputation has fared the best over time. By the age of 34 Saltus had published three novels, two works of philosophical reflection, and a biography of Balzac. Crane's accomplishments were contained within a life of less than 30 years, and he did not live long into the twentieth century. Both men raged against illusion and shared a grim suspicion that man was essentially alone in the universe.

This sense of loneliness in a universe at best indifferent to man's ideals and strivings is a predominant and powerful theme in Crane's prose and poetry. Its roots lay in his youthful rebellion not only against Victorian proprieties but also against his father, a Methodist minister. Nothing seemed safe from Crane's withering prose assault. In *Maggie: A Girl of the Streets* (1893) Crane painted—not without sympathy—an impressionistic picture of the underside of American life, a side that anti–fin de siècle thinkers such as Nordau pre-

ferred to leave under the covers. Crane was not unusual in turning to the
city for fictional material. Others in the 1890s found the urban environment,
and especially its immigrant inhabitants, to be fertile ground for analysis.
The allure of the city, the immigrant, and the worker lay in their presumed
enthusiasms and struggles, which were seen as contrasting powerfully with
the pale interior of the bourgeois drawing room. Jacob Riis's reputation as a
reformer was enhanced through his photographic evocations of New York
City immigrants in *How the Other Half Lives* (1890). Riis did not capture his
subjects unaware; in fact, he sometimes paid them to strike particular poses.

Like Riis, Crane was familiar with the urban netherworld, and he did not
seek to represent it with a naive verisimilitude. Crane knew that he was a
writer of fiction. The poor in Crane's stories are his own creations, buffeted
about by forces and circumstances too large for them to comprehend; it is
unclear whether they learn anything of value in the end. Almost all of Crane's
characters live in a self-deceiving manner. The alcoholic mother rages about
the moral laxity of her daughter, Maggie; Pete boasts about what a square

Stephen Crane in 1899. *Courtesy of Stephen Crane Collection, Clifton Waller Barrett Library, Special Collections Department, University of Virginia Library*

guy he is while treating Maggie in a poor fashion. Maggie alone maintains a desire for something better; she goes to the melodrama and there is enthused by the "culture and refinement" of the heroine. In the process Maggie comes to deceive herself into believing that such attributes might "be acquired by a girl who live[s] in a tenement house and work[s] in a shirt factory." In Crane's view, such hopes are specious. Maggie's fortunes plummet; escape from the monsters of poverty and desire comes only with death.[23]

In Crane's most famous work, *The Red Badge of Courage* (1895), the horror of war is presented in telling detail—especially impressive since Crane had not experienced war prior to writing the book. A few years later, as a correspondent covering the Greek war for independence and then the Spanish-American War, Crane would be pleased that his vicarious rendition of the experience of fighting had an air of veracity. In *The Red Badge of Courage* Crane does not identify what battle is being fought, nor does he describe the motives that some presumed might explain why the Civil War had been fought (e.g., to reunite the union, to end slavery). The novel simply stands as a response to the question "Is life worth living?"—or, at the very least, as an ironic play on that notion.

Henry Fleming is one of the few characters in *The Red Badge of Courage* with a proper name; most of the others are merely described. Henry is hardly idealistic about the war; he simply wants to partake of the excitement and to bask in the glory of successfully proving himself a man. He gets more than he bargained for. Once the din of the guns is heard, reason and courage, ideals and hopes vanish amid the smoke and suffering. Henry flees in cowardice. In the end he receives a wound—ironically, at the hands of one of his compatriots—which gives him a certain credibility and the courage to brave the fire of the opposing side. In one sense *The Red Badge of Courage* may be read as a moral tale of a young man's journey from cowardice to heroism, from yearning to acceptance: "He turned now with a lover's thirst to images of tranquil skies, fresh meadows, cool brooks—an existence of soft and eternal peace." Yet the book also illustrates the banality of idealism and heroism. The entire novel is about deceptions, about men imposing their own constructions on the resistant stuff of reality, usually failing to realize that lofty ideals and the grit of the outside world rarely jibe.[24]

Nowhere is this theme more compellingly and sadly played out than in Crane's short story "The Blue Hotel" (1897–98). Forced by a snowstorm to take refuge in the Palace Hotel in Nebraska, "a shaky and quick-eyed Swede" quickly becomes a prisoner to his illusions about the West.[25] He is terribly frightened that he will be killed in a barroom brawl or fall victim to a gunslinger. The Swede holds on to these fears because he has read many Western thrillers. In reality the gents of the Palace Hotel are a sturdy and not unkind group. But in the midst of a card game, the Swede's paranoia convinces him that one of the players is cheating, which leads to a vicious fight, later followed by still another altercation that claims the Swede's life. In this story Crane suggests that one's illusions can lead one astray; in distorting reality, illusions can bring forth disastrous consequences. That it is better to live without illusions and expectations seems to be Crane's simple message.

Other of Crane's works of fiction deal with the unrelenting fury of the environment and the weakness of men's illusions in dealing with its harsh realities. In the short story "The Open Boat," based on Crane's own experiences during a shipwreck off the coast of Florida, four men adrift on a rough sea hope and dream about the possibility of being rescued. The opening line of the story represents their longing for a God who will offer them sustenance in a cruel environment: "None of them knew the color of the sky." The characters are certain that they are living life to the fullest by suffering and imagining salvation. They work as a group, riveted together by their shared fate. Like *Red Badge*, the story is cast in the familiar iron of camaraderie and heroism. Three of the four survive, but none of them, one assumes, will shed the illusions they hold about justice and truth. Throughout the story the men mistake a glimmer of light for a rescue station, or a tourist bus for a rescue vehicle. They are, in the end, dangerously adrift. The most capable of the four, the one who by all odds should survive the ordeal, dies in the frenzied attempt to reach land. The other three wash up on the shore and come to believe that "they could . . . be interpreters." But what will they interpret? The tiresome story of survival against the odds, of human solidarity, of divine intervention? In the view of Crane, these narratives only represented ideals that blind men; such notions were nothing more than the antique bric-a-brac of the Victorian drawing room of the mind. For the quite consciously modern Stephen Crane, in rebellion against a world where God was absent and where pain and suffering existed in surplus, the only response could be to face the music, to dance to the harsh tune of a world that did not correspond to one's ideals and hopes. The world, in sum, was not a kind place. Crane captured this idea in his poetry:

> Many workmen
> Built a huge ball of masonry
> Upon a mountain-top
> Then they went to the valley below,
> And turned to behold their work,
> "It is grand," they said;
> They loved the thing.
>
> Of a sudden, it moved:
> It came upon them swiftly;
> It crushed them all to blood.
> But some had opportunity to squeal.[26]

Edgar Saltus

Edgar Saltus shared Crane's rage against a world bereft of meaning, a world soaked in the happy but insipid colors of progress. His written expressions of his measured anger bring to mind the ethereal purple prose associated with the English decadent movement. The lilt and flow of the words, for Saltus, were at times as alluring as the ideas to be expressed. Perhaps that accounts for the failure of his novels to endure. But in his many works of fiction, and especially in his philosophical criticism, Edgar Saltus distilled the fin de siècle mood of pessimism.[27]

The exact sources, biographical or otherwise, for Saltus's deep sense of ennui and pessimism are difficult to discern. Perhaps his wealthy upbringing and his mother's doting spoiled him early. It is clear that Saltus led a troubled and tempestuous life. His first marriage was a failure, and his subsequent romantic liaisons proved unsuccessful. Saltus escaped to Paris to search out the peculiar pleasures of aestheticism, then in vogue. He adopted the dandified, aloof persona of the aesthete—distanced from the world, bored by its pretensions, delighting only in other's foibles. Yet there is a contradiction at the heart of Saltus's apparent stance of ennui. After all, for someone who reveled in the sensitivities of boredom, he was a peripatetic writer, unceasingly promoting not only his fiction but also his vision of life.

In both *The Philosophy of Disenchantment* (1885) and *The Anatomy of Negation* (1889) Saltus took his readers on a grand tour along the rocky terrain of pessimism. He presented thumbnail sketches of the heroes of despair, focusing in the first volume on the thought of German philosophers Arthur Schopenhauer and Eduard von Hartmann. In the final chapter of *The Philosophy of Disenchantment* (on the familiar theme "Is Life an Affliction?") Saltus stated in no uncertain terms that only the "obtuse" would find meaning and hope in life. In contrast, for one like Saltus, "who commiserates with all mankind, and sympathizes with everything that is, life never appears otherwise than as an immense and terrible affliction."[28]

In the face of the "immense nausea" that constituted living, Saltus did not counsel suicide, although self-afflicted death certainly had its emotional and rational appeal. Instead, Saltus seemed to prefer von Hartmann's sturdy attitude of looking squarely into the abyss of existence and refusing to flinch. Happiness represented a dangerous illusion, feeding on itself and, in the psychic economy of desire, only increasing the possibility of future bouts with disappointment. Fascination with Buddhist philosophy led Saltus to recommend, in his roundabout manner, the transcendence of the everyday world of desire. Only through negation or resignation would one find surcease from the woes of the world.

How deeply Saltus himself held these attitudes is hard to gauge. In a playful manner, or at least in the spirit of the modernist notion of distance and irony, Saltus noted in a revised edition of *The Anatomy of Negation* that his exquisitely detailed exposition of pessimism and despair was intended to "divest his reader of one or two idle preoccupations, and to leave him serener in spirit, and of better cheer than before." But this observation runs aground on the shoals of the concluding passage of the book, which well summarizes Saltus's general philosophy of pessimism:

Nature, who is unconscious in her immorality, entrancing in her beauty, savage in her cruelty, imperial in her prodigality, and appalling in her convulsions, is not only deaf, but dumb. There is no answer to any appeal. The best we can do, the best that has ever been done, is to recognize the implacability of the laws that rule the universe, and contemplate as calmly as we can the nothingness from which we are come and into which we shall all disappear. The one consolation that we hold, though it is one which may be illusory too, consists in the belief that when death comes, fear and hope are at an end. Then wonder ceases; the insoluble no longer perplexes; space is lost; the infinite is blank; the farce is done.[29]

This sense of despair, of the weakness of the human in the grip of implacable natural laws or the irony of circumstances, appears in one of Saltus's better novels, *The Truth about Tristrem Varick* (1888). Here Saltus presents these themes in the form of a problem central to the modernist mentality: the distance between our perceptions and the realities that invariably elude our comprehension. Victorian fiction had considered this problem but had offered different conclusions. Reality in sentimental fiction was comfortable with high ideals. In most fiction of the period, morality was allowed to triumph over evil, or at least to impose its signature on the chaotic pages of reality. No such victories were to be won in Crane or in Saltus.

The story that Saltus wraps around his character Tristrem Varick is terribly complex but has a clear and depressing conclusion. Varick is a righteously moral young man. After successfully contesting a will that gave his father's fortune to charity, Varick turns around and without hesitation awards his legacy back to its originally intended recipient. In time, love's illusions cast a spell on Varick that leads to his decline. He comes to believe that his beloved Viola, who has given birth to a baby, had been seduced or raped by his onetime best friend, Royal Weldon. He chases Viola across the European continent to ask her to marry him, but he is unable to find her. Varick subsequently takes revenge against Weldon by plunging an exquisitely slim stiletto into his dastardly heart. The crime goes undetected: only a single drop of blood gushes from the precise and tiny incision. Varick rushes to his beloved to tell her that she has been avenged and is now free to accept his love. Alas, his perceptions are tinted by his illusions. Viola had actually been in love with Weldon, and she shrieks in horror at the news of his demise. Crushed by the shock of recognition, Varick turns himself in to the police. But he must work hard to convince them that Weldon's death was actually due to foul play and that he, Varick, is both sane and guilty of murder. Like Cervante's Don Quixote, Varick is a mad knight of truth whose escapades result in nothing more than a comedy of errors. Saltus no doubt would have counseled Varick to accept a philosophy of pessimism and to shun the emotions that bring forth painful complications.[30] What other possibilities could exist in a world that plays tricks on our conceits of reason, honor, truth, and morality?

Reluctant Modernism

Crane and Saltus undermined the presumptions upon which reluctant modernism was constructed by embracing a philosophical position that was devoid of hope, that eschewed the proprieties of progress and the niceties of culture. They chose, perhaps like their Puritan ancestors, to confront the world as it presented itself, with all of its chaos, uncertainty, and horror. They found that the illusions of progress, science, and hope led only to despair and ignorance. Of course, irony abounds. Crane's refusal, his great naysaying, brought him few delights; he died young and in poverty but, one suspects, not entirely unhappy. He had remained true to the beliefs that inform his fiction and poetry. Crane proudly resigned himself to fate in one poem:

> If I should cast off this tattered coat,
> And go free into the mighty sky;
> If I should find nothing there
> But a vast blue,
> Echoless, ignorant—
> What then?[31]

What then, indeed? This question perplexed American intellectuals during the years from 1880 until 1900. Confronted by the undeniable fact of evolutionary change, cognizant of the difficulty of forcing experience to fit neatly into rational schemes of interpretation, and also painfully aware that the Victorian ideals that had sustained an earlier generation were in a state of decline, American intellectuals attempted to find a useful answer. This endeavor was more than an intellectual game; the stakes were too high. To fail to arrive at a useful answer, in the minds of these thinkers, was to become lost in an abyss of inactivity, a slough of determinism or fatalism, or a frightening cage of relativism.

Not surprisingly, few thinkers were able or willing to embrace Saltus's "anatomy of negation" or Crane's "Echoless and ignorant" world. This should not lead to the conclusion that intellectuals during these years longed only to escape from an unpleasant and upsetting reality. They were not ostriches burying their heads in the sands of illusion. In their own ways, and in various degrees, American intellectuals dealt with the demons of modernity that Crane and Saltus understood so well. They did so, however, by believing that between the precipice of modernity and the certitude of Victorian ideals lay a comforting middle ground.

American scientists willingly accepted evolutionary ideals, as did anthropologists. For most, the acceptance of change complicated traditional, idealistic pictures of the world. In their embrace of the most modern of notions, of change and transformation, these thinkers attempted to use the most powerful of modern ideas to bolster traditional beliefs in progress and truth, in God and certitude. Their successes were as pronounced as their failures. Similarly, in philosophy, American thinkers accepted the temporality of experience, but also proudly announced the power of the mind to make useful connections among diverse experiential data. In revolt against formalism, American philosophers developed systems that accepted the unceasing reality of change and that accounted for the transiency of morals, in a language conversant with science. They also sought a synthesis that would allow the individual to play a meaningful role as interpreter and creator.

In taking such positions, American intellectuals in this era were not simply engaging in a form of "innovative nostalgia," which one historian considers to have been predominant among the generation of intellectuals who defined the progressive era in America. Nor were they necessarily guilty of what another historian refers to as a form of nostalgic elitism.[32] Although there were elements of the latter mind-set in the thought of Newman Smyth, Lewis Henry Morgan, Charlotte Perkins Gilman, Charles Peirce, and many of the other intellectuals whose ideas have graced the pages of this book, it must be remembered that these thinkers were desperately struggling to understand a world of change and uncertainty. They were trying as honestly and fruitfully as they could to come to grips with the world of modernity, as represented by social dislocation on a scale hitherto unimagined, by the god of science and its angels of change and transformation, and by the material riches and dangerous desires concomitant with the advent of consumer culture.

Neither heroic nor cowardly, these intellectuals used their ideas to bring order out of chaos, to adapt to changing ideals without overthrowing older ones. They paved the streets for much of modernist thought but preferred to see their roads as incessantly leading in a progressive direction. They recognized what William James would later posit as one of the psychological laws of thought, common to the intellectual as well as to the bricklayer: new ideas are not swallowed whole. Rather, they comprehended, new truths are assimilated into our old stock of beliefs. New ideals and beliefs do arise, but slowly and often hesitantly. We are all, in this Jamesian sense, reluctant modernists; to be otherwise might lead to disastrous consequences—to philosophies of relativism, to abject ennui, or to mindless activity. In the end the ideas of the reluctant modernists of the period 1880–1900 were marked by the Jamesian belief that "our knowledge grows *in spots.*"[33] Even if unexciting in comparison with the glamorous modernity and the adversarial strength of Crane and Saltus, of Veblen and Adams, this middle-of-the-road approach to the climate of a changing intellectual and material world was the common coin of the realm for American intellectuals of the period.

Chronology

1859   Charles Darwin's *Origin of Species* published; challenges traditional conceptions of religion and genesis of the species.

1878   Charles S. Peirce originates idea of pragmatism in "How to Make Our Ideas Clear."

1879   Henry George's reform ideas appear in *Progress and Poverty.*

1881   President James A. Garfield is assassinated. Oliver Wendell Holmes, Jr., publishes *The Common Law.* George Beard diagnoses extent of neurasthenia in America in *American Nervousness.*

1882   Ralph Waldo Emerson dies.

1883   William Graham Sumner's *What Social Classes Owe to Each Other* and Lester Frank Ward's *Dynamic Sociology* published; each offers different conception of value of social reform.

1884   Haymarket Massacre in Chicago. American Historical Association is formed. Construction begins on Home Insurance building of Chicago, the first skyscraper. New York and Boston are connected by telephone.

1885   Mark Twain publishes *Huckleberry Finn.* William Dean Howells issues *The Rise of Silas Lapham.* Josiah Royce publishes *The Religious Aspect of Philosophy.*

1886   American Federation of Labor is formed. First settlement house opens on New York's Lower East Side. Franz Boas settles in the United States.

1887   Dawes Severalty Act divides up Indian lands.

1888   First "Kodak" hand-held camera becomes available. Edward Bellamy's *Looking Backward* published.

1889   Mark Twain publishes *A Connecticut Yankee in King Arthur's Court*.

1890   Sherman Antitrust Act is passed. William James's *Principles of Psychology* published. Battle of Wounded Knee. Jacob Riis's photographic essay *How the Other Half Lives* reveals poverty in New York City.

1892   People's (Populist) party is formed.

1893   World's Columbian Exposition begins in Chicago. Thomas Alva Edison invents kinetoscope. Frederick Jackson Turner delivers his paper "The Significance of the Frontier in American History."

1894   "Coxey's Army" marches on the Capitol to demand jobs during a period of severe depression. Pullman strike occurs in Chicago.

1895   Stephen Crane publishes *The Red Badge of Courage*.

1896   William McKinley is elected president over William Jennings Bryan. Supreme Court rules in *Plessy v. Ferguson* that "separate but equal" for blacks and whites is constitutional. Harold Frederic publishes *The Damnation of Theron Ware*.

1898   Spanish-American War marks America's official entry into role of imperial power. Charlotte Perkins Gilman publishes *Women and Economics*.

1899   Thorstein Veblen publishes *The Theory of the Leisure Class*. John Dewey publishes *School and Society*.

1900   Stephen Crane dies. Andrew Carnegie's *The Gospel of Wealth* published.

1901   The U. S. Steel Company, America's first billion-dollar corporation, is formed.

Notes and References

Preface

1. Quoted from the James Family Papers, Houghton Library, Harvard University; used by permission.

2. William James to Henry James, 16 July 1894, James Family Papers; Joyce Walker, *The Making of a Modernist: Gertrude Stein from Three Lives to Tender Buttons* (Amherst: University of Massachusetts Press, 1984), xi–xii.

3. May, *The End of American Innocence* (New York: Quadrangle, 1959), 30–51.

4. This point is pursued in George Cotkin, *William James, Public Philosopher* (Baltimore and London: Johns Hopkins University Press, 1990). See also T. J. Jackson Lears, *No Place of Grace: Antimodernism and the Transformation of American Culture, 1880–1920* (New York: Pantheon, 1981).

5. Robert H. Wiebe, *The Search for Order, 1877–1920* (New York: Hill & Wang, 1967).

Chapter One

1. Quoted in Robert Young, "Darwin's Metaphor: Does Nature Select?" in Young, *Darwin's Metaphor: Nature's Place in Victorian Culture* (Cambridge: Cambridge University Press, 1985), 101.

2. Young, *"Darwin's Metaphor,"* 102–3.

3. On the importance of the design argument to the debate over Darwinism in America, see David N. Livingstone, "The Idea of Design: The Vicissitudes of a Key Concept in the Princeton Response to Darwin," *Scottish Journal of Theology* 37 (1984): 329–57.

4. George M. Marsden, "Everyone One's Own Interpreter? The Bible, Science, and Authority in Mid-Nineteenth-Century America," in *The Bible in America:*

Essays in Cultural History, ed. Nathan O. Hatch and Mark A. Noll (New York and Oxford: Oxford University Press, 1982), 79–100; Holmes, "Agassiz's Natural History," *Atlantic* 1 (1858): 326.

5. The reception of Darwin's ideas in America is discussed in Edward J. Pfeiffer, "United States," in *The Comparative Reception of Darwinism*, ed. T. F. Glick (Austin and London: University of Texas Press, 1972), 168–206; Jon H. Roberts, *Darwinism and the Divine in America: Protestant Intellectuals and Organic Evolution, 1859–1900* (Madison: University of Wisconsin Press, 1988); Ed Caudill, "A Content Analysis of Press Views of Darwin's Evolution Theory, 1860–1925," *Journalism Quarterly* 64 (1987): 782–86, 946; Jacques Barzun, "Cultural History as Synthesis," in *The Varieties of History: From Voltaire to the Present*, ed. Fritz Stern (Cleveland and New York: World Publishing Co., 1956), 396.

6. Peter J. Bowler, "Scientific Attitudes to Darwinism in Britain and America," in *The Darwinian Heritage*, ed. David Kohn (Princeton, N.J.: Princeton University Press, 1985), 641–81.

7. Charles S. Peirce, "The Century's Great Men in Science," *Annual Report of the Smithsonian Institution* (Washington, D.C.: Government Printing Office, 1901), 694–95.

8. Josiah Parsons Cooke, *Scientific Culture and Other Essays* (1881; reprint, New York: D. Appleton & Co., 1885), 8, 69; Cooke, *The Credentials of Science: The Warrant of Faith* (New York: Robert Carter and Brothers, 1888), 252 passim.

9. Charles E. Rosenberg, *No Other Gods: On Science and American Social Thought* (Baltimore and London: Johns Hopkins University Press, 1976), 3.

10. James Woodrow, "Evolution," in *American Philosophical Addresses, 1700–1900*, ed. Joseph L. Blau (New York: Columbia University Press, 1946), 488–513. On Woodrow and Winchell, see Roberts, *Darwinism and the Divine*, 225–29. On Zahm and the Catholic reception of evolution, see John Rickards Betts, "Darwinism, Evolution, and American Catholic Thought, 1860–1900," *Catholic Historical Review* 45 (1959): 179–83.

11. Hodge, *What Is Darwinism?* (New York: Scribner, Armstrong & Co., 1874). Portions of this work will be found in *Darwinism and the American Intellectual: A Book of Readings*, ed. R. J. Wilson (Homewood, Ill.: Dorsey Press, 1967), 47–70.

12. Francis Bowen, "Remarks on the Latest Form of the Development Theory," in *Memoirs of the American Academy of Arts and Sciences*, n.s. 8 (1860), 98–107; Bowen, *Modern Philosophy: From Descartes to Schopenhauer* (New York: Charles Scribner's Sons, 1877), vii; Bowen, "Malthusianism, Darwinism, and Pessimism" (1877) and "The Human and Brute Mind" (1880), both in *Gleanings from a Literary Life, 1838–1880* (New York: Charles Scribner's Sons, 1880), esp. 368–72, 328–50. An excellent analysis of Bowen's philosophy is in Bruce Kuklick, *The Rise of American Philosophy: Cambridge, Massachusetts, 1860–1930* (New Haven, Conn., and London: Yale University Press, 1977), 28–45.

13. Asa Gray, *Darwiniana: Essays and Reviews Pertaining to Darwinism* (1876), ed. A. Hunter Dupree (Cambridge: Harvard University Press, 1963), 5. The standard biography of Gray is Dupree, *Asa Gray: 1810–1888* (Cambridge: Belknap Press of Harvard University, 1959).

14. Quoted in Young, *Darwin's Metaphor*, 107.

15. Gray, *Darwiniana*, 311.

16. All quotes and material in the section on Wright are from his *Studies in Science and Religion* (Andover, Mass.: W. F. Draper, 1882).

17. Asa Gray, "Natural Selection and Natural Theology," *Nature* 27 (5 April 1883), 528.

18. Wright, *Studies in Science and Religion*, 139. A recent interpretation of Wright finds him an inconsistent Darwinist whose views on evolution were obscure at best, increasingly fundamentalist, and antimodernist as the years went on. See Ronald L. Numbers, "George Frederick Wright: From Christian Darwinist to Fundamentalist," *Isis* 79 (1988): 624–45.

19. The fullest analysis of McCosh is in J. David Hoeveler, Jr., *James McCosh and the Scottish Intellectual Tradition: From Glasgow to Princeton* (Princeton, N.J.: Princeton University Press, 1981), esp. 180–211.

20. McCosh, *The Religious Aspect of Evolution* (New York: Charles Scribner's Sons, 1890), vii, 96–97.

21. All quotes are from McCosh, *Development: What It Can Do and What It Cannot Do* (New York: Charles Scribner's Sons, 1883), 10, 20, 24 ff.

22. Archibald Alexander Hodge, *Outlines of Theology: Rewritten and Enlarged* (1878; reprint, New York: A. C. Armstrong and Son, 1894), 36, 39–41. Van Dyke's position is outlined in James R. Moore, *The Post-Darwinian Controversies* (Cambridge and London: Cambridge University Press), 244.

23. The rise of religious modernism is discussed in Sydney E. Ahlstrom, *A Religious History of the American People* (New Haven, Conn., and London: Yale University Press, 1972), 731–84; William R. Hutchison, *The Modernist Impulse in American Protestantism* (Oxford: Oxford University Press, 1982), esp. 76–100; Stow Persons, "Religion and Modernity, 1865–1914," in *Religion in American Life* (Princeton, N.J.: Princeton University Press, 1961), 1: 372–86.

24. The best analysis of Beecher is William G. McLoughlin, *The Meaning of Henry Ward Beecher: An Essay on the Shifting Values of Mid-Victorian America, 1840–1870* (New York: Knopf, 1970). See also Clifford E. Clark, Jr., *Henry Ward Beecher: Spokesman for Middle-Class America* (Urbana: University of Illinois Press, 1978); and Lyman Abbott, *Henry Ward Beecher* (Boston: Houghton Mifflin, 1903). Beecher's fullest discussion of evolution in relation to religion is in his *Evolution and Religion* (New York: Fords, Howard & Hurlbert, 1885), 139–40.

25. Lyman Abbott, *The Theology of an Evolutionist* (Boston: Houghton Mifflin, 1897), 20.

26. Octavius B. Frothingham, *Recollections and Impressions, 1822–1890* (New York: G. P. Putnam's Sons, 1891), 275, 279, 281.

27. Newman Smyth, *The Religious Feeling: A Study for Faith* (New York: Scribner, Armstrong & Co., 1877). More needs to be written on Smyth. Helpful are Hutchison, *Modernist Impulse*, 84–90 passim, and Neil Coughlan, *Young John Dewey: An Essay in American Intellectual History* (Chicago and London: University of Chicago Press, 1973), 43–47, 50–53, 56–60.

28. Quotations are from Smyth, *Through Science to Faith* (New York: Charles Scribner's Sons, 1902).

29. On this voluntaristic turn, see the excellent work by Robert J. Richards, *Darwin and the Emergence of Evolutionary Theories of Mind and Behavior* (Chicago and London: University of Chicago Press, 1987).

30. Alpheus S. Packard, "On the Inheritance of Acquired Characters in Animals with a Complete Metamorphosis," *Proceedings of the American Academy of Arts and Sciences*, n.s., 21 (1894): 340.

31. E. D. Cope, *The Theology of Evolution: A Lecture* (Philadelphia: Arnold & Co., 1887), 25; Cope, *The Origin of the Fittest: Essays on Evolution* (New York: D. Appleton & Co., 1886).

32. Joseph LeConte, *Evolution: Its Nature, Its Evidences, and Its Relation to Religious Thought* (New York: D. Appleton & Co., 1897, 2d ed., rev.), 346. All quotations from LeConte come from this work unless otherwise noted. Also see LeConte, "A Note on the Religious Significance of Science," *Monist* 10 (January 1900), 161–66.

33. On these controversies, see Lester D. Stephens, *Joseph LeConte: Gentle Prophet of Evolution* (Baton Rouge and London: Louisiana State University Press, 1982), 181–83. For LeConte's religious views, see "A Brief Confession of Faith Written in 1890—Slightly Revised and Added to in 1897," LeConte Family Papers, Bancroft Library, University of California, Berkeley.

34. Moore's impressive analysis is in *Post-Darwinian Controversies*, 19–122. See also James Turner, *Without God, Without Creed: The Origins of Unbelief in America* (Baltimore and London: Johns Hopkins University Press, 1985).

35. Typical of this characterization are Paul A. Carter, *The Spiritual Crisis of the Gilded Age* (DeKalb: Northern Illinois University Press, 1871); D. H. Meyer, "American Intellectuals and the Victorian Crisis of Faith," in *Victorian America*, ed. Daniel Walker Howe (Philadelphia: University of Pennsylvania Press, 1976), 59–77.

36. Norton, "The Church and Religion," *North American Review* 106 (1868): 380, 390.

Chapter Two

1. For an analysis of this notion as the centerpiece of the modernist ethos, see Marshall Berman, *All That Is Solid Melts into Air* (New York: Simon & Schuster, 1982).

2. Statistics and information about the rise of the modern university system will be found in Burton J. Bledstein, *The Culture of Professionalism: The Middle Class and the Development of Higher Education in America* (New York: W. W. Norton & Co., 1976), 271 passim. See also Laurence R. Veysey, *The Emergence of the American University* (Chicago and London: University of Chicago Press, 1965); and Hugh Hawkins, *Between Harvard and America: The Educational Leadership of Charles W. Eliot* (New York: Oxford University Press, 1972). See the excellent essays on the rise of the university system by Veysey, Hollinger, Bender, Ross, and others collected in the following volumes: Thomas L. Haskell, ed., *The Authority of Experts: Studies in History and Theory* (Bloomington: Indiana University Press, 1984); and Alexandra Oleson and John Voss, eds., *The Organization of Knowledge in Modern America, 1860–1920* (Baltimore and London: Johns Hopkins University Press, 1979).

3. On the divisions within these disciplines, see Dorothy Ross, "The Development of the Social Sciences," in *Organization of Knowledge*, 107–38. On the split between amateurs and professionals in history, see David D. Van Tassell, "From Learned Society to Professional Organization: The American Historical Association, 1884–1900," *American Historical Review* 89 (1984): 929–56.

4. The professionalization of the Harvard philosophy department is well documented by Bruce Kuklick, *The Rise of American Philosophy: Cambridge, Massachusetts, 1860–1930* (New Haven and London: Yale University Press, 1977); and Daniel J. Wilson, *Science, Community, and the Transformation of American Philosophy, 1860–1930* (Chicago and London: University of Chicago Press, 1990).

5. For James's most famous statement of his frustrations with the course of academic philosophy in America, see "The Ph.D. Octopus," in *Essays, Comments, and Reviews* (Cambridge and London: Harvard University Press, 1987), 67–74.

6. Hall, "Philosophy in the United States," *Mind*, o.s. 7 (1880), 89–105; James, "The Teaching of Philosophy in Our Colleges" (1876), in *Essays in Philosophy* (Cambridge: Harvard University Press, 1978), 3–6; Royce, "The Freedom of Teaching," *Overland Monthly* (1883), 235.

7. In John Dewey, *The Middle Works, 1889–1924*, ed. Jo Ann Boydston (Carbondale and Edwardsville: Southern Illinois University Press, 1977), 4: 3.

8. Hall, "The New Psychology," *Andover Review* 3 (1885): 247–48.

9. Both essays are in John Dewey, *The Early Works: 1882–1898*, 1. Quote is from page 115.

10. White, *The Origins of Dewey's Instrumentalism* (New York: Columbia University Press, 1943), 18.

11. Dewey, "The New Psychology," in *The Early Works of John Dewey, 1882–1898*, 60.

12. Quoted in Merle Curti, *The Growth of American Thought* (New York and London: Harper & Brothers, 1943), 571.

13. Dewey, "The New Psychology," 59–60.

14. James, *The Principles of Psychology* (1890; reprint, Cambridge and London: Harvard University Press, 1981), 1: 233.

15. Hall, "The Muscular Perception of Space," *Mind* 3 (1878): 433–50. The best analysis of Hall is Dorothy Ross, *G. Stanley Hall: The Psychologist as Prophet* (Chicago and London: University of Chicago Press, 1972).

16. James, "Are We Automata?" (1879), in *Essays in Psychology* (Cambridge: Harvard University Press, 1983), 51.

17. In John Dewey, *The Early Works: 1882–1898*, 5: 96–110.

18. James, *Principles*, 1: 125-26.

19. Howison, "The Limits of Evolution" (1895), in John Wright Buckham and George Malcolm Stratton, *George Holmes Howison: Philosopher and Teacher, A Selection from His Writings with a Biographical Sketch* (Berkeley: University of California Press, 1934), 153–89.

20. Peirce, "Evolutionary Love" (1893), in *Collected Papers of Charles Sanders Peirce: Pragmatism and Pragmaticism*, ed. Charles Hartshorne and Paul Weiss (Cambridge: Harvard University Press, 1960), 5: 190–215.

21. James, *The Varieties of Religious Experience* (1902; reprint, Cambridge: Harvard University Press, 1981), 266.

22. Quoted in J. D. Y. Peel, *Herbert Spencer: The Evolution of a Sociologist* (New York: Basic Books, 1971), 137.

23. Sumner, "The Absurd Effort to Make the World Over" (1894), in *Social Darwinism*, intro. and notes by Stow Persons (Englewood Cliffs, N.J.: Prentice-Hall, 1963), 179–80. Many see such views as expressions of a prevalent philosophy of social

Darwinism, stressing the harshness of the economic world and supporting a dog-eat-dog mentality. In point of fact, while a Darwinian frame of reference was used to bolster laissez-faire and determinist viewpoints, it was rarely employed to sanction vicious competition. See Robert C. Bannister, *Social Darwinism: Science and Myth in Anglo-American Social Thought* (Philadelphia: Temple University Press, 1979).

24. See the insightful discussion in Thomas Haskell, *The Emergence of Professional Social Science: The American Social Science Association and the Nineteenth-Century Crisis of Authority* (Urbana: University of Illinois Press, 1977), 39–47.

25. Charles E. Rosenberg, *The Trial of the Assassin Guiteau: Psychiatry and Law in the Gilded Age* (Chicago: University of Chicago Press, 1968).

26. James to Thomas W. Ward, March(?) 1869, in *The Letters of William James*, ed. Henry James (Boston: Atlantic Monthly Press, 1920), 1: 152–53.

27. James, "The Dilemma of Determinism" (1884), in *The Will to Believe* (1897; Cambridge: Harvard University Press, 1979), 117.

28. James, "Great Men and Their Environment," in *The Will to Believe*, 170.

29. James, "The Dilemma of Determinism," in *The Will to Believe*, 130, 136.

30. Peirce, "The Doctrine of Necessity Examined" (1892), in *Collected Papers of Charles Sanders Peirce*, 41. Also, for a brilliant analysis of James and Peirce on the problem of determinism, see John E. Smith, "Two Defenses of Freedom: Peirce and James," in *Tulane Studies in Philosophy: The Idea of Freedom in American Philosophy*, ed. Donald S. Lee (New Orleans: Tulane University Press, 1987), 35, 51–64.

31. Royce, *The Religious Aspect of Philosophy: A Critique of the Bases of Conduct and of Faith* (1885; reprint, Gloucester, Mass.: Peter Smith, 1965), 422–23.

32. Royce, *Religious Aspect*, 217. On the ideal of community in Royce, see R. Jackson Wilson, *In Quest of Community* (New York: Oxford University Press, 1970), 144–70; and Jean B. Quandt, *From the Small Town to the Great Community* (New Brunswick, N.J.: Rutgers University Press, 1970).

33. Royce, "The Conception of God," 44, and Howison, "The City of God," 91. Both in *The Conception of God* (1898; reprint, St. Claire, Mich.: Scholarly Press, 1971).

34. Royce, "The Absolute and the Individual," in *The Conception of God*, 137.

35. James T. Kloppenberg, *Uncertain Victory* (New York and Oxford: Oxford University Press, 1986); Sanford Schwartz, *The Making of Modernism* (Princeton, N.J.: Princeton University Press, 1985).

36. This argument is made most strongly by Richard Rorty, for example, in "Pragmatism, Relativism, and Irrationalism," in *Consequences of Pragmatism* (Minneapolis: University of Minnesota Press, 1982), 160–75.

37. Peirce, "How to Make Our Ideas Clear," in *Writings of Charles S. Peirce*, ed. Christian J. W. Kloessel (Bloomington: Indiana University Press, 1982), 3: 257–76. See the excellent discussion of Peirce in John E. Smith, *The Spirit of American Philosophy* (New York: Oxford University Press, 1963), 3–37.

38. James, *Pragmatism* (1898; reprint, Cambridge: Harvard University Press, 1975), 124.

39. James, "Philosophical Conceptions and Practical Results," in *Pragmatism*, 261.

40. James, *Pragmatism*, 99.

41. Herbert W. Schneider, *A History of American Philosophy* (New York: Columbia University Press, 1963), 388–414.

42. Robert C. Solomon, *In the Spirit of Hegel* (New York: Oxford University Press, 1983), 10–11.

43. Much of the discussion of Hegelian ideas in America is culled from the impressive work of David John Watson, "Idealism and Social Theory: A Comparative Study of British and American Adaptations of Hegel, 1860–1914," Ph.D. diss, University of Pennsylvania, 1975.

44. Quoted from Harris, *Hegel's Logic: A Book on the Genesis of the Categories of the Mind* (1890), in Watson, "Idealism and Social Theory," 17.

45. See Harris, "Edward Bellamy's Vision" (1889), in William H. Goetzmann, ed., *The American Hegelians* (New York: Knopf, 1973), 199.

46. All material on Harris is from Watson, "Idealism and Social Theory," 122–133.

47. Schneider, *A History of American Philosophy*, 409.

48. Quoted in Neil Coughlin, *Young John Dewey* (Chicago and London: University of Chicago Press, 1975), 29.

49. Morris, *Hegel's Philosophy of the State and of History: An Exposition* (Chicago: S. C. Griggs & Co., 1887).

50. Hall, "Notes on Hegel and His Critics," *Journal of Speculative Philosophy* 12 (1878), 102. The best discussion of Hall is Dorothy Ross, *G. Stanley Hall*, 46, 152, passim. On the similarities between Hegelianism and Darwinism, see David F. Bowers, "Hegel, Darwin, and the American Tradition," in *Foreign Influences in American Life*, ed. Bowers (Princeton, N.J.: Princeton University Press, 1944), 146–71.

51. Dewey, "Psychology as Philosophic Method" (1886), 167.

52. Dewey, "Christianity and Democracy" (1892), in *The Early Works, 1882–1898*, 4: 9.

53. See Coughlin, 61–62.

54. On the public philosopher, see George Cotkin, *William James, Public Philosopher* (Baltimore and London: Johns Hopkins University Press, 1990).

55. Lewis S. Feuer, "John Dewey and the Back to the People Movement in American Philosophy," *Journal of the History of Ideas* 20 (1959): 545–68.

56. Royce, "Pessimism and Modern Thought" (1881), in Royce, *Fugitive Essays* (Freeport, N.Y.: Books for Libraries Press, 1968), 186.

57. James, "The Philippine Tangle" (1899), in James, *Essays, Comments, and Reviews* (Cambridge: Harvard University Press, 1987), 158.

58. James, "On a Certain Blindness in Human Beings" (ca. 1898), in James, *Talks to Teachers on Psychology* (Cambridge: Harvard University Press, 1983), 133–34.

59. James, "The Philippines Again" (1899), in *Essays, Comments, and Reviews*, 161.

Chapter Three

1. Lewis Henry Morgan, *Ancient Society* (New York: Henry Holt & Co., 1877), 12.

2. Hinsley, *Savages and Scientists: The Smithsonian Institution and the Development of American Anthropology, 1846–1910* (Washington, D.C.: Smithsonian Institution Press, 1981), 151–52.

3. The history of the BAE is fully discussed in Regna Diebold Darnell, "The

Development of American Anthropology: From the Bureau of American Anthropology to Franz Boas," Ph.D. diss., University of Pennsylvania, 1969, 33–139. Tylor's comments about the BAE will be found in his "How the Problems of American Anthropology Present Themselves to the English Mind," *Transactions of the Anthropological Society of Washington, D.C.* 34 (1885): 81–94. See also Lévi-Strauss, "The Work of the Bureau of American Ethnology and Its Lessons," in *Structural Anthropology*, trans. Monique Layton, 2 vols. (New York: Basic Books, 1976), 49–59.

4. Ward, *Dynamic Sociology or Applied Social Science*, 2 vols. (New York: Greenwood Press, 1968), 11.

5. Powell, "From Barbarism to Civilization," *American Anthropologist* n.s., 1 (1888): 121. The list quoted is partial.

6. Quoted in Hinsley, *Savages and Scientists*, 104.

7. Quoted in Hinsley, *Savages and Scientists*, 242. (McGee never used periods to separate his initials.)

8. Robert F. Berkhofer, Jr., *The White Man's Indian* (New York: Vintage Books, 1979), 51.

9. Morgan, *Ancient Society*, 491. An enlightening discussion of Victorian beliefs on institutional progress will be found in George W. Stocking, Jr., *Victorian Anthropology* (New York: Free Press, 1987).

10. McGee, "The Science of Humanity," *American Anthropologist*, o.s., 10 (1897): 255–56.

11. Quoted in Hinsley, *Savages and Scientists*, 246.

12. McGee, "The Trend of Human Progress," *American Anthropologist*, n.s., 1 (1899): 447.

13. Walter Houghton, *The Victorian Frame of Mind* (New Haven and London: Yale University Press, 1957), 20–21.

14. Welling, "The Law of Malthus," *American Anthropologist*, o.s., 1 (1888): 12.

15. Powell, "Competition as a Factor in Human Evolution," *American Anthropologist*, o.s., 1 (1888), 320–23.

16. George W. Stocking, Jr., "From Physics to Ethnology," in *Race, Culture, and Evolution: Essays in the History of Anthropology* (New York: Free Press, 1968), 151.

17. Boas, "The Aims of Ethnology" (1888), in Boas, *Race, Language and Culture* (New York: Free Press, 1966), 637.

18. On the Mason-Boas debate, see George W. Stocking, Jr., ed., *The Shaping of American Anthropology: A Franz Boas Reader* (New York: 1974), 1–5; John Buettner-Janusch, "Boas and Mason: Particularism versus Generalization," *American Anthropologist* 59 (1957): 318–24.

19. Stocking, *Shaping*, 61–62, 66. Emphasis added.

20. Marvin Harris, *The Rise of Anthropological Theory* (New York: Thomas Y. Crowell Co., 1968), 335; Stocking, "Franz Boas and the Culture Concept," in *Race, Culture, and Evolution*, 228.

21. Boas, "The Limitations of the Comparative Method of Anthropology" (1896), in Boas, *Race, Language and Culture*, 276.

22. Morton White, *Social Thought in America: The Revolt Against Formalism* (Boston: Beacon Press, 1968).

23. On the institutionalization of anthropology, see Regna Darnell, "The Pro-

fessionalization of American Anthropology: A Case Study in the Sociology of Knowledge," *Social Science Information* 10 (1971), 83–103.

24. Quoted in Darnell, "Development of American Anthropology," 209.

25. Analysis and background information on Cushing will be found in, Curtis Hinsley, Jr., "Ethnographic Charisma and Scientific Routine: Cushing and Fewkes in the American Southwest, 1879–1893," in *Observers Observed: Essays on Ethnographic Fieldwork*, ed. George W. Stocking, Jr. (Madison: University of Wisconsin Press, 1983): 53–69; and Joan Mark, "Frank Hamilton Cushing and an American Science of Anthropology," *Perspectives in American History* 10 (1976): 449–86.

26. Cushing to Spencer F. Baird, 18 July 1880, in Cushing, *Zuni: The Selected Writings of Frank Hamilton Cushing*, ed. Jesse Green (Lincoln and London: University of Nebraska Press, 145.

27. Cushing, *Nation of the Willows* (Flagstaff, Ariz.: Northland Press, 1965), 58.

28. Cushing, *Nation of the Willows*, 69.

29. Hinsley, "Ethnographic Charisma," 53–59.

30. Fletcher is insightfully analyzed in Joan Mark, *A Stranger in Her Native Land: Alice Fletcher and the American Indians* (Lincoln and London: University of Nebraska Press, 1988). Fletcher and other women anthropologists are discussed in Nancy Oestreich Lurie, "Women in Early American Anthropology," in *Pioneers of American Anthropology*, ed. June Helm (Seattle and London: University of Washington Press, 1966), 29–82.

31. Lurie, "Women in Early American Anthropology," 52–53.

32. Joan Mark, "Francis La Flesche: The American Indian as Anthropologist," *Isis* 73 (1982): 497–510; Margot Liberty, "Native American Informants: The Contribution of Francis LaFlesche," in *American Anthropology: The Early Years*, ed. John V. Murra (St. Paul, Minn.: West Publishing, 1978), 99–110.

33. The history of pre–Civil War racism is strongly discussed in William Stanton, *The Leopard's Spots* (Chicago: University of Chicago Press, 1960). For the postwar period, see Idus Newby, *Jim Crow's Defense: Anti-Negro Thought in America* (Baton Rouge: Louisiana State University Press, 1965).

34. Robert F. Berkhofer, Jr., *The White Man's Indian*.

35. Quoted in Lee Clark Mitchell, *Witness to A Vanishing America: The Nineteenth-Century Response* (Princeton, N.J.: Princeton University Press, 1981), 219.

36. Quoted in Leonard Dinnerstein, Roger L. Nichols, and David M. Reimers, *Natives and Strangers: Ethnic Groups and the Building of America* (New York: Oxford University Press, 1979), 226.

37. Ronald L. Takaki, *Iron Cages: Race and Culture in Nineteenth Century America* (New York: Knopf, 1979).

38. Adams is quoted in Frederic Cople Jaher, *Doubters and Dissenters* (Glencoe, N.Y.: Free Press, 1964), 152. On immigration, see John Higham, *Strangers in the Land: Patterns of American Nativism, 1865–1925* (New York: Atheneum, 1963).

39. For a discussion of "evolutionary racialism" as a mode of formalistic analysis, see George W. Stocking, Jr., "The Critique of Racial Formalism," in *Race, Culture, and Evolution*, 161–94.

40. Quoted in Harris, *Anthropological Theory*, 256.

41. See the excellent discussion of Brinton's racism in John S. Haller, Jr., *Out-*

casts from Evolution: Scientific Attitudes of Racial Inferiority, 1859–1900 (Urbana: University of Illinois Press, 1971), 114–20. See also Regna Darnell, "Daniel Brinton and the Professionalization of American Anthropology," in *American Anthropology: The Early Years,* 69–85.

42. Brinton, "The Aims of Anthropology," *Proceedings of the 44th Meeting of the American Association for the Advancement of Science* (1896): 12.

43. Haller, *Outcasts,* 106.

44. R. Berkeley Miller, "Anthropology and Institutionalization: Frederick Starr at the University of Chicago, 1892–1923," *Kroeber Anthropological Society Papers* (1978): 51.

45. William Culp Darrah, *Powell of the Colorado* (Princeton, N.J.: Princeton University Press, 1951), 260.

46. Material on the World's Fair is culled from the brilliant analysis of Robert W. Rydell, *All the World's a Fair: Visions of Empire at American International Expositions, 1876–1916* (Chicago and London: University of Chicago Press, 1984). The McKinley quote is from page 4. See also Alan Trachtenberg, *The Incorporation of America: Culture & Society in the Gilded Age* (New York: Hill & Wang, 1982), 208–34.

47. Rydell, *All the World's a Fair,* 57.

48. Rydell, *All the World's a Fair,* 66, 235.

49. Recent analyses of the novel's ambiguities are Everett Carter, "The Meaning of *A Connecticut Yankee*" (1978), in *On Mark Twain: The Best from American Literature,* ed. Louis J. Budd and Edwin H. Cady (Durham, N.C.: Duke University Press, 1987): 185–208; Andrew Jay Hoffman, *Twain's Heroes, Twain's Worlds* (Philadelphia: University of Pennsylvania Press, 1988), 79–141; and Takaki, *Iron Cages,* 166–70. Carter makes the most convincing argument that Twain intended to portray Hank Morgan in a favorable manner. See also Mitchell, *Witnesses to a Vanishing America,* 264–66.

50. Twain, *A Connecticut Yankee in King Arthur's Court* (1889; reprint, New York: New American Library, 1963), 26.

51. Twain, *A Connecticut Yankee,* 316.

52. See the various essays published by Boas on heredity and environment, in Boas, *Race, Language and Culture,* 28–59, 60–85.

Chapter Four

1. Figures on the rise of women within the educational system may be found in Louise Michele Newman, ed., *Men's Ideas / Women's Reality: Popular Science, 1870–1915,* (New York: Pergamon Press, 1985), 62.

2. Cynthia Eagle Russett, *Sexual Science: The Victorian Construction of Womanhood* (Cambridge: Harvard University Press, 1989), 191.

3. Quoted in Russett, *Sexual Science,* 206. See also Rosalind Rosenberg, *Beyond Separate Spheres: Intellectual Roots of Modern Feminism* (New Haven, Conn: Yale University Press, 1982), 1–27.

4. Unless otherwise noted, all Clarke quotes are from Edward H. Clarke, *Sex in Education; or, A Fair Chance for the Girls* (1873; reprint, New York: Arno Press, 1972).

5. Carroll Smith-Rosenberg, *Disorderly Conduct: Visions of Gender in Victorian America* (New York: Oxford University Press, 1985), 13.

6. Hardaker's essay is in Newman, *Men's Ideas / Women's Realities*, 34–39.

7. Hall, *Adolescence* (1903), quoted in Russett, *Sexual Science*, 61.

8. See Smith-Rosenberg, "The Hysterical Woman: Sex Roles and Role Conflict in Nineteenth-Century America," *Disorderly Conduct*, 197–216.

9. Allen, "Plain Words on the Woman Question" (1889), in Newman, *Men's Ideas / Women's Realities*, 129.

10. Jordan, "The Higher Education of Women" (1902), in Newman, *Men's Ideas / Women's Realities*, 96–104.

11. Quoted in Julia Ward Howe, ed., *Sex and Education* (1874; reprint, New York: Arno Press, 1972), 104.

12. Morais, "A Reply to Miss Hardaker on the Woman Question" (1882), in Newman, *Men's Ideas / Women's Realities*, 39–47.

13. The essay by Tweedy is in Newman, *Men's Ideas / Women's Realities*, 132–36. Also, Lynn Gordon, "The Gibson Girl Goes to College: Popular Culture and Women's Higher Education in the Progressive Era, 1890–1920," *American Quarterly* 39 (1987): 216.

14. Thompson, *The Mental Traits of Sex: An Experimental Investigation of the Normal Mind in Men and Women* (Chicago: University of Chicago Press, 1903), 176.

15. Livermore, "Woman Suffrage," *North American Review* 143 (1886): 380.

16. Arguments for and against suffrage are perceptively discussed in Aileen S. Kraditor, *The Ideas of the Woman Suffrage Movement, 1890–1920* (Garden City, N.Y.: Anchor Books), 66–70.

17. Stanton et. al., *The Woman's Bible* (1895; reprint, Arno Press, New York, 1972), 184.

18. Kraditor, *Ideas of the Woman Suffrage Movement*, 68–69, 110. Some historians view the expediency argument as coexisting throughout the movement with a natural-rights or Enlightenment perspective on women's right to vote. See also Nancy F. Cott, *The Grounding of Modern Feminism* (New Haven and London: Yale University Press, 1987), 16–50.

19. Grand, "The New Aspect of the Woman Question," *North American Review* 158 (1894): 272.

20. Eileen Boris, *Art and Labor: Ruskin, Morris, and the Craftsman Ideal in America* (Philadelphia: Temple University Press, 1986), 120–21.

21. Dee Garrison, "The Tender Technicians: The Feminization of Public Librarianship, 1876–1905," in *Clio's Consciousness Raised*, ed. Mary Hartman and Lois Banner (New York: Harper Torchbooks, 1974), 158–78.

22. Material on women in the medical profession will be found in Regina Markell Morantz-Sanchez, *Sympathy & Science: Women Physicians in American Medicine* (New York: Oxford University Press, 1985); Morantz and Sue Zschoche, "Professionalism, Feminism, and Gender Roles: A Comparative Study of Nineteenth-Century Medical Therapeutics," *Journal of American History* 67 (1980): 568–88; and Regina Markell Morantz, "Feminism, Professionalism, and Germs: The Thought of Mary Putnam Jacobi and Elizabeth Blackwell," *American Quarterly* 34 (1982): 459–78.

23. See the excellent essay by Toby Quitsland, "Her Feminine Colleagues: Pho-

tographs and Letters Collected by Frances Benjamin Johnston in 1900," in *Women Artists in Washington Collections* (College Park: University of Maryland Art Gallery, 1979), 97–109.

24. Quitsland, "Her Feminine Colleagues," 100; Frank W. Crane, "American Women Photographers," *Munsey's Magazine* 11 (1894): 398–408.

25. Thomas, "Should the Higher Education of Women Differ from That of Men?" (1901), in *The Education of Women in America: Selected Writings of Catherine Beecher, Margaret Fuller, and M. Carey Thomas*, ed. Barbara M. Cross (New York: Teachers College Press, 1965), 145–54.

26. Quitsland, "Her Feminine Colleagues," 102.

27. Quitsland, "Her Feminine Colleagues," 124; Anne Tucker, ed., *The Woman's Eye* (New York: Knopf, 1973), 29–30.

28. Quitsland, "Her Feminine Colleagues," 102.

29. William Innes Homer, ed., *A Pictorial Heritage: The Photographs of Gertrude Käsebier* (Wilmington: Delaware Art Museum, 1979), 17.

30. Tucker, *The Woman's Eye*, 13–27.

31. Cone, "Women in Literature," in *Women's Work in America*, ed. Annie Nathan Meyer (New York: Henry Holt & Co., 1891), 17–27.

32. Mary Kelley, *Private Woman, Public Stage: Literary Domesticity in Nineteenth-Century America* (New York: Oxford University Press, 1984), 280, 334–35.

33. Tompkins, *Sentimental Designs: The Cultural Work of American Fiction, 1790–1860* (New York: Oxford University Press, 1985), 120–23.

34. Jewett, *The Country of the Pointed Firs and Other Stories* (New York: W. W. Norton & Co., 1968), 129.

35. Mary E. Wilkins, *Pembroke* (New York: Harper & Bros., 1894). The work of Jewett and Wilkins Freeman is perceptively discussed in Larzer Ziff, *The American 1890s: Life and Times of a Lost Generation* (Lincoln and London: University of Nebraska Press, 1979), 275–305.

36. Chopin, *The Awakening* (1899; reprint, New York: W. W. Norton & Co., 1976). Particularly useful in this edition are the text and commentary organized by Margaret Culley.

37. Wharton, *The House of Mirth* (New York: Scribners, n.d.), 7, 12.

38. On Richards, see Dolores Hayden, *The Grand Domestic Revolution* (Cambridge and London: MIT Press, 1981), 151–79; Gwendolyn Wright, *Moralism and the Model Home: Domestic Architecture and Cultural Conflict in Chicago, 1873–1913* (Chicago and London: University of Chicago Press, 1980), 150–60; Ruth Schwartz Cowan, "Ellen Swallow Richards: Technology and Women," in *Technology in America: A History of Individuals and Ideas*, ed. Carroll W. Pursell, Jr. (Cambridge: MIT Press, 1986), 142–50.

39. As William Leach puts it, "mid-nineteenth-century feminism took much of its power from the tradition of female nurture." Women approached the arena of reform in a spirit of acting on their moral imperative to improve the public family. See Leach, *True Love and Perfect Union: The Feminist Reform of Sex and Society* (New York: Basic Books, 1980), 112.

40. Harvey Levenstein, "The New England Kitchen and the Origins of Modern American Eating Habits," *American Quarterly* 32 (1980): 369–86.

41. On Talbot, see Wright, *Moralism and the Model Home*, 159–69. See also Rosenberg, *Beyond Separate Spheres*, 35–36.

42. Hayden, *Grand Domestic Revolution*, 185–86.

43. Rosenberg, *Beyond Separate Spheres*, 49.

44. Wood, "The Ideal and Practical Organization of the Home," *Cosmopolitan* 26 (1899), 659–64. Other essays, under the same title, appeared in the May and June issues of *Cosmopolitan*.

45. On Gilman's neurasthenia, see Mary A. Hill, *Charlotte Perkins Gilman: The Making of a Radical Feminist, 1860–1896* (Philadelphia: Temple University Press, 1980), 143–64. See also Gilman, *The Living of Charlotte Perkins Gilman: An Autobiography* (New York: Arno Press, 1972), 90–106.

46. The text of "The Yellow Wallpaper" will be found in Ann J. Lane, ed. *The Charlotte Perkins Gilman Reader* (New York: Pantheon Books, 1980), 3–19. Gilman was proud that her fictional rendition of a common cure for neurasthenia helped to change the minds of some physicians on the treatment's validity. See Gilman, "Why I Wrote 'The Yellow Wallpaper,'" ibid., 19–20.

47. See Degler's introduction to Gilman's *Women and Economics* (1898; reprint, New York: Harper & Row Torchbooks, 1966), vi–xxxv. Further quotes from this work of Gilman's are from this edition.

48. Hayden, *Grand Domestic Revolution*, 183.

Chapter Five

1. Clifford Geertz, *The Interpretation of Cultures* (New York: Basic Books, 1973), 5.

2. Henry F. May, *The End of American Innocence* (New York: Knopf, 1959). Also excellent on the cultural custodians is Lewis Perry, *Intellectual Life in America* (New York: Franklin Watts, 1984), 261–316.

3. Wendell, *A Literary History of America* (1900: reprint, New York: Greenwood Press, 1968), 471–79, 530.

4. Thomas Bender, *New York Intellect* (New York: Knopf, 1987), 206–22.

5. Quoted in Richard Ellman, *Oscar Wilde* (New York: Knopf, 1988), 183–84.

6. On Howells, see Kenneth S. Lynn, *William Dean Howells: An American Life* (New York: Harcourt Brace Jovanovich, 1970); Daniel H. Borus, *Writing Realism: Howells, James, and Norris in the Mass Market* (Chapel Hill and London: University of North Carolina Press, 1989). On Bok, see his autobiography, *The Americanization of Edward Bok* (New York: Charles Scribner's Sons, 1921).

7. Joan Shelley Rubin, "Self, Culture, and Self-Culture in Modern America: The Early History of the Book-of-the-Month Club," *Journal of American History* 71 (1985): 797–99.

8. Richard Crowder, *Those Innocent Years: The Legacy and Inheritance of the Victorian Era, James Whitcomb Riley* (Indianapolis: Bobbs-Merrill Co., 1957), 121.

9. Helen Lefkowitz Horowitz, *Culture & the City: Cultural Philanthropy in Chicago from the 1880s to 1917* (Chicago and London: University of Chicago Press, 1989), esp. 1–26.

10. For Washington's speech, see his *Up from Slavery* (1901), in *The Booker T. Washington Papers: The Autobiographical Writings*, ed. Louis R. Harlan and John W. Blassingame (Urbana: University of Illinois Press, 1972), 1: 347–49. For James's, see his "Robert Gould Shaw: Oration by Professor William James," in *Essays in Religion and Morality* (Cambridge: Harvard University Press, 1982), 64–74.

11. Lawrence W. Levine, *Highbrow / Lowbrow: The Emergence of Cultural Hierarchy in America* (Cambridge: Harvard University Press, 1988), 190 ff.

12. John Y. Cole, "Storehouses and Workshops: American Libraries and the Uses of Knowledge," in *The Organization of Knowledge in Modern America 1860–1920* (Baltimore and London: Johns Hopkins University Press, 1979), 364–85.

13. Quoted in Michael Harris, "The Purpose of the American Public Library: A Revisionist Interpretation of History," *Library Journal* 98 (1973): 2513.

14. Dee Garrison, "Immoral Fiction in the Late Victorian Library," in *Victorian America*, ed. Daniel Walker Howe (Philadelphia: University of Pennsylvania Press, 1976), 141–59.

15. Cole, "Storehouses and Workshops," 368–69. Peter Mikelson, "American Society and the Public Library in the Thought of Andrew Carnegie," *Journal of Library History* 10 (1975): 117–38.

16. Antin, *The Promised Land* (Boston and New York: Houghton Mifflin, 1912), 341.

17. London, *Martin Eden* (New York: Macmillan, 1909), 106 ff.

18. Bellamy, *Looking Backward* (1888; reprint, New York: New American Library, 1960), 26–27.

19. Quoted in Arthur Lipow, *Authoritarian Socialism in America: Edward Bellamy and the Nationalist Movement* (Berkeley: University of California Press, 1982), 120.

20. DuBois, *The Souls of Black Folks* (New York: Dodd, Mead & Co., 1979), 3.

21. Gompers, *Seventy Years of Life and Labor* (London: Horst & Blackett Ltd., 1925), 2 vols. On Gompers, see George Cotkin, "Caught in Cultures: Samuel Gompers and the Problem of the Working-Class Individual in Culture," *Mid-America: An Historical Review* 66 (1984): 41–48. Quotes from Washington are from *Up from Slavery* (1901), in *The Booker T. Washington Papers*, 1:211–385.

22. A different interpretation of Washington's memory of the dinner is offered in William E. Cain, "Forms of Self-Representation in Booker T. Washington's *Up from Slavery*," *Prospects* 12 (1987): 201–22.

23. Alun Munslow, "Andrew Carnegie and the Discourse of Cultural Hegemony," *Journal of American Studies* 22 (1988): 213–24.

24. Agnes Rush Burr, *Russell Conwell and His Work* (Philadelphia: John C. Winston Co., 1926), 423–24.

25. Hollinger, *Morris R. Cohen and the Scientific Ideal* (Cambridge: MIT Press, 1975), 22, 50–51.

26. *International Socialist Review* 9 (1909): 910. Daniel Bell first raised this issue; see his *Marxian Socialism in the United States* (Princeton, N.J.: Princeton University Press, 1967), 86–87.

27. See the brilliant analysis of Whitaker's novels and the dime novel in general in Michael Denning, *Mechanic Accents: Dime Novels and Working-Class Culture in America* (London and New York: Verso, 1987), 169.

28. On the department store, see Benson, "Palace of Consumption and Machine

for Selling: The American Department Store, 1880–1940," *Radical History Review* 21 (1979): 199–221; and Neil Harris, "Museums, Merchandising, and Popular Taste: The Struggle for Influence," in *Material Culture and the Study of American Life*, ed. Ian M. G. Quimby (New York: W. W. Norton, 1978), 140–74.

29. Dreiser, *Sister Carrie* (1900; reprint, New York: Penguin Books, 1983), 22–23.

30. Quoted in William R. Leach, "Transformations in a Culture of Consumption: Women and Department Stores, 1890–1925," *Journal of American History* 71 (1984): 335.

31. T. J. Jackson Lears, "From Salvation to Self-Realization: Advertising and the Therapeutic Roots of the Consumer Culture, 1880–1930," in *The Culture of Consumption*, ed. Richard Wightman Fox and T. J. Jackson Lears (New York: Pantheon Books, 1983), 17.

32. Leach, "Women and Department Stores," 337.

33. Much of my analysis of the *Wizard of Oz* as a text on the power of consumption is drawn from Stuart Culver, "What Manikins Want: *The Wonderful Wizard of Oz*" and *"The Art of Decorating Dry Goods Windows," Representations* 21 (1988): 97–116.

34. Baum, *The Wonderful Wizard of Oz* (1900; reprint, New York: New American Library, 1984), 32–33.

35. Culver, "What Manikins Want," 103.

36. Quoted in Thomas S. Hines, *Burnham of Chicago: Architect and Planner* (Chicago and London: University of Chicago Press, 1979), 120, 115.

37. John F. Kasson, *Amusing the Millions: Coney Island at the Turn of the Century* (New York: Hill & Wang, 1978), 18.

38. William James to Henry James, 22 September 1893, in *The Letters of William James*, ed. Henry James (Boston: Atlantic Monthly Press, 1920), 1: 348.

39. Quoted in Alan Trachtenberg, *The Incorporation of America: Culture and Society in the Gilded Age* (New York: Hill & Wang, 1982), 213.

40. Kasson, *Amusing the Millions*, 8.

41. Not all cultural analysts found this shift unproblematic. See Daniel Horowitz, "Consumption and Its Discontents: Simon N. Patten, Thorstein Veblen, and George Gunton," *Journal of American History* 67 (September 1980), 301–17.

42. Lewis Erenberg, *Steppin' Out: New York Nightlife and the Transformation of American Culture, 1890–1930* (Chicago: University of Chicago Press, 1981).

43. William James to his wife, Alice, 31 July 1896, in *The Letters of William James*, 2: 43–44.

44. John Higham, "The Reorientation of American Culture in the 1890s," in *Writing American History: Essays in Modern Scholarship* (Bloomington: Indiana University Press, 1970), 73–102.

45. On the cult of heroism, see George Cotkin, *William James: Public Philosopher* (Baltimore and London: Johns Hopkins University Press, 1990), 95–122.

46. On Eakins, see Elizabeth Johns, *Thomas Eakins: The Heroism of Modern Life* (Princeton, N.J.: Princeton University Press, 1983); William James, "What Makes a Life Significant," in *Talks to Teachers* (Cambridge: Harvard University Press, 1983), 154–55.

47. Kenneth Cmiel, *Democratic Eloquence: The Fight over Popular Speech in Nineteenth-Century America* (New York: William Morrow and Co., 1990), 249.

48. Robert Dallek, *The American Style of Foreign Policy: Cultural Politics and Foreign Affairs* (New York: New American Library, 1983), 43–44.

49. Lary May, *Screening Out the Past: The Birth of Mass Culture and the Motion Picture Industry* (New York and Oxford: Oxford University Press, 1980); Daniel J. Czitrom, *Media and the American Mind: From Morse to McLuhan* (Chapel Hill, N.C.: University of North Carolina Press, 1982), 30–59.

Chapter Six

1. Adams, *The Education of Henry Adams: An Autobiography* (Boston and New York: Massachusetts Historical Society, 1918), 266. All quotes from this work are from this edition.

2. Adams, "The Tendency of History" (1894), in Adams, *The Degradation of the Democratic Dogma* (New York: Harper Torchbook, 1969), 129.

3. Adams, *The Education of Henry Adams*, 451.

4. Adams, "A Letter to American Teachers of History" (1910), in *Degradation*, 208.

5. Adams, *Mont-Saint-Michel and Chartres* (1905; reprint, Princeton, N.J.: Princeton University Press, 1981), 161.

6. On Veblen, see Joseph Dorfman, *Thorstein Veblen and His America* (1934; reprint, New York: Augustus M. Kelley, 1972).

7. Veblen, *The Theory of the Leisure Class* (1899; reprint, Boston: Houghton Mifflin, 1973). All quotes from this work are from this edition.

8. Veblen, "The Economic Theory of Women's Dress" (1894), in *Essays in Our Changing Order*, ed. Leon Ardzrooni (New York: Viking Press, 1954), 69.

9. Veblen, "Arts and Crafts" (1902), in Ardzrooni, *Essays*, 194–99.

10. Veblen, *The Theory of Business Enterprise* (1904; reprint, New York: Mentor Books, 1932), esp. 144–89.

11. Quoted in Morton White, *Social Thought in America: The Revolt Against Formalism* (Boston: Beacon Press, 1957), 196.

12. Emerson, "The American Scholar" (1837), in *Documents in the History of American Philosophy*, ed. Morton White (New York: Oxford University Press, 1972), 162.

13. Louis H. Sullivan, *Kindergarten Chats and Other Writings* (1901–1902; rev. 1918; reprint, New York: Wittenborn Art Books, 1947), 130.

14. Sullivan, *Kindergarten Chats*, 107–11.

15. Santayana, "The Genteel Tradition in American Philosophy" (1911), in White, *Documents*, 406.

16. Sullivan, "The Tall Office Building Artistically Considered" (1896), in Sullivan, *The Public Papers*, ed. Robert Twombly (Chicago and London: University of Chicago Press, 1988), 107, 112–13.

17. Sullivan, "The Tall Office Building," 81; Frank Lloyd Wright, *Genius and the Mobocracy* (New York: Sloan and Pearce, 1949), 79–80.

18. Sullivan, *Kindergarten Chats*, 114.

19. Sullivan, *Kindergarten Chats*, 113.

20. Sullivan, *Kindergarten Chats*, 153–54.

21. Mark Twain, *The Mysterious Stranger and Other Stories* (New York: Harper & Row, 1922), 140.

22. Max Nordau, *Degeneration* (1895; reprint, New York: Howard Freitag, 1968), 560. On Nordau's American reception, see Linda L. Maik, "Nordau's *Degeneration:* The American Controversy," *Journal of the History of Ideas* 50 (1989): 607–23.

23. Stephen Crane, *Maggie: A Girl of the Streets* (1893), in *Crane: Prose and Poetry* (New York: Library of America, 1984), 37.

24. Crane, *The Red Badge of Courage* (1895), in *Prose and Poetry*, 212.

25. Crane, "The Blue Hotel" (1897–98), in *Prose and Poetry*, 799.

26. Crane, "The Black Riders and Other Lines" (n.d.), in *Prose and Poetry*, 885, 909, 1309.

27. On Saltus, see Claire Sprague, *Edgar Saltus* (New York: Twayne, 1968). So deep is the decline of Saltus's reputation that he is not even mentioned in the standard work on literature in the 1890s, Ziff's *The American 1890s* (1966, Lincoln and London, University of Nebraska Press, 1979).

28. Edgar Everton Saltus, *The Philosophy of Disenchantment* (Boston: Houghton Mifflin and Co., 1885), 233.

29. Saltus, *The Anatomy of Negation* (Chicago: Belford, Clarke & Co., 1889), 218.

30. Saltus, *The Truth about Tristrem Varick* (New York: Belford Clark, 1888).

31. Crane, "The Black Riders and Other Lines," in *Prose and Poetry*, 1323.

32. Robert M. Crunden, *Ministers of Reform* (Urbana: University of Illinois Press, 1984), x; Jackson Lears, *No Place of Grace* (New York: Pantheon, 1981).

33. William James, *Pragmatism* (Cambridge: Harvard University Press, 1975), 82.

Bibliographic Essay

Many works have focused on the intellectual and cultural life of this watershed period in American thought. Dated but still useful are Henry Steele Commager, *The American Mind: An Interpretation of American Thought and Character Since the 1880s* (New Haven, Conn.: Yale University Press, 1950); Stow Persons, *American Minds: A History of Ideas* (New York: Holt, Rinehart & Winston, 1958), especially chapters 12 to 19; and the introductory chapter in Perry Miller, ed., *American Thought: Civil War to World War I* (New York: Holt, Rinehart & Winston, 1954). More recent treatments will be found in Lewis Perry, *Intellectual Life in America: A History* (New York: Franklin Watts, 1984); Alan Trachtenberg, *The Incorporation of America: Culture and Society in the Gilded Age* (New York: Hill & Wang, 1982); and T. J. Jackson Lears, *No Place of Grace: Antimodernism and the Transformation of American Culture, 1880–1920* (New York: Pantheon, 1981). For a synthetic interpretation of the political and social context of the era, see Robert H. Wiebe, *The Search for Order, 1877–1920* (New York: Hill & Wang, 1967).

On the various interpretive aspects of Darwin's text, see Robert Young, *Darwin's Metaphor: Nature's Place in Victorian Culture* (Cambridge: Cambridge University Press, 1985), and George Levine, *Darwin and the Novelists: Patterns of Science in Victorian Fiction* (Cambridge: Harvard University Press, 1988). The best work on the reception of Darwinism in America is Jon H. Roberts, *Darwinism and the Divine in America: Protestant Intellectuals and Organic Evolution, 1859–1900* (Madison: University of Wisconsin Press, 1988). Also see Edward J. Pfeiffer, "United States," in *The Comparative Reception of Darwinism*, ed. Thomas F. Glick (Austin: University of Texas Press, 1972), 168–206. Very impressive on the variety of thinkers who reconciled Darwin with religion is James R. Moore, *The Post-Darwinian Controversies* (Cambridge: Cambridge University Press, 1979). Also useful is Neal C. Gillespie, *Charles Darwin and the Problem of Creation* (Chicago: University of Chicago Press, 1979). Some analysts are less certain about the case of reconciliation between Darwinism and religion. See Ronald

174

L. Numbers, "George Frederick Wright: From Christian Darwinist to Fundamentalist," *Isis* 79 (1988): 624–45. A recent work contends that liberal churchmen actually undermined the power of religious thought by being too open to scientific and modern strains of thought; see James Turner, *Without God, Without Creed* (Baltimore: Johns Hopkins University Press, 1985). Another recent book insightfully contends that Darwinian ideals were weapons in the arsenal for a vision of consciousness as an active agent. See Robert J. Richards, *Darwin and the Emergence of Evolutionary Theories of Mind and Behavior* (Chicago: University of Chicago Press, 1987).

A useful route into the scientific and religious controversies of the era is through biography. See J. David Hoeveler, Jr., *James McCosh and the Scottish Intellectual Tradition: From Glasgow to Princeton* (Princeton, N.J.: Princeton University Press, 1981); Lester D. Stephens, *Joseph Le Conte: Gentle Prophet of Evolution* (Baton Rouge: Louisiana State University Press, 1982); and David N. Livingstone, *Nathaniel Southgate Shaler and the Culture of American Science* (Tuscaloosa: University of Alabama Press, 1987). Older but still authoritative biographies are A. Hunter Dupree, *Asa Gray: 1810–1888* (Cambridge: Belknap Press of Harvard University Press, 1959) and Edward Lurie, *Louis Agassiz: A Life in Science* (Chicago: University of Chicago Press, 1960).

The importance of Neo-Lamarckian evolutionary theory and of the American School theorists is emphasized in Peter J. Bowler, *The Eclipse of Darwinism: Anti-Darwinian Evolution Theories in the Decades Around 1900* (Baltimore: Johns Hopkins University Press, 1983), and George W. Stocking, Jr., *Race, Culture, and Evolution: Essays in the History of Anthropology* (New York: Free Press, 1968). For many years debate has raged about the effect of Darwinism on social theory. The classic statement on social Darwinism will be found in Richard Hofstadter, *Social Darwinism in American Thought* (Boston: Beacon Press, 1962). A strong revisionist view argues that social Darwinism was negligible in America. See Robert C. Bannister, *Social Darwinism: Science and Myth in Anglo-Saxon Social Thought* (Philadelphia: Temple University Press, 1979).

Anyone interested in the history of American philosophy must begin with Bruce Kuklick, *The Rise of American Philosophy: Cambridge, Massachusetts, 1860–1930* (New Haven, Conn.: Yale University Press, 1977), in which the process of professionalization is stressed. See also Daniel J. Wilson, *Science, Community, and the Transformation of American Philosophy, 1860–1930* (Chicago: University of Chicago Press, 1990). Excellent introductions to various philosophers of the period will be found in Herbert W. Schneider, *A History of American Philosophy* (New York: Columbia University Press, 1946), and Elizabeth Flower and Murray G. Murphey, *A History of Philosophy in America*, 2 vols. (New York: Capricorn Books, 1977). Strong interpretations of American philosophy and psychology in this period are Cornel West, *The American Evasion of Philosophy: A Genealogy of Pragmatism* (Madison: University of Wisconsin Press, 1989); James Hoopes, *Consciousness in New England: From Puritanism and Ideas to Psychoanalysis and Semiotic* (Baltimore: Johns Hopkins University Press, 1989); and John M. O'Donnell, *The Origins of Behaviorism: American Psychology, 1870–1920* (New York: New York University Press, 1985). Perceptive on the rejection of formalism and the elucidation of process and experience by philosophers is Morton White, *Social Thought in America: The Revolt Against Formalism* (Boston: Beacon Press, 1957). Excellent in placing American philosophers within the context of European thought is

James T. Kloppenberg, *Uncertain Victory: Social Democracy and Progressivism in European and American Thought, 1870–1920* (New York: Oxford University Press, 1986). On Hegelianism in America, see David John Watson, "Idealism and Social Theory: A Comparative Study of British and American Adaptations of Hegel, 1860–1914" (Ph.D. diss., University of Pennsylvania, 1975); and William H. Goetzmann, ed., *The American Hegelians: An Intellectual Episode in the History of Western America* (New York: Alfred A. Knopf, 1973).

Treatments of the philosophers of the period are George Cotkin, *William James: Public Philosopher* (Baltimore: Johns Hopkins University Press, 1990); Neil Coughlan, *Young John Dewey: An Essay in American Intellectual History* (Chicago: University of Chicago Press, 1975); Dorothy Ross, *G. Stanley Hall: The Psychologist as Prophet* (Chicago: University of Chicago Press, 1972); John Clendenning, *The Life and Thought of Josiah Royce* (Madison: University of Wisconsin Press, 1985); and Robert S. Guttchen, *Felix Adler* (New York: Twayne, 1974).

Three excellent works covering American anthropology of the period are Curtis M. Hinsley, Jr., *Savages and Scientists: The Smithsonian Institution and the Development of American Anthropology, 1846–1910* (Washington, D.C.: Smithsonian Institution Press, 1981); Stocking, *Race, Culture, and Evolution* (already cited); and Regna Diebold Darnell, "The Development of American Anthropology: From the Bureau of American Anthropology to Franz Boas" (Ph.D. diss., University of Pennsylvania, 1969). On the importance of evolutionary models to anthropological thought, see Marvin Harris, *The Rise of Anthropological Theory* (New York: Thomas Y. Crowell, 1968); J. W. Burrow, *Evolution and Society: A Study in Victorian Social Theory* (Cambridge: Cambridge University Press, 1970); and George W. Stocking, Jr., *Victorian Anthropology* (New York: Free Press, 1987).

On racism and anthropological thought, see John S. Haller, Jr., *Outcasts from Evolution: Scientific Attitudes on Racial Inferiority, 1859–1900* (Urbana: University of Illinois Press, 1971); William Stanton, *The Leopard's Spots: Scientific Attitudes toward Race in America: 1815–59* (Chicago: University of Chicago Press, 1960); Reginald Horsman, "Scientific Racism and the American Indian in the Mid-Nineteenth Century," *American Quarterly* 27 (1975): 152–68; Robert F. Berkhofer, Jr., *The White Man's Indian* (New York: Vintage, 1979); Ronald T. Takaki, *Iron Cages: Race and Culture in Nineteenth-Century America* (New York: Alfred A. Knopf, 1979); John Higham, *Strangers in the Land: Patterns of American Nativism, 1865–1925* (New York: Atheneum, 1967); and Glenn C. Altschuler, *Race, Ethnicity, and Class in American Social Thought, 1865–1919* (Arlington Heights, Ill.: Harlan Davidson, 1982). To understand how racism and anthropology were intertwined and communicated to the public, see Robert W. Rydell, *All the World's a Fair: Visions of Empire at American International Expositions, 1876–1916* (Chicago: University of Chicago Press, 1984).

Indispensable on Boas is George W. Stocking, Jr., ed., *The Shaping of American Anthropology: A Franz Boas Reader* (New York: Basic Books, 1974). Other biographical treatments of key figures in American anthropology are Carl Resek, *Lewis Henry Morgan: American Scholar* (Chicago: University of Chicago Press, 1960); Bernhard J. Stern, *Lewis Henry Morgan: Social Evolutionist* (New York: Russell & Russell, 1967); William Culp Darrah, *Powell of the Colorado* (Princeton: Princeton University Press, 1951); Joan Mark, "Frank Hamilton Cushing and an American Science of Anthropology,"

Perspectives in American History 10 (1976): 449–60; Curtis M. Hinsley, Jr., "Ethnographic Charisma and Scientific Routine: Cushing and Fewkes in the American Southwest, 1879–1893," in *Observers Observed: Essays on Ethnographic Fieldwork*, ed. George W. Stocking, Jr. (Madison: University of Wisconsin Press, 1983), 53–69; and Joan Mark, *A Stranger in Her Native Land: Alice Fletcher and the American Indians* (Lincoln: University of Nebraska Press, 1988).

Excellent works on women and the possibilities of an intellectual life in this period are Cynthia Eagle Russett, *Sexual Science: The Victorian Construction of Womanhood* (Cambridge: Harvard University Press, 1989); Rosalind Rosenberg, *Beyond Separate Spheres: Intellectual Roots of Modern Feminism* (New Haven: Yale University Press, 1982); and Carroll Smith-Rosenberg, *Disorderly Conduct: Visions of Gender in Victorian America* (New York: Oxford University Press, 1985). Two works that strongly argue for antagonism on the part of male intellectuals and artists toward women are Bram Dijkstra, *Idols of Perversity: Fantasies of Feminine Evil in Fin-de-Siècle Culture* (New York: Oxford University Press, 1986), and Sandra Gilbert and Susan Gubar, *No Man's Land: The War of Words* (New Haven: Yale University Press, 1988).

Critical documents on women's capacity for the intellectual life will be found in Louise Michele Newman, ed., *Men's Ideas / Women's Reality: Popular Science, 1870–1915* (New York: Pergamon Press, 1985); Edward H. Clarke, *Sex in Education; or, A Fair Chance for the Girls* (1873; reprint, New York: Arno Press, 1972); and Julia Ward Howe, ed., *Sex and Education: A Reply to Dr. E. H. Clarke's "Sex in Education"* (1864; reprint, New York: Arno Press, 1972). To understand the political ideas of women's suffrage, begin with Aileen S. Kraditor, *The Ideas of the Woman Suffrage Movement, 1890–1920* (Garden City, N.Y.: Anchor Books, 1971); and Nancy F. Cott, *The Grounding of American Feminism* (New Haven: Yale University Press, 1987). Also helpful is Elisabeth Griffith, *In Her Own Right: The Life of Elizabeth Cady Stanton* (New York: Oxford University Press, 1984).

On women in the professions, see Margaret W. Rossiter, *Women Scientists in America: Struggles and Strategies to 1940* (Baltimore: Johns Hopkins University Press, 1982); Regina Markell Morantz-Sanchez, *Sympathy & Science: Women Physicians in American Medicine* (New York: Oxford University Press, 1985); Roberta Frankfort, *Collegiate Women: Domesticity and Career in Turn-of-the-Century America* (New York: New York University Press, 1977); Dee Garrison, "The Tender Technicians: The Feminization of Public Librarianship, 1876–1905," in *Clio's Consciousness Raised*, ed. Mary Hartman and Lois Banner (New York: Harper Torchbooks, 1974), 158–78; and Toby Quitsland, "Her Feminine Colleagues: Photographs and Letters Collected by Frances Benjamin Johnston in 1900," in *Women Artists in American Collections* (College Park: University of Maryland Art Gallery, 1979).

There are many challenging interpretations to be found on American women writers. For a strongly positive evaluation, one that undermines the canon of the great male writers, see Jane Tompkins, *Sensational Designs: The Cultural Work of American Fiction, 1790–1860* (New York: Oxford University Press, 1985). For the other side, see Ann Douglas, *The Feminization of American Culture* (New York: Alfred A. Knopf, 1977). Also helpful are Judith Fryer, *Felicitous Space: The Structures of Edith Wharton and Willa Cather* (Chapel Hill: University of North Carolina Press, 1986); R. W. B. Lewis, *Edith Wharton: A Biography* (New York: Harper & Row, 1977); Sharon

O'Brien, *Willa Cather: The Emerging Voice* (New York: Fawcett Columbine, 1987); and Kate Chopin, *The Awakening* (New York: W. W. Norton, 1976; text and commentary organized by Margaret Culley).

On the domestic science and architecture movements, see Delores Hayden, *The Grand Domestic Revolution* (Cambridge: MIT Press, 1981); Gwendolyn Wright, *Moralism and the Model Home: Domestic Architecture and Cultural Conflict in Chicago, 1873–1913* (Chicago: University of Chicago Press, 1980); Kathryn Kish Sklar, *Catharine Beecher: A Study in American Domesticity* (New Haven: Yale University Press, 1973); and Ruth Schwartz Cowan, "Ellen Swallow Richards: Technology and Women," in *Technology and America: A History of Individuals and Ideas*, ed. Carroll W. Pursell, Jr. (Cambridge: MIT Press, 1986), 142–50). On Charlotte Perkins Gilman, see Mary A. Hill, *Charlotte Perkins Gilman: The Making of a Radical Feminist, 1860–1896* (Philadelphia: Temple University Press, 1980); and the introductory essay by Carl N. Degler in Gilman's *Women and Economics* (New York: Harper Torchbooks, 1966). Also see the unusual reading of "The Yellow Wallpaper" in Walter Benn Michaels, *The Gold Standard and the Logic of Naturalism* (Berkeley: University of California Press, 1987).

The ideals and work of the cultural custodians are discussed in Helen Lefkowitz Horowitz, *Culture & the City: Cultural Philanthropy in Chicago from the 1880s to 1917* (Chicago: University of Chicago Press, 1989); Henry F. May, *The End of American Innocence* (New York: Alfred A. Knopf, 1959); David D. Hall, "The Victorian Connection" in *Victorian America*, ed. Daniel Walker Howe (Philadelphia: University of Pennsylvania Press, 1976), 81–94; John Tomsich, *A Genteel Endeavor: American Culture and Politics in the Gilded Age* (Stanford, Calif.: Stanford University Press,1971); and Thomas Bender, *New York Intellect* (New York: Alfred A. Knopf, 1987). A fine biography of an individual cultural arbiter is Kenneth S. Lynn, *William Dean Howells: An American Life* (New York: Harcourt Brace Jovanovich, 1970).

A recent and controversial interpretation of American culture in the nineteenth century is Lawrence Levine, *Highbrow / Lowbrow: The Emergence of Cultural Hierarchy in America* (Cambridge: Harvard University Press, 1988). On how sculpture helped to build a shared public culture, see Michelle H. Bogart, *Public Sculpture and the Civic Ideal in New York City, 1890–1930* (Chicago: University of Chicago Press, 1989). Autobiographies, essays, and fiction are a good means of discerning cultural ideals and assimilation. See Jack London, *Martin Eden* (New York: Macmillan, 1909); Mary Antin, *The Promised Land* (Boston: Houghton Mifflin, 1912); W. E. B. DuBois, *The Souls of Black Folk* (New York: Dodd, Mead, 1979); Samuel Gompers, *Seventy Years of Life and Labor*, 2 vols. (London: Horst and Blackett, 1925); and Booker T. Washington, *Up from Slavery*, in *Booker T. Washington Papers: The Autobiographical Writings*, vol. 1., ed. Louis Harlan and John W. Blassingame (Urbana: University of Illinois Press, 1972). On Washington, see Louis R. Harlan, *Booker T. Washington: The Making of a Black Leader, 1856–1901* (New York: Oxford University Press, 1982) and August Meier, *Negro Thought in America, 1880-1915* (Ann Arbor: University of Michigan Press, 1971).

The literature on the myth of success in America is immense: see John W. Cawelti, *Apostles of the Self-Made Man* (Chicago: University of Chicago Press, 1965); Irvin G. Wyllie, *The Self-Made Man in America* (New York: Free Press, 1954); Richard Huber, *The American Idea of Success* (New York: McGraw Hill, 1971); Agnes Rush Burr, *Russell*

Conwell and His Work (Philadelphia: John C. Winston, 192(
"The Nursery Tales of Horatio Alger," *American Quarterly*
penetration of these ideals into the working class in Am(
Mechanic Accents: Dime Novels and Working-Class Culture
1987); and George Cotkin, "Caught in Cultures: Samuel (
the Working-Class Individual in Culture," *Mid-America* 6(

The rise of a consumerist culture is examined in M
Imitation and Authenticity in American Culture, 1880-1940
North Carolina Press, 1989); Lears, *No Place of Grace* (a
Incorporation of America (already cited); and Richard Wigh
Lears, eds., *The Culture of Consumption* (New York: Panth(
the creation of a culture of desire in America are William
in a Culture of Consumption: Women and Department S
American History 71 (1984): 319–42; Stuart Culver, "Wha
derful Wizard of Oz and *The Art of Decorating Dry Goods*
(1988): 97–116; Remy G. Saisselin, *The Bourgeois and* (
N.J.: Rutgers University Press, 1984); John F. Kasson,
Island at the Turn of the Century (New York: Hill & Wa
Steppin' Out: New York Nightlife and the Transformation o
University of Chicago Press, 1981); Lary May, *Screening* (
Culture and the Motion Picture Industry (New York: Oxf(
and Daniel J. Czitrom, *Media and the American Mind: Fr(
Hill: University of North Carolina Press, 1982). On how
continued to exert cultural force well into the 1920s
Rubin, "Self, Culture, and Self-Culture in Modern An
the Book-of-the-Month Club," *Journal of American Histor*

To understand modernism and the fin de siècle in Am
with works examining the European context. See Carl (
Politics and Culture (New York: Alfred A. Knopf, 1980);
Years: The Origins of the Avant-Garde in France, 1885 to Wor
1968); Frederick R. Karl, *Modern and Modernism: The S*
1925 (New York: Atheneum, 1985); Lionel Trilling, *Bey*
court Brace Jovanovich, 1965); and Peter Gay, *Freud, Je*
and Victims in Modernist Culture (New York: Oxford Univ
the essays by David A. Hollinger and Daniel Joseph Sir
ernist Culture in America," *American Quarterly* 39 (1(
Henry Adams is Ernest Samuels's three-volume biogr
single volume, *Henry Adams* (Cambridge: The Belknap
Press, 1989). Also see David Contosta, *Henry Adams and*
ton: Little, Brown, 1980); and William H. Jordy, *He*
(New Haven: Yale University Press, 1952).

Especially helpful for understanding Veblen are Jos(
and His America (New York: Viking, 1947) and John P.
Thorstein Veblen and Modern Social Theory (New York: (
begin with Robert Twombly, *Louis Sullivan: His Life &*
Chicago Press, 1986). Also see William H. Jordy, *Progr*

Ideals
York:
Americ
drew,
(Urba
1890s:
1979);
& Gir
Brazill
and Ste
Sprag(

the *Turn of the Century*, vol. 4 of *American Buildings and Their Architects* (New)xford University Press, 1972); Sherman Paul, *Louis Sullivan: An Architect of n Thought* (Englewood Cliffs, N.J.: Prentice-Hall, 1962); and David S. An- *ouis Sullivan and the Polemics of Modern Architecture: The Present against the Past* ı: University of Illinois Press, 1985). On Crane, see Larzer Ziff, *The American *he Life and Times of a Lost Generation* (Lincoln: University of Nebraska Press, ohn Berryman, *Stephen Crane: A Critical Biography* (New York: Farrar, Straus ıx, 1977); R. W. Stallman, *Stephen Crane: A Biography* (New York: George r, 1968); and Michael Fried, *Realism, Writing, Disfiguration: On Thomas Eakins ›en Crane* (Chicago: University of Chicago Press, 1987). On Saltus, see Claire , *Edgar Saltus* (New York: Twayne, 1968).

Index

182

The Author

George Cotkin received his B.A. from Brooklyn College and his M.A. and Ph.D. from Ohio State University. He is a professor of history at California Polytechnic State University in San Luis Obispo. A specialist in American intellectual and cultural history, Cotkin is the author of *William James: Public Philosopher* (1990). His essays include "Truth or Consequences" (*Reviews in American History*, 1990); "Ralph Waldo Emerson and William James as Public Philosophers" (*The Historian*, 1986); "The Photographer in the Beat-Hipster Idiom: Robert Frank's *The Americans*" (*American Studies*, 1985); "Fathers and Sons, Texts and Contexts: Henry James, Sr., and William James" (*American Quarterly*, 1984); and "The Socialist Popularization of Science in America, 1900 to the First World War" (*History of Education Quarterly*, 1984). During the academic year 1991–92, Cotkin, with the support of a National Endowment for the Humanities Fellowship, will be researching and writing a book to be titled *Public Philosophy in America*.